A highly readable, factually accurate, and attractively presented synopsis of the life and contribution of the major shapers of the Christian faith. *The 40 Most Influential Christians Who Shaped What We Believe Today* is a wonderful introduction to the history of the Christian church; it engages its readers, carrying them beyond the basics into an understanding of the progress and contours of · Christian intellectual life. It is simply an informative, beneficial, and delightful read.

—John D. Hannah, Dallas Theological Seminary,
Distinguished Professor of Historical Theology,
Research Professor of Theological Studies

THE 40 MOST INFLUENTIAL CHRISTIANS

WHO SHAPED WHAT WE BELIEVE TODAY

DARYL AARON

BETHANY HOUSE PUBLISHERS
a division of Baker Publishing Group
Minneapolis, Minnesota

© 2013 by Daryl Aaron

Published by Bethany House Publishers
11400 Hampshire Avenue South
Bloomington, Minnesota 55438
www.bethanyhouse.com

Bethany House Publishers is a division of
Baker Publishing Group, Grand Rapids, Michigan

Printed in the United States of America

Library of Congress Cataloging-in-Publication Data
Aaron, Daryl.
    The 40 most influential Christians who shaped what we believe today / Daryl Aaron.
        pages cm
    Includes bibliographical references.
    Summary: "Brief accessible accounts of the people who significantly formed the core beliefs of the Christian faith"—Provided by publisher.
    ISBN 978-0-7642-1084-6 (pbk. : alk. paper)
    1. Church history. 2. Christians. I. Title. II. Title: Forty most influential Christians who shaped what we believe today.
BR145.3.A27 2013
270.092´2—dc23   2013010865

Cover design by Eric Walljasper

13 14 15 16 17 18 19   7 6 5 4 3 2 1

*This book is dedicated to
my past and present colleagues
in the Biblical and Theological Studies Department
of Northwestern College.*

*It has been my immense privilege to serve with
you for sixteen years and counting.
You too have been and are very influential Christians—
in the lives of thousands of students as well as my own.*

CONTENTS

ACKNOWLEDGMENTS

I would like to express my gratitude to Dr. John Hannah for his gracious willingness to read this manuscript and offer a generous endorsement. This is especially meaningful to me because Dr. Hannah is the one who sparked my interest in the whole area of historical theology, the subject matter of the book. I took the first History of Doctrine course that he offered at Dallas Theological Seminary (in the fall of 1977!). That in turn prompted me to undertake an additional graduate program in the History of Ideas at the University of Texas at Dallas. Dr. Hannah was also my favorite teacher. He was indeed a very influential Christian who shaped what I believe and how I teach today.

I would also like to thank Andy McGuire, my editor at Bethany House. He has guided and encouraged me now through three books. I greatly appreciate all that he has done, as well as the rest of the very capable staff at Bethany House.

A Chronology of These Influential Christians

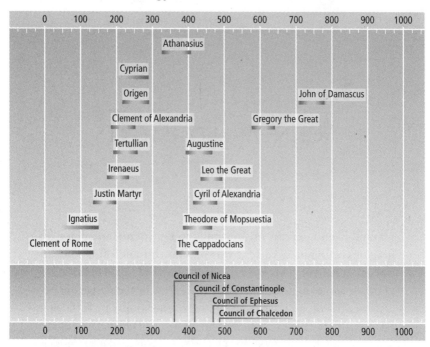

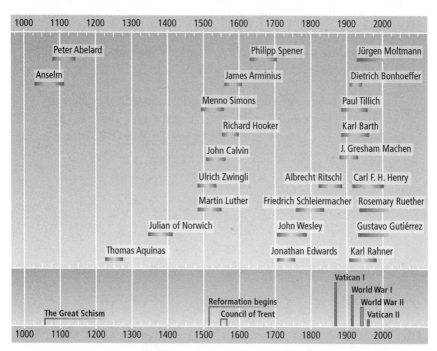

INTRODUCTION

Theology is often not a very popular topic among Christians. The term sometimes conjures up visions of overly educated individuals who have overly lofty thoughts about things that are totally irrelevant to pretty much everything. But this reflects a misunderstanding of what theology is as well as the vital importance of theology to our own spiritual health and that of our churches.[1] Similarly, the idea of any kind of "history of theology" is sometimes not highly regarded and is often misunderstood by many Christians. The thinking is, "The Bible was complete in the first century. What we believe is based on the Bible. Therefore, how can there be a history or development of that? Isn't that just going beyond the Bible?"

There is something both right and wrong in this thinking. What is right and important to note is that the earliest generations of Christians, all the way back to the first century, had a *basic* belief system: There is only one true God—Yahweh, the God of Israel. Sin has separated all people from God, who is holy. God fulfilled his Old Testament promises of a Messiah who happens to be the Son of God, God himself (fully and eternally), and who also became a human. This unique individual, Jesus Christ, died to pay the penalty for sin, was buried, and was resurrected in victory over sin and death (1 Corinthians 15:1–9). This same Jesus returned to

---

1. I have tried to address this briefly in *Understanding Theology in 15 Minutes a Day* (Minneapolis: Bethany House, 2012), chapter 1.

heaven but will one day come back to earth. This is also what most Christians believe today in continuity with first-century Christians.

So what the first-century Christians knew and believed was *necessary*—those truths are the heart of the Christian faith—but it was not *sufficient*. How could it be when the object is the *infinite* being and mind of God himself? For example, the first-generation Christians believed that Jesus was fully God and fully human, but they had not yet considered how that could possibly be. They also believed that Jesus' heavenly Father was also God, as was the Spirit, who was sent on a broader mission on the Day of Pentecost. This did not mean that they believed in three gods—they were still strictly and fervently monotheists—but they had not yet thought through how there could be three but still one. They believed that Jesus died for sin, but they had not yet fully considered the significance of this. How exactly did he die for sin? For whose sin? Is forgiveness of sin *all* his death accomplished? And so on and so on. These are the questions and issues that later generations of Christians took up. Their suggested answers were sometimes wrong and rejected by the majority of Christians; this was called *heresy*. But little by little, Christians were coming to grips with the deeper truths of God and becoming spiritually healthier as a result.

So the idea of development of theology or doctrine is not wrong or dangerous; rather, it is to be expected. It does *not* involve *expanding* on Scripture, that is, going beyond it; the Word of God is sufficient, meaning God has given us everything that we need to know (2 Timothy 3:16–17). Rather, it involves *explaining* Scripture, that is, going deeper into it. Scripture is sufficient, but our understanding of it is not sufficient.[2] Even now in the twenty-first century we are only really "scratching the surface" of the infinitely deep and high things of God (Job 11:7–9; Isaiah 55:8–9).

So theology is a good thing and the history of theology is a good thing because they both help us to understand God better, and that is a very good thing. There are a few other benefits that come

---

from studying the history of theology that could be mentioned: First, it helps us to be discerning by being able to recognize theological errors that have been made in the past. Second, it helps us to distinguish between what is just a passing fad in Christianity today from what is timeless and enduring biblical truth. Third, it should impress upon us the sovereignty and mercy of God who has preserved his truth despite false teaching and fleeting trends. Fourth, it promotes a healthy humility as we realize that great thinkers have made great errors in the past and that our understanding of the Bible today is in large part due to hundreds of years of thought on the part of others. As many have said, we modern Christians are standing on the shoulders of giants. Fifth and finally, in an age when the concept of truth—especially universal, timeless truth—is being denied, the history of theology reminds us that, for centuries, God's people have not only believed in universal truth, but also that the most *vital* truth has been recorded and preserved in the Bible. And it is just as relevant today as when it was written.

Regarding the title of this book, you may be thinking, *Really? THE 40 MOST Influential Christians?! Come on!* Please understand that I am not under the illusion that I have nailed the definitive top 40 list of theologians. (Actually, it is the top 42; I snuck a couple of bonus Gregorys into chapter 10.) I thought a more accurate title would be *40 of the Most Influential Christians Who Shaped What We Believe Today, in the Humble Opinion of One Particular Writer*, but that seemed a little unwieldy to the publisher. Good arguments can be made that some of these should not have made it while others should have.

Some of them are blatantly obvious: Tertullian, Athanasius, Augustine, Aquinas, Luther, Calvin, Edwards, etc. Other names are perhaps rather unfamiliar: Clement, Cyprian, Cyril, Julian, Richard Hooker, Rosemary Ruether, etc. In fact, just because I have chosen to include some of these theologians does not mean that I am necessarily a fan of their theologies. A few of them, in my opinion, have been more harmful than helpful. "Influential" does not necessarily mean "accurate." But all of them, from Anselm to Zwingli, who lived in important centers of theology from

Antioch to Zurich, advanced theological thinking or contributed to a certain Christian tradition in significant ways. All of these individuals *did* play important and influential roles in the overall story of the development of Christian theology. It is that story that I am also trying to tell.

Regarding format, each chapter will be divided into three main sections with two subparts: **context** (*theological* and *biographical*), **contribution** (*theological* and *bibliographical*), and **conclusion** (*theological* and *personal*).

First, we will discuss the **context** of these great Christian thinkers. All thinking takes place within a historical context, and in this case also a *theological* one. The question is, What was taking place in the historical setting that prompted these Christians to think and write about what they did? Very often this setting was theological controversy, and in some cases outright heresy. It is rather amazing how often great strides forward in Christians' understanding of the Bible and its theological teachings came about as a result of heresy. Some self-professing Christian would come up with an idea that was rather novel (to put it mildly), and many others in the Christian community would respond, "That is intriguing, but it doesn't sound like what we have traditionally believed." The result was that Christians would be pushed back to the Word of God to check out the new idea and come to a deeper understanding of what God's Word really taught, and a deeper understanding of what they had believed all along. This realization should also impress us with our great God, who, far from being sidetracked or frustrated by false teaching, actually uses it to accomplish his sovereign purposes. This kind of God deserves our ultimate trust and sincere worship. So first we will become acquainted with the historical-theological context of these great Christian thinkers. We will also consider these thinkers' *biographical* context, that is, some highlights of their personal lives. Sometimes these are just as interesting and significant as their thought and writings.

The second main section of each chapter will be their **contribution**. The *theological* contribution will be a brief overview of their main ideas that advanced or challenged our understanding of the

Word, ways, and works of God. The *bibliographical* contribution will be a notation of their main writings and a few quotations from those writings—letting these great Christian thinkers speak for themselves.

The **conclusion** will briefly wrap up that Christian thinker's *theological* contribution and occasionally suggest some *personal* applications—lessons we can learn from their lives.

We are going to begin this story in the second century AD. The pre-story is that the canon of the Bible has been completed. Christians accepted the books of the Old Testament as authoritative, that is, the very Word of God—inspired, to be accepted and believed. By the end of the first century, all of the books of the New Testament had been written and also acknowledged, at least informally, as authoritative and equivalent to the Old Testament (although more was to happen along these lines in the next three centuries, as we will see).[3] Also, by the end of the first century, all of the apostles—the *personal* authoritative source of God's truth following the ascension of Jesus—had died.

As the Church entered the second century, it had the complete written Word of God and a body of truth based on the Word of God—known as the "teachings of the apostles"—but only an elementary understanding of it all. So God continued to work through his people to build on the foundation of the apostles and prophets (Ephesians 2:20) in order to take believers in Jesus deeper into the infinite person and mind of God.

What is most important in what follows is not getting to know these great Christian thinkers better, nor is it understanding theology better (in and of itself); rather, what is most important is getting to know God better. After all, our Savior, Jesus Christ, commanded us to "Love the Lord your God with all your heart and all your soul and all your mind" (Matthew 22:37). These are the stories of Christians who were trying to do that and trying to help others do it as well.

3. For more, see Daryl Aaron, *Understanding Your Bible in 15 Minutes a Day* (Minneapolis: Bethany House, 2012), 101–104.

1

CLEMENT OF ROME

First Apostolic Father

Context

The last apostle, John, died at the end of the first century, ending what is known as the "apostolic period." At this time, all of the books that would eventually make up the New Testament had been written by the apostles and a few others closely associated with them. So by the end of the first century, God had given, through inspiration, all of his Word that he intended for people to have (Old Testament and New Testament).

The period immediately following, beginning in the second century, is called the "post-apostolic" period. Immediately, Christians began reflecting on and writing about the teachings of the apostles as recorded in the books of the New Testament and the rest of Scripture. Some of these individuals actually knew the apostles and were indeed their disciples. The writings from this period are known as the "works of apostolic fathers" and include the following: the *Epistle of Clement* (or, *1 Clement*[1]), seven epistles of

1. This distinguishes it from *2 Clement*, which was not written by Clement.

Ignatius, the *Epistle of Polycarp*, the *Didache* (or, *Teaching of the Apostles*), the *Epistle of Barnabas*, and the *Shepherd of Hermas*.[2] The authors of the last three are not known.[3] Some Christians in the early centuries even regarded some of the apostolic fathers on the same level of authority as the works of the apostles themselves. However, by the end of the fourth century, none of these books were considered canonical—inspired by God and divinely authoritative.

Generally speaking, the writings of the apostolic fathers were more practical and pastoral than theological, at least in the sense of any deep reflection and speculation on what the apostles taught. The church was still in its infant stages and just trying to find its way in the complex setting of the second-century Roman Empire. That deeper reflection would come soon, but not quite yet. Very early on there were pressing problems and threats that needed to be addressed. These were the primary concerns of the apostolic fathers. We will consider just two of them: Clement and his epistle in this chapter, and Ignatius and his seven epistles in chapter 2.

The writer of *Clement* was the bishop of the church in Rome in the last decade of the first century, and therefore generally known as Clement of Rome. He *may* be the Clement mentioned in Philippians 4:3. Not much is known about him otherwise.

Contribution

No author is named in the letter, but there is universal agreement that Clement of Rome did write it. It was written from Rome to the church in Corinth (chapter 1) around AD 96. This, then, is the first Christian document that we have following the writings of the apostles themselves.

In these earliest post-apostolic writings, we clearly see acknowledgment of foundational Christian truths. For example, Clement

---

2. A few others are sometimes added.
3. The *Epistle of Barnabas* is pseudonymous, that is, the name of Barnabas was falsely attached to it.

used the "triadic formula"—referring to Father, Son, and Holy Spirit as God—reflecting his belief in the doctrine of the Trinity even though Christians did not yet use the word *Trinity* for this truth (e.g., chapter 58).[4] Clement clearly understood that the death of Christ was for salvation (e.g., 7), and he would agree with Paul that we "are not justified by ourselves, nor by our . . . works which we have wrought in holiness of heart; but by that faith through which, from the beginning, Almighty God has justified all men . . ." (32).[5] Clement and other apostolic fathers faithfully passed on these fundamental truths that they had received and been taught by the apostles themselves.

Clement's main contribution to Christian thought is in the area of church unity and leadership. Threats to unity were of great concern to Jesus himself (John 17:20–23) and to the apostles (Ephesians 4:1–6; 1 Peter 3:8–9). In fact, that was one of Paul's concerns when he wrote to the Corinthians—division within the church (1 Corinthians 1:10ff.). This was also Clement's concern when he wrote to the same church some forty years later. For some reason, some of the younger Christians there were rebelling against the leaders of the church, and some of those leaders had been forced from their positions. The result was a crisis of leadership and division in the church.

Some New Testament background regarding church leaders would be helpful at this point. The New Testament refers to the primary office of church leadership as *episkopos* (e.g., Philippians 1:1; 1 Timothy 3:1–2; Titus 1:7; 1 Peter 2:25), from which we get the term *Episcopalian*. The Greek word literally means "overseer," but in some older English versions, such as the King James Version, and in translations of the Fathers, such as Clement, it is translated

---

4. J. B. Lightfoot, *The Apostolic Fathers* (Grand Rapids: Baker, 1976), 38.

5. Unless otherwise noted, quotations from the works of the apostolic fathers are taken from *Ante-Nicene Fathers: Translations of the Writings of the Fathers Down to AD 325*, ed. Alexander Roberts and James Donaldson (WORD*search* Database, 2006; Peabody, MA: Hendrickson, 1994), with minor updating of the language (e.g., "ye" to "you"). The numbers cited in the parentheses refer to the chapter from which the quote was taken. *Clement* has 65 (short) chapters.

as "bishop." The New Testament also referred to a church leader as *presbuteros* (e.g., Acts 14:23; Titus 1:5). This word literally means "elder," and from it we get the term *Presbyterian*. However, this is *not* something different from an overseer. Rather, they are two different titles for the *same* office or leadership position in a local church. This is clear because both are sometimes used in the same context (e.g., Acts 20:1, 28; Titus 1:6–7). Clement showed that he understood this in the same way because he used both *episkopos* and *presbuteros* for this church leadership position (e.g., chapter 44).

Now, back to Clement's concern regarding the crisis of leadership and division in the Corinthian church. He urged his readers to find their unity in Christ, but more specifically in those who had been appointed to oversee their church. For example, he wrote, "Let us reverence the Lord Jesus Christ . . . let us esteem *those who have the rule over us* [overseers/bishops]; let us honor the presbyters [elders] among us . . ." (21). Clement also called upon the troublemakers to repent and submit to their elders (57; cf. Hebrews 13:17).

His reasoning for expecting Christians to submit to their leaders was this: God had chosen and appointed Jesus; Jesus had chosen and appointed the apostles; the apostles had chosen and appointed their successors, elder-overseers/bishops (including Clement himself). Therefore, this pattern should be repeated through the succeeding generations of church leaders (42). This idea eventually came to be known as "apostolic succession." Clement's motive here was good: to preserve the truth of the apostolic message (just as Paul was doing in 2 Timothy 2:2) and to preserve order and unity in the church. Church elders do indeed have authority in a local church. But the very *same* authority as the *apostles*? As we will see, the concept of apostolic succession continued to develop and eventually presented some significant problems for the church.

Clement planted another related seed that began to sprout very quickly and eventually resulted in the clear distinction between the "clergy" and the "laity," and the elevation of the former over the latter. In chapter 40 he wrote, "For [the Lord's] own peculiar services are assigned to the [Old Testament Jewish] high priest, and their own proper place is prescribed to the priests, and their own special ministrations pass on to the Levites. The layman is bound by the laws that pertain to laymen." In this last sentence he used the Greek word *laikos*—from which we get the word *laity*—for the first time in Christian literature. What he is obviously doing is drawing from the Old Testament way of serving God—through one high priest along with many priests and Levites *exclusively*—and applying it to the New Testament church. Even though this is certainly not what Clement had in mind, the analogy quickly developed into the belief that Christian bishops were the "priests," and they *alone* were qualified to do the ministry of Jesus Christ. The Christian priesthood is designated to serve God; everybody else does something less.

Others took this even further: The bishop of the church in Rome (now known as the pope) is the highest bishop of all, the Christian *high priest*. This idea is known as the "supremacy of the papacy." The former pope Benedict XVI found support from this in Clement: "Thus, we could say that Clement's *Letter* was a first exercise of the Roman primacy after St. Peter's death."[6] Why would Pope Benedict say this? Because Clement was bishop of *Rome*, but he seemed to be exercising some authority over the church in *Corinth* by telling them how to deal with matters there.

Conclusion

Clement's primary concern reflected the very clear concern of other New Testament writers—the preservation of the unity of the church. Clement also understood, as did other New Testament writers, the importance of local church leadership for the sake of preserving biblical truth and biblical unity. All of this demonstrates

6. Pope Benedict XVI, *Great Christian Thinkers: From the Early Church through the Middle Ages* (Minneapolis: Fortress, 2011), 4. "Roman primacy" refers to the superiority of the bishop of Rome—the pope—over all other clergy in what is now known as the Roman Catholic Church.

what *should* still be important to local churches today. On the other hand, Clement illustrates the danger of saying something that is picked up by others and taken far beyond what was originally intended. This happened all too often in the flow of church history, as we will see.

2

IGNATIUS OF ANTIOCH

Eager Martyr

Context

The gospel of Jesus Christ spread rapidly after Jesus' ascension (Acts 2:41, 47; 6:7; 9:31), and Christianity was firmly entrenched throughout the Roman Empire very early on. Christianity was not officially condemned; nevertheless, Christians immediately faced significant persecution. Jesus had warned of just this certainty (Matthew 16:24; John 15:20; 16:33; 17:14), as had Paul (2 Timothy 3:12) and Peter (1 Peter 3:14–17; 4:16). The second apostolic father we will consider experienced this personally. In fact, he died as a martyr.

Ignatius was the bishop of Antioch in Syria, the city in which the followers of Jesus were first called "Christians" (Acts 11:26), which was initially a derogatory term—something like "little Christs." The dates of Ignatius' life are a bit obscure, but he probably died in the second decade of the second century. Not much else is known about his life other than what he himself wrote about in his letters. We know that he was arrested due to his faith in Christ and

23

was sent from Antioch, across Asia Minor (present-day Turkey), to Rome, where he expected to be executed.

Contribution

During his trip to Rome he wrote seven letters: to the churches in Magnesia; Tralles; Ephesus (from which Christians had come to visit him along the way); Philadelphia; Smyrna; and Rome, his destination; as well as a personal letter to Polycarp, the bishop of Smyrna. One New Testament scholar said that these letters are "one of the finest literary expressions of Christianity during the second century."[1] Even though they are not deeply theological, "It may be fair to say that these letters contain the first real theology in Christianity [beyond the apostles' own writings]."[2] As we saw previously, the apostolic fathers were not primarily theologians, but rather pastors who were doing their best to encourage Christians in the early days of the church, which found itself in a challenging environment.

A major theme that runs throughout Ignatius's letters is a strong affirmation that Jesus Christ is fully God and (especially) fully human, and the related idea that the denial of this, especially Christ's genuine humanity, was a significant threat to vital Christian truth as well as the unity of the church.

Like Clement, Ignatius clearly understood that his Savior, Jesus Christ, was none other than God himself. He referred to Jesus as "Christ our God" (Smyrnaeans 10). There is no reflective thought regarding *how* Jesus could be fully God along with the Father and the Spirit, but neither was this a pressing concern at this point. What was important in those early days was to believe it, not to be able to explain it.

But of greater concern to Ignatius was that Jesus was genuinely human. Some Christians had come to believe that Jesus was truly

1. Bruce Metzger, *The Canon of the New Testament: Its Origin, Development, and Significance* (Oxford: Clarendon, 1987), 4.

2. Roger Olson, *The Story of Christian Theology: Twenty Centuries of Tradition & Reform* (Downers Grove, IL: InterVarsity, 1999), 46.

God but not truly human—he only *appeared* to be human. This view is called *Docetism*, one of the "Christological heresies" in the early centuries. The term comes from the Greek word *dokeō*, which means "to appear to be." This probably reflected the influence of an aspect of Greek philosophy known as dualism, the assumption that what is spirit is good by definition, and what is physical or material is evil by definition. The obvious implication is that God, who is spirit and therefore good, would not and could not be associated with what is physical and necessarily evil. God would *never* "incarnate" himself (put on flesh) by becoming genuinely human.

However, this was *not* what the apostles taught—just the opposite! For example, the title "Son of Man" is applied to Jesus over eighty times in the New Testament (and was Jesus' favorite way of referring to himself). He was born of a woman (Luke 2:7) and had a family tree (Matthew 1:1–16: Luke 3: 23–38). Jesus referred to himself as a "man" (John 8:40), as did Paul (Romans 5:15; 1 Timothy 2:5). As a matter of fact, the apostle John had already addressed the denial of Christ's humanity. He called it the "spirit of the antichrist" (1 John 4:2–3; 2 John 7–11).

Ignatius passed on this apostolic teaching. For example, he wrote, "There is one Physician [Jesus Christ] who is possessed both of *flesh* and spirit . . . God existing in *flesh* . . . both *of Mary* and of God . . . [who] *became also man*, of Mary the virgin. For '*the Word was made flesh*' [quoted from John 1:14]. Being incorporeal [without a body], He was *in the body*; being impassible [incapable of suffering and dying], He was in a passible *body*; being immortal, He was in a *mortal body* . . ." (Ephesians 7, emphasis added).

One of the reasons that this was so strongly addressed by John and Ignatius was this: If Jesus was not really human, then he did not really suffer, die, and rise from the dead with a real human body. To deny the humanity of Jesus, then, is to deny the gospel (1 Corinthians 15:1–4), and to deny the gospel is to forfeit any hope of salvation. For this reason, the denial of Jesus' humanity was a serious threat to Christians and why Ignatius had to warn his readers about it.

Like Clement, Ignatius was concerned for church unity, and Docetism was a significant threat to that. So, repeatedly in his letters, he warned Christians to "flee from division and wicked doctrines" (Philadelphian 2). Also, like Clement, Ignatius believed that the bishop played an important role in the preservation of unity and doctrinal purity. Statements such as the following appear over and over again in Ignatius: "Do nothing without the bishop" (Philadelphians 7) and "See that you all follow the bishop, even as Jesus Christ does the Father. . . . Wherever the bishop shall appear, there let [the church] also be; even as, wherever Jesus Christ is, there is the Catholic Church"[3] (Smyrnaeans 8).

There is something vital here. Church leaders do indeed play a critical role in passing on biblical truth and protecting the church from error (2 Timothy 1:13; 4:2; Titus 1:5, 9, 13; 2:1). However, Ignatius seems to water the seed planted by Clement that resulted in the elevation of one bishop/overseer over the many presbyters/elders and other church leaders. For example, he wrote, "Your bishop presides in the place of God, and your presbyters in the place of the assembly of the apostles" (Magnesians 6). Ignatius's motive was good: the preservation of unity and truth. The problem, however, is that bishops, indeed all church leaders, are human, fallible, sinful, and, as history soon demonstrated, could themselves be the promoters of false teaching and the cause of disunity. Clement's and Ignatius's views would continue to evolve into an unbiblical elevation of the clergy, giving them power and status that God never intended for them to have.

Conclusion

Ignatius exhorted his readers to believe in the true humanity of Christ, but his positive pastoral advice also came from this: If Jesus Christ, in addition to being God, is also fully human, then

---

3. Ignatius was the first person to attach the word *catholic* to the church, not to be confused with the Roman Catholic Church. The word *catholic* means "general" or "universal." The concept of the "catholic church" became an important one in the early centuries—there is *one* church, even though there are many Christians who are spread around the world. This is a wonderful and vital truth of the body of Christ (1 Corinthians 12:12–13; Galatians 3:28; Ephesians 4:3–4).

Christians should gladly identify with him, be devoted to him, and imitate him, even to the point of being willing, even eager, to suffer and die, just as Jesus did. This is not some kind of abstract theological commitment on the part of Ignatius. He was going to his own martyrdom, and he was *joyful* about it, so much so that he did not want any well-meaning Christians trying to prevent it in any way (Romans 4). "Ignatius's thinking about his death reveals a man who rightly knew that Christian believing demands passionate engagement of the entire person, even to the point of death."[4] Ignatius's willingness and eagerness to suffer and die indicated that his faith in Christ, who also suffered and died, was sincere, not just empty profession.

Ignatius reminds us of several important things: First, false teaching is dangerous to spiritual health and must be rejected; biblical truth is vital and must be believed. Second, belief in biblical truth is more than just intellectual; it should also affect how we live, and maybe even how we die!

---

4. Michael A. G. Haykin, *Rediscovering the Church Fathers: Who They Were and How They Shaped the Church* (Wheaton: Crossway, 2011), 33. Interestingly, the word *martyr* comes from the Greek word *martus*, which literally means "witness" (e.g., Acts 1:8). There was a close association between being a witness for Christ and dying for Christ!

3

JUSTIN MARTYR

First Apologist

Context

Very soon, outside threats against Christianity brought about the next category of Christian writers, the apologists. By the middle of the second century it had become clear that Christianity was distinct from Judaism, and it began to pose a threat not only to Judaism but also to the Roman Empire, due to its zealous evangelism and explosive growth. Christians were viewed as idolaters by the Jews because they worshiped a human (Jesus) rather than the one, true, invisible God, and they were viewed as atheists by the Romans because they would not worship the emperor or the Roman gods.

New threats to the church also began to emerge. There were attacks from *outside* Christianity in two forms: 1) Pagan (non-Jewish and non-Christian) philosophers attacked Christianity for religious or philosophical reasons, and 2) the Roman Empire attacked Christianity for legal or political reasons. There were also attacks from *inside* Christianity from those who claimed to be Christian but taught some things that were very different from what the apostles had taught. Due to all of these threats, there was no time for theological disputes among orthodox Christians.[1] That would come soon enough, but in the meantime, the very survival of Christianity continued to be at stake.

Therefore, from about AD 150 to 300, the efforts of Christian writers were focused on defending Christianity against pagans and heretics. This activity in general, called *apologetics*, refers to the reasoned defense of the Christian faith. Those who did this during this historical period were known as the *apologists*. We will discuss five of these: Justin Martyr, Irenaeus, Tertullian, Clement of Alexandria, and Origen.

Justin was one of the most important early apologists. He was born around AD 100 in Palestine but to Greek parents. He sought truth through philosophy—from Stoicism to Platonism with a few more in between. At this point, as he himself tells the story, he met an old man by the sea who drew his attention to Christ through the Old Testament. Justin was also impacted by the courageous way in which Christians were willing to die for their faith. As a result, Justin became a Christian. He continued studying and teaching philosophy, but now with the conviction that Christianity was the superior philosophy. He ended up teaching in Rome, where he was arrested for believing in and teaching an illegal religion and also for refusing to sacrifice to Roman gods. He was executed in 165, and the church has come to know him as Justin Martyr.

Contribution

Three of his works survive. Justin's *First Apology* (written around 155) and *Second Apology* (around 160) are defenses of the Christian

---

1. The term *orthodox* literally means "right thinking." As applied to Christianity, it refers to those beliefs or doctrines that were consistent with the teachings of the apostles and that won the support of the overwhelming majority of Christians.

faith addressed to the emperor, Antonius, and the Roman senate respectively. *Dialogue with Trypho* is a conversation with Trypho, a Jewish philosopher, in which Justin tries to convince him that Judaism anticipated Christianity and that Christianity has fulfilled and surpassed Judaism. This is where he describes his own conversion. These works are a giant theological step beyond those of the apostolic fathers.

We will focus on two theological contributions from Justin, both of which were helpful and harmful at the same time. The first is how he used philosophy generally in his defense of Christianity. The second is how he used philosophy specifically with regard to understanding the person of Jesus Christ.

Justin continued studying and teaching philosophy after his conversion, but now he was arguing for Christianity from a Christian perspective. As noted above, Justin believed that Christianity was the superior philosophy and that previous philosophies only anticipated Christian truth. For example, he believed that Plato and others had gotten ideas from the Old Testament. This is why he felt justified in continuing to use Greek philosophy (although he was also critical of it in places).

Justin attempted to demonstrate, using the Greeks' own way of thinking, that Christianity was not foolishness at all—just the opposite.[2] With regard to the Romans, Justin argued that Christians were no threat to the empire—again, just the opposite. He accused the empire of persecuting Christians simply because they were Christians, regardless of their behavior.[3] Justin pointed out that those who accepted the title *Christianos* were, in fact, good for the empire since they lived according to high moral standards and were therefore excellent citizens and no threat to Rome. In fact, it was exactly in this moral sense that Christianity demonstrated itself as the ultimate philosophy. In Greek philosophy, virtues such as love and truth were abstract ideals. In Christianity, however, those ideals had become concrete realities in the person of Jesus himself,

2. For the apostle Paul's way of putting this, see 1 Corinthians 1:18–24.
3. This had previously been anticipated by the apostle Peter in 1 Peter 4:14, 16.

who *was* the ultimate reality, and who showed virtues such as love and truth in how he lived. It was because of Jesus that his followers also lived morally superior lives and were even willing to die for what they believed (*First Apology*, 15; *Dialogue with Trypho*, 93).

This contribution from Justin was helpful because he showed that Christianity is intellectually reasonable, and not only can it "hold its own," but it actually shows its superiority in the realm of philosophy. He also does not apologize for supporting his arguments with Scripture. Later Christian theologians would continue to use this philosophical way of thinking as they struggled to understand and discuss challenging concepts about God. On the other hand, too much reliance on philosophy can damage biblical Christianity. Justin can rightly be accused of relying a bit too much on philosophical thinking. After all, as Paul noted, "the message of the cross is foolishness" to Greeks (1 Corinthians 1:18). Some of God's things are beyond human logic. As we will see, other apologists followed Justin in an abundant use of philosophy in their theology (e.g., Origen), while others were quite critical of philosophy of any kind (e.g., Tertullian).

Justin's second theological contribution was his use of philosophy specifically to explain who Christ is. The concept of *Logos* was very important in Greek philosophy. This Greek word means "word," "thought," or "reason." In Platonic philosophy specifically (which Justin tended to prefer), God is spirit (nonphysical), infinite, and perfect—the highest form of existence. As such, he is necessarily separated from everything else, especially what is physical, finite, and imperfect—the universe—and needed a "go-between" to have anything to do with it. This intermediary was the Logos, which connected God and the world and through which God could act in the world.

Justin picked up this idea and used it to explain Christ. It was his way of saying, "What philosophers have long thought of as the Logos is what we Christians now understand specifically to be Christ." As Justin notes, this indeed is a biblical concept: "In the beginning was the Word [*logos*], and the Word was with God, and the Word was God" (John 1:1). But what exactly does this mean?

For Justin, the Logos was originally something *within* God, an aspect of his being—his wisdom or reason. When God first created, this divine wisdom was expressed—put into words: "Let there be . . ." (Genesis 1:3, 6). Justin quotes Proverbs 8:25 as support. Wisdom (the Logos) is speaking and says, "Before the mountains were settled in place, before the hills [at creation], I was given birth [or generated, i.e., expressed]." It was through the Logos, then, that God created the material realm. In Old Testament history, it was the Logos *specifically* who appeared, for example, to Abraham (Genesis 18), Moses at the burning bush (Exodus 3), and the Hebrew prophets. Ultimately, the divine Logos was incarnated in the person of Jesus Christ: "The Word became flesh and made his dwelling among us" (John 1:14). So before time, God was a unity, and wisdom/Logos was a part of his being. For the work of creation, he expressed his wisdom/Logos (like a thought is expressed through speech) for the first time and became triune through the expression of his wisdom/Logos and Spirit.

Justin really began the challenging discussion that eventually led to Trinitarian theology. Already Christians believed that Yahweh, the God of the Old Testament, was God, and so was Jesus Christ. But how could that be? What exactly is the relation between Yahweh God and Jesus? How could the infinite God who is spirit become a finite man with a physical body, like Jesus? Christians had not yet asked these tough but important questions. Justin got the ball rolling, and that was a good thing.

However, there are some problems with how Justin went about this. For example, Greek philosophy taught that the "seed" of the divine Logos was really present in *all* human beings in the form of whatever reason or wisdom they possessed. Justin agreed but distinguished Christ by saying that the Logos was only *perfectly* found in him, whereas it was imperfect and incomplete in other humans.

The implication is stated by Justin in one of his more famous statements: "I confess that I both boast and with all my strength strive to be found a Christian; not because the teachings of Plato are different from those of Christ, but because they are not in all respects similar, as neither are those of the others, Stoics, and poets, and historians. For each man spoke well in proportion to the share he had of the seed of the *logos*, seeing what was related to it" (*Second Apology*, 13). According to Justin, Plato was essentially a proto-Christian! It is just that, since Christ has now come, believers in him now have access to *all* truth through him. But can *pagan* philosophy in any way be categorized as Christian?

Another problem with Justin's thought is that it was inconsistent. Most of the time God seems to be a unity, with the Logos being merely an extension of God (his wisdom) or even a creation of God (not God at all). At other times God seems to be a duality—Father and Son—or even a foursome—including the Spirit *and angels* (*First Apology*, 6). Occasionally Justin even talks about "two Gods."[4] Generally, Justin tended to subordinate the Logos/Son to the Father. As we will see, many theologians to follow would continue to do that.

Conclusion

Justin advanced the cause of Christian truth, especially in the challenging area of Trinitarianism, but he also introduced some theological problems that later Christians were going to have to deal with. But Justin is also to be admired for his defense of the intellectual credibility and truthfulness of Christianity and, like Ignatius and many others, for his willingness to die for the truth that he was so convinced of.

4. Jonathan Hill, *The History of Christian Thought* (Downers Grove, IL: InterVarsity, 2003), 23.

4

IRENAEUS

Ardent Anti-Gnostic

Context

Philosophy had a profound impact upon early Christianity. Pagan philosophers used it to attack Christianity, and Christian philosophers (like Justin Martyr) used it to defend Christianity. Greek philosophy also infiltrated Christian thought with devastating effects. One important form of second-century Greek philosophy that affected Christianity in this way was Gnosticism. The term comes from the Greek word *gnōsis*, which means "knowledge." Gnostic Christians believed that salvation was through a secret knowledge that only an elite few could obtain.[1] Another aspect of Gnostic thought is *dualism*.[2] This is the idea that what is spirit is, by definition, good, and what is material is, by definition, evil. An implication is that God, who is spirit and perfectly good, is

---

1. It is possible that Peter (in 2 Peter), Jude, and John (in 1 John) were dealing with an early form of this influence on first-century Christians.
2. We have encountered this concept already in connection with Ignatius.

not the creator of anything material and, in fact, is far removed from the world and totally uninvolved in it. Then who did create the world? In Gnostic thought, the creator is the "Demiurge."[3] God had created a realm of spiritual beings—the Greeks called them "emanations" or "aeons"; we might think of them as angels.[4] These beings were like a series of waves rippling out from God. Those closest to God were very powerful and very good; those further removed were less powerful (although still very powerful) and even capable of evil. The Demiurge was one of the far-removed emanations who was capable of such an evil act as creating the material realm. The "God" of the Old Testament was actually the Demiurge, not the eternal, infinitely perfect Supreme Being. All of this was a significant challenge to orthodox Christian belief, and it was this that was taken on by another apologist, Irenaeus.

Not a lot is known about Irenaeus. He was probably born in the early-middle part of the second century somewhere in Asia Minor (present-day Turkey). He seems to be one of the first significant Christian writers to be born into a Christian family. He is probably best known as a disciple of Bishop Polycarp, who himself was a disciple of the apostle John. Irenaeus eventually moved to Lyon in Gaul (present-day France), and then became bishop of Lyon. According to tradition, he died as a martyr, probably at the beginning of the third century, although the exact nature of his death is uncertain.

Contribution

Irenaeus wrote several books, but the only one that has survived (in the form of a Latin translation of the original Greek) bore the

3. The term comes from two Greek words that together basically mean "creator of people."

4. In some forms of Gnostic Christian theology, Christ was one of these emanations, probably the very highest and closest to God, but not *fully* God. He was the "enlightener," the one who came to reveal the secret knowledge (*gnōsis*) necessary for salvation.

unwieldy title *On the Refutation and Overthrow of the Knowledge Falsely So-called*. It has come to be known as *Against Heresies*. It is a rambling five-volume work that he wrote when he discovered the effects of Gnosticism on the church in Lyon. Irenaeus clearly understood Gnosticism to be a significant threat to Christianity, but also to be absurd and foolish. His refutation of it included not only reason but also ridicule. For example, of one Gnostic teacher he wrote, "Iu, Iu! Pheu, Pheu!—for well may we utter these tragic exclamations at such a pitch of audacity in the coining of names as he has displayed without a blush, in devising a nomenclature for his system of falsehood" (1.11.4). What?! A more contemporary paraphrase could be something like this: "Eewww! Yuck! Gag! Retch! Such outbursts of outrage are the right response to the contemptible conceit he shows in unashamedly using ridiculous rhetoric in his preposterous proposals." Irenaeus described second-century Gnosticism in such detail that much of what is known about it came from his book.

We will consider three of Irenaeus's considerable contributions to Christian thought: his view of God, especially over and against that of the Gnostics; his view of humanity and the humanity of Jesus, especially as it relates to salvation; and his view of Scripture, especially as it relates to the issue of authority for what is to be taught and believed by Christians.

In contrast to Gnosticism, Irenaeus affirmed that the God of Christianity is the one, true God who created *all* things. Even though he did not elaborate on it, he also understood the Son and Spirit to be equal with the Father in their divine being. He referred to them as the "two hands" of the Father by which he created and continues to act in the world. He also referred to the Son as the Logos, but, unlike Justin, did *not* mean that the Son was merely an intermediary between God and the world—just the expression of God's wisdom rather than fully God himself. One of Irenaeus's more famous statements is this: "The Father is the invisible of the Son, but the Son is the visible of the Father" (4.6.6). Also, unlike Justin, who considered God to be far-removed from the world, Irenaeus used the imagery of God holding the world in the palm of his hand to emphasize his intimate involvement in it and close presence to all who inhabit it (e.g., 4.19.2).

Irenaeus believed in the full deity and full humanity of Jesus Christ. It is in the area of humanity in general but also the humanity of Jesus specifically that Irenaeus contributed some unique ideas. In the sixth day of creation, God said, "Let us make man in our image, in our likeness" (Genesis 1:26). Irenaeus understood this to mean that God created humanity initially with the divine "image," but intended for the divine "likeness" to be attained through a process of growth—not just during an individual's lifetime, but through the whole flow of human history.[5] Indeed, Adam and Eve were really created like children, especially in a moral sense; they were immature and childish. Everything that God does is for the purpose of helping humanity to "grow up," even bad things like suffering and death. He used the imagery of God as the potter who desires to mold humans until they are eventually "pure gold and silver" (4.39.2). Irenaeus downplayed the significance of Adam's and Eve's initial sin as childish misbehavior.

Jesus' humanity fits into this in a rather unique way. He was the most important means by which God would help humans to grow to maturity. In fact, since Jesus was divine as well as human, he was God's means of injecting divinity into humanity so that we can enjoy both the divine image and likeness, or, as the apostle Peter wrote, so that we "may participate in the divine nature, having escaped the corruption in the world caused by evil desires" (2 Peter 1:4). As Irenaeus put it: "For it was for this end that the Word of God was made man, and He who was the Son of God became the Son of man, that man, having been taken into the Word, and receiving the adoption, might become the son of God. For by no other means could we have attained to incorruptibility and immortality, unless we had been united to incorruptibility and immortality. But

5. Many early Christian thinkers distinguished between the divine "image" and "likeness" in some sense. It is probably better to understand them as referring to the same thing.

how could we be joined to incorruptibility and immortality, unless, first, incorruptibility and immortality had become that which we also are . . . ?" (3.19.1). Or, more succinctly, "How shall man pass into God, unless God has passed into man?" (4.33.4). This is an early expression of what came to be known as the doctrine of *theosis*, deification, or divinization.

Irenaeus's thought in this area has come to be known as the theory of recapitulation, which basically means a "re-heading" and refers to Jesus becoming the new head of humanity. All of this was in stark contrast to the Gnostic denial of the true humanity of Jesus Christ. Their dualism made it necessary for them to deny the incarnation—that God really took on a human nature including a physical body. In Irenaeus's theology, the incarnation was not only true but *crucial*. In fact, the *entire* human life of Jesus was a part of God's plan of salvation. Based on Romans 5:12–21, Irenaeus taught that Adam was the original head of humanity, but due to his sin, everything went wrong for all humans. However, Jesus became the new head of humanity, and due to his perfect life, everything can now go right for humans. What Adam got wrong for all of us, Jesus got right for all of us. When Adam was tempted, he yielded to it; when Jesus was tempted, he conquered it. Jesus' death was just the culmination of his work of salvation through his entire life. He demonstrated his willingness to obey his Father throughout life, even to the point of death. "God recapitulated in [Christ, the *Logos*] the ancient formation of man, that He might kill sin, deprive death of its power, and vivify man . . ." (3.18.7). Irenaeus's understanding of the life and work of Jesus was adopted by many Christian thinkers after him and really became the controlling idea for quite some time.

One criticism of Irenaeus is his downplaying the unique significance of the death of Jesus. He really did not emphasize the death of Jesus that much. It was only important as a part of Jesus' entire life, all of which had saving value. On the other hand, Jesus himself said that he came not to *live* his life, but rather "to *give* his life as a ransom for many" (Mark 10:45; cf. Matthew 26:28). The apostles also emphasized that it was the *death* of Jesus that provides salvation (Romans 3:23–25; Galatians 3:13; Ephesians 2:13; Hebrews 2:9; 13:12; 1 Peter 1:18–19; 3:18; 1 John 1:7).

The third theological contribution of Irenaeus that we will consider has to do with authority, tradition, and Scripture. This also relates to his refutation of Gnostic Christians who made the claim that what they taught was traced back to Christ and the apostles but passed along *secretly*. Irenaeus's question was, if the apostles had taught Gnosticism, why had they not *openly* passed it on to the churches that they founded? In contrast, what was abundantly clear was that churches throughout the empire publicly and consistently taught what orthodox Christians had believed all along (3.3.1). This was known as "tradition," or literally, "what is handed down" from the apostles through the generations of churches and Christians. It was this oral tradition that was eventually written down in Scripture. "Orthodox Christianity and Gnosticism are two religions, with two different sets of Scriptures. The question is: which religion and which set of Scriptures goes back to Christ and the apostles? It is this question which is answered by Irenaeus's argument—and it is hard to see how it could be answered otherwise."[6]

Irenaeus was one of the first to speak of the documents that make up our New Testament as "Scriptures," that is, equivalent in truthfulness and authority to the Hebrew Scriptures (the Old Testament). He was also the first to refer to them as the "New" covenant or testament (4.9.1). He specifically mentions twenty-three of the twenty-seven books of the New Testament.[7] These newer books had not yet been "officially" recognized as the Word of God (and would not be for several more centuries), but a basis of truth was needed in order to fight false teaching. Irenaeus understood this basis to be the apostolic teachings passed along both in oral and written form.

---

6. Tony Lane, *A Concise History of Christian Thought*, rev. ed. (Grand Rapids: Baker, 2006), 13.

7. All except Philemon, James, Jude, and 3 John; Paul Wegner, *The Journey from Texts to Translations* (Grand Rapids: Baker, 1999), 139.

Conclusion

Irenaeus should be commended for creating "a prototype of Christian theology and what is probably (even if cumbersome) the most thorough of all the earliest explanations of the Christian faith."[8] It is unclear how much immediate impact he had, specifically in relation to the onslaught of Gnosticism, but his thought provided a significant contribution to Christian theologians who would soon follow.

8. William Anderson, *A Journey Through Christian Tradition*, 2nd ed. (Minneapolis: Fortress Press, 2010), 23.

5

TERTULLIAN

Latin Lawyer

Context

This apologist has been considered one of the best theological minds of the second century. He was the first to write in Latin, rather than Greek, and therefore had a profound impact on the theology of the Latin or Western church. As we will see, he also anticipated and set the stage for the great Trinitarian councils and creeds that would come several centuries later.

Tertullian was born sometime in the middle of the second century (150–160) into a Roman family living in Carthage in North Africa. He was trained as a lawyer and became a Christian as an adult. Immediately, he used his sharp legal mind to begin to defend Christianity from its many detractors from outside the church and also to criticize those with whom he disagreed inside the church. Eventually he embraced a sect of Christianity known as Montanism (after its founder, Montanus), which was characterized by belief in ongoing divine revelation beyond that recorded in the Old and

New Testaments, belief in the imminent return of Christ, and commitment to a vigorous and ascetic morality in light of the impending end of the world. This sect was eventually condemned by the orthodox catholic church, and Tertullian then turned his written wrath on the orthodox church. The time (c. 220–225) and manner of his death is unknown. Some suggest that he died of natural causes at an advanced age. Others suggest that he died as one of the martyrs he so admired. One of his more famous statements is, "The oftener we are mown down by [persecutors], the more in number we grow; the blood of Christians is seed" (*Apology*, 50).

Contribution

Tertullian's writing style and rhetoric have been described as having the exactness of a legal document, but also as witty, mocking, sarcastic, polemical, brutal, black-and-white, and uncompromising. He was "incapable of being dull" and "an apologist who never apologized."[1] Despite his brilliance, Tertullian seems to have fallen short of being charitable to those with whom he disagreed, as Scripture commands (2 Timothy 2:24–25; Titus 3:2; 1 Peter 3:15). One writer suggests that what Tertullian most anticipated in heaven was a good view of the enemies of Christianity suffering in hell.[2]

He was also amazingly prolific, producing more than thirty books on a wide range of topics. One important topic was Christian morality and how to deal with Christians who live anything less than highly moral lives. This is the subject of *On Repentance*, which he wrote while still loyal to the orthodox catholic church. His acute moral sensitivity is actually what attracted him to Montanism. He wrote *On Modesty* after switching his allegiance to this sect. He also wrote numerous books on practical Christian issues, for example, *On Prayer*, *On Baptism*, *On Fasting*, and *On the Apparel of Women.*

1. Quoted by Tony Lane, *A Concise History of Christian Thought*, 15.
2. Jonathan Hill, *The History of Christian Thought*, 33. He quotes Tertullian's *On Spectacles*, 30.

As an apologist, he continued in the lines of Justin and Irenaeus by defending Christianity, but he also took giant intellectual steps beyond them. In stark contrast to Justin, however, Tertullian condemned the use of philosophy by Christians. In *Prescription Against Heretics*, he famously asked, "What indeed has Athens to do with Jerusalem? What concord is there between the Academy and the Church? What is there between heretics and Christians?" (7). He went so far as to suggest that philosophy always leads to heresy. The "prescription" was to totally avoid philosophy as a means of understanding Scripture and the things of God. In reality, Tertullian's own thought had been clearly influenced by philosophy, specifically Stoicism. There is a lesson to be learned here: Tertullian's warning is well-taken. We must be careful not to let mere human wisdom control our understanding of biblical truth (Colossians 2:8; 1 Timothy 6:20). There are things taught in Scripture that are beyond our perfect understanding and explanation. However, Tertullian also demonstrated that there are factors in all of our lives that do indeed influence our interpretation of Scripture, even though we do not want them to. To deny this is to be naïve. To acknowledge it is to be on guard against these factors and dependent upon the Holy Spirit to overcome them and lead us into truth.

Like Irenaeus, Tertullian attacked false teaching in general and specifically Gnosticism, for example, in his *Prescription Against Heretics*, *Against Hermogenes*, and *Against Valentinians*. Tertullian's longest work was the five-volume *Against Marcion*. Tertullian's object of scorn here was a very influential second-century teacher whose understanding of Christianity was influenced by Gnosticism. For example, Marcion distinguished between the God of the Old Testament—who was angry and vengeful, favorable only to Jews, and unworthy of worship—and the God of the New Testament—who was loving and gracious, the Father of Jesus Christ, and alone worthy of worship. He rejected the Old Testament entirely and also parts of the New Testament that he thought were too Jewish, for example, Matthew, Mark, and Hebrews. He accepted most of Luke's writings and Paul's epistles with the exception of the Pastoral Epistles (1 and 2 Timothy, Titus).

Probably Tertullian's greatest contribution was regarding the doctrine of the Trinity, and much of this came in his book *Against Praxeas*. Praxeas's concern was to uphold monotheism—that there is only one true God—over and against ditheism (the Father and Son are two gods) or tritheism (the Spirit is yet a third god). The term *monarchianism* is applied to this concern; it means "sole rule," that is, there is only one ultimate ruler over all things, not two or three. Praxeas ended up suggesting that the one true God operates in three different roles or modes—Father, Son, and Spirit. This view is called "modalism." The idea is attractive because it makes this "mystery" of God less mysterious. Each one of us is one person with many roles. I am a son, brother, husband, father, teacher, writer, handyman, etc. But is this an adequate understanding of the being of God—one divine person with multiple roles?

Tertullian coined the term *patripassianism* for this view. It means "the suffering of the Father" and was used by Tertullian to refute the idea. If modalism is correct, then the Father was the one who suffered and died on the cross, since the Father *is* the Son. The problem is that God cannot die. Furthermore, according to modalism, when Jesus cried out, "My God, my God, why have you forsaken me?" (Matthew 27:46), he was really talking to himself since the Son *is* the Father (*Against Praxeas*, 30). When Jesus said, "Not my will, but yours be done" (Luke 22:42), he was really saying, "Not my will, but mine be done." Modalism simply does not make sense of these and other Gospel narratives in which the three Persons of the Godhead are present and interacting (e.g., the baptism of Jesus and the High Priestly Prayer of Jesus in John 17).

Tertullian did more than refute Praxeas's views; he also stated a positive doctrine of the Trinity. In doing so, he coined or introduced terms that were not only helpful in stating the doctrine but also became the terms that would be used for centuries to come. For example, Tertullian was the first to use the word *trinitas*—Trinity. He introduced into the discussion the term *substantia* (substance), which refers to essential qualities that make something what it is. Tertullian also employed the word *persona*. This Latin word literally means "mask," such as an actor would wear in order to portray a character in a play. Docetists[3] used this imagery, saying that, as one actor could portray multiple roles in a play just by switching masks, so God, who is one individual, can play multiple roles. However, Tertullian used *persona* to emphasize the *multiple* characters in the play, not the *one* actor who portrayed them. The audience would perceive that the characters were different by their *relationships*, as seen in the way that they act and interact on stage. The same actor could *not* play two roles on the stage *at the same time*. But this is exactly what God has done on the stage of creation, history, and salvation, as demonstrated in the Gospel narratives noted above. Jesus was being baptized; the Father was verbally identifying Jesus as his beloved Son, and the Spirit was descending as a dove on Jesus (Matthew 3:16–17). How could one actor do all three things *at the same time*? Rather, God was demonstrating that, in addition to his unity, there are also distinctions in that unity; those distinctions are evident through their relationships and can be called "persons." This is also implied in the very terms *Father* and *Son*. How could a father be his own son or a son his own father? Yet Jesus said, "I and [My] Father are one" (John 10:30).[4] So, to use Tertullian's helpful terminology, God is *una substantia, tres personae*—one "substance" and three "persons."

However, Tertullian did not want to be accused of promoting tritheism. So he addressed the concern of modalistic monarchians such as Praxeas by insisting that there was indeed only one true God who alone ruled over all. Unfortunately, the way he did this set the stage for some problems. Whereas Justin seemed to imply that the Son and Spirit were simply extensions or expressions of the wisdom of God, thus depersonalizing them, Tertullian was unambiguous about both the eternal deity and personhood of

3. We were introduced to Docetism in chapter 2.
4. The Greek and Latin grammar of this verse also indicate that by "one," Jesus meant one essence or nature (deity), not one person.

the Son and Spirit. But to avoid accusations of being tritheistic, Tertullian argued that both monotheism—there is only one God—and monarchianism—there is only one ruler—are true because there is one divine *source* of all—God the *Father*. The Son and Spirit, then, find their source in the Father and are the Father's means of creating and working in his creation. The unfortunate implication is that the Son and Spirit are really subordinate to the Father since the Father, as their source, is really greater than them. But Tertullian's point was that it is the *Father alone* who is the "monarch." This way of thinking came to be known as *subordinationism*. Tertullian used the imagery of the Father as the root, the Son as the tree, and the Spirit as the fruit (*Against Praxeas*, 8). The problem was that this suggested inequality within the being of God. Many theologians followed Tertullian in this; others profoundly rejected it.

Tertullian used the same terminology he introduced in his discussion of the nature of God in his discussion of Jesus Christ, and in doing so also clarified the issue more than those who preceded him. Whereas God is one "substance" and three "persons"—Father, Son, and Spirit—Jesus Christ is one "person" and two "substances"—deity and humanity. As Tertullian argued, one of the reasons that Jesus *had* to be truly human is because God cannot die; only a true human with a true physical body can die. If, as Gnostic Christians claimed, Jesus only *appeared* to be human, then his death only *appeared* to be real, and, if so, there is no true sacrifice for sin and no salvation. It was the true human nature of Jesus, not his divine nature, that suffered and died on the cross.

To his credit, Tertullian admitted that much of this was beyond human reason, but, for him, that was exactly what made it believable: "But, after all, you will not be 'wise' unless you become a 'fool' to the world, by believing the 'foolish things of God.' . . . The Son of God died; it is by all means to be believed, because it is absurd. And He was buried, and rose again; the fact is certain, because it is impossible" (*On the Flesh of Christ*, 5). Amazing truths such as these could never be the invention of the human mind and must therefore be divine reality.

Conclusion

Tertullian's thought was brilliant but did not come to fruition until several centuries later. Why? First, he was probably ignored by orthodox Christians in the West because of his defection to Montanism and criticism of the orthodox catholic church. Second, he was overlooked by Eastern Christians because he wrote in Latin rather than Greek. Nevertheless, his ideas and his terminology were taken up in the great church councils and reflected in the great creeds of the church, as we will see. Even though Tertullian's writing style was rather harsh and mean-spirited, his thoughts were immensely important in the development of theology, especially in the all-important areas of God as Trinity and Jesus Christ as the God-man.

6

CLEMENT OF ALEXANDRIA

Alexandrian Academic

Context

Gnosticism was rampant in the second century, especially in Egypt. It also had a profound impact on Christianity at that time and in that place. As we have seen, it came about by liberally applying Greek philosophy to Christianity. Justin Martyr thought that philosophy and Christianity worked well together; in fact, he said Christianity is nothing other than the ultimate philosophy. Tertullian went in the opposite direction: Christianity and philosophy were mutually exclusive; in fact, philosophy led to heresy. Our next two late-second–early third-century Christian thinkers—Clement and Origen, both from Egypt—veered back in the direction of Justin, and not only allowed philosophy to affect their theology, but also explicitly advocated for this being a good and necessary thing.

Not much detail is known about the life of Titus Flavius Clemens, who came to be known as Clement of Alexandria. It seems that he was born into a pagan family in the middle second century and converted to Christianity. He was taught by various Christian teachers, the last being Pantaenus, who was the head of the Christian school in Alexandria, Egypt. Eventually, Clement succeeded him in this position toward the end of the second century. When persecution was threatening Christians in Egypt in the early years of the third century, Clement fled and died in Asia Minor sometime before 216.

Contribution

Five of Clement's written works have survived. *Exhortation to the Heathen* is an apologetic work against paganism, but it is here that Clement also argues for the appropriate use of philosophy in Christian thought. *The Instructor* focuses on Jesus Christ as the *Logos* who is the divine instructor. This is primarily a guide for the new Christian regarding obedience, simple living (over against uncontrolled desires), and living according to reason, wisdom, and the things taught by the *Logos*. In *Miscellanies* (also known by the Greek title, *Stromata*), Clement blends philosophy with many other sources into a complex yet fairly comprehensive Christian theology/ philosophy. It is called *Miscellanies* because it is a little bit of a lot of things, which a quick survey of the chapter titles of its eight books reveals. These three are Clement's primary works. Lesser important works are *Who Is the Rich Man That Shall Be Saved?* which is an interpretation of Jesus' words to the rich young ruler in Matthew 19:16–26, and fragments of *The Writings of Theodotus*.

With regard to philosophy and Christianity, Clement was particularly enamored by Platonism. He did acknowledge Paul's warning against philosophy in Colossians 2:8 but applied it, not to philosophy in general, but to *bad* philosophy, such as Epicureanism, which challenged Platonic thought by denying any involvement of the gods in human affairs, denying immortality of humans, and affirming pleasure as the highest good. Rather, Clement believed that there were many parallels between Platonic philosophy and biblical truth, for example, the belief in one ultimate Supreme Being, the immortality of the soul, and the priority of spiritual realities over material realities.

Like Justin before him, Clement saw Greek philosophy as containing divine truth, which borrowed from the Hebrew Scriptures and anticipated the Christian Scriptures:

> Accordingly, before the advent of the Lord, philosophy was necessary to the Greeks for righteousness. And now it becomes helpful to piety; being a kind of preparatory training to those who attain to faith through demonstration. . . . For God is the cause of all good things; but of some primarily, as of the Old and the New Testament; and of others by consequence, as philosophy. Perchance, too, philosophy was given to the Greeks directly and primarily, till the Lord should call the Greeks. For this was a schoolmaster to bring the Greek mind to Christ, as the law [the Old Testament] did for the Hebrews. Philosophy, therefore, was a preparation, paving the way for him who is perfected in Christ. (*Miscellanies* 1.5)

In addition, philosophy is good because it provides a way of thinking—logically and critically—that can be beneficially applied to ideas in general and the interpretation of Scripture specifically:

> [P]hilosophy, being the search for truth, contributes to the comprehension of truth; not as being the cause of comprehension, but a cause along with other things, and co-operator; perhaps also a joint cause. . . . [S]o while truth is one, many things contribute to its investigation. But its discovery is by the Son. . . . [I]f philosophy contributes remotely to the discovery of truth, by reaching, by diverse essays, after the knowledge which touches close on the truth, the knowledge possessed by us, it aids him who aims at grasping it, in accordance with the Word, to apprehend knowledge. . . . Perspicuity accordingly aids in the communication of truth, and logic in preventing us from falling under the heresies by which we are assailed. But the teaching, which is according to the Savior, is complete in itself and without defect, being "the power and wisdom of God"; and the Greek philosophy does not, by its approach, make the truth more powerful; but rendering powerless the assault of sophistry against it, and frustrating the treacherous plots laid against the truth, is said to be the proper "fence and wall of the vineyard" (*Miscellanies*, 1.20).

As Roger Olson notes, "This is ironic in light of Tertullian's denunciation of philosophy as the *cause* of heresies among Christians! For Clement, philosophy could serve as a *curative* of heresies among them."[1]

Another effect of Greek philosophy on Clement's thought was that of denigrating the material/physical realm and praising the soulish/spiritual realm. It was in the latter that a person's rationality would be found. This did not, however, cause Clement to go as far as dualism; he did believe that God created the material realm, not some lesser Demiurge, and denied that the material realm was evil by definition. Neither did he opt for Docetism; he clearly affirmed the full deity and full humanity/physicality of Jesus. His high view of the Person of Jesus Christ is seen in this statement from *The Instructor*: "Now, O you, my children, our Instructor is like His Father God, whose son He is, sinless, blameless, and with a soul devoid of passion; *God in the form of man*, stainless, the minister of His Father's will, the Word [*Logos*] *who is God*, who is in the Father, who is at the Father's right hand, and with the form of God *is God*" (1.2, emphasis added). Notice his description of Christ as having "a soul devoid of passion." This reflects the influence of Greek philosophy and is an important part of Clement's ideal for all Christians.

This ideal Christian was called by Clement the "true Gnostic." He is not bowing to Gnosticism here, but rather expressing that all Christians should move completely beyond pursuing physical pleasures and satisfying material desires, and attain to a purely rational state of existence in which the exercise of wisdom results in goodness and virtue. Clement defines the term as follows: "He is the Gnostic, who is after the image and likeness of God, who imitates God as far as possible, deficient in none of the things which contribute to the likeness as far as compatible, practicing self-restraint and endurance, living righteously, reigning over the passions, bestowing of what he has as far as possible, and doing good both by word and deed" (*Miscellanies*, 2.19). When he says

1. Olson, *The Story of Christian Theology*, 88.

"reigning over the passions," he really means completely devoid of passions or emotions. Why? Because that is how God is, at least according to Greek philosophy. The term for this, as we have seen before, is "impassibility." The supreme being of Greek philosophy was just this—emotionless, unmoved, unruffled, perfectly in control of himself, and perfectly rational in all things. This was also Clement's conception of God. What about biblical descriptions of, for example, the wrath or love of God? Clement explained these as figures of speech that describe not God as he really is, but God as he is perceived by humans. In reality, God has no such emotions.

Jesus Christ is our "instructor" in the sense that he embodies this ideal and leads us into it. This is very much like the concept of "divinization"—sharing in the divine nature—that would become a hallmark of Eastern Orthodox Christian thought.[2]

Conclusion

So how much should philosophy and theology interact? Maybe a balance between Tertullian and Clement is desirable. As Tertullian noted, God's thoughts and actions are not *completely* understandable by small human minds (Isaiah 55:8–9). So we should be careful to avoid "dumbing down" biblical truths into categories of human comprehension or forcing biblical truths into philosophical categories and ideas (Clement, at points, being guilty of the latter). On the other hand, as Clement rightly notes, God has given us brains (though limited) to use and truth to think about and understand (though imperfectly). Philosophy *can* be helpful in sharpening our thinking abilities and is useful for that benefit.

The debate about philosophy and theology would continue to rage. Clement's inclination toward Greek philosophy was passed on and taken even further by his student and our next Christian thinker, Origen.

2. See chapter 4.

7

ORIGEN

Egyptian Enigma

Context

Theological hero or heretic? That is the question regarding Origen.
He is universally recognized as an amazing intellect, but there is a
split decision regarding whether his intellect led him in the right
way or astray. Either way, he had a huge influence on theology.

Unlike most of those we have considered so far, much is known
about the life of Origen. He was born into a Christian family in
Alexandria, Egypt, around 185. He was given an excellent education and showed great intellectual giftedness early on. He was also
very devoted to his Christian faith. When his father was arrested
as a Christian and executed, young Origen wanted to join him in
martyrdom, but his mother hid his clothes, preventing him from
leaving the safety of their home.[1] Modesty prevented martyrdom.
When persecution forced Clement to leave Alexandria, Origen was
asked to succeed him as the head of the Christian school, which

1. Eusebius, *Ecclesiastical History*, 6.2.

he did when he was only eighteen years old! He too was the object of persecution and came to be nicknamed *Adamantius*, meaning "unyielding" or "unbreakable."

Very quickly, his fame as an intellectual and teacher began to spread. He had studied and mastered many philosophical systems but eventually decided to devote himself strictly to the study of Scripture. Not only was he devoted to Christianity in an intellectual sense, but also in a spiritual and moral sense. He lived a very strict, ascetic lifestyle, partly out of poverty, but also in order to be pleasing to God. Eusebius, an ancient historian, records that, in his desire to be holy, Origen took Matthew 19:12 in a very literal sense and made himself a eunuch for the kingdom of heaven's sake.[2]

Eventually, Origen moved to Caesarea in Judea where he was ordained as a priest. This prompted Demetrius, the bishop of Alexandria and former student of Origen, to turn against his teacher, probably motivated by jealousy of Origen's growing fame and influence. He persuaded his fellow Egyptian bishops to condemn Origen due to some of his teachings, and excommunicate him. The local bishops in Judea, however, continued to support Origen, he continued his work, and his fame and influence continued to spread.

In 249 the new emperor, Decius, initiated a new wave of persecution of Christians, particularly directed at their leaders. As a result, Origen was arrested and tortured in order to force him to recant. However, "Unbreakable" remained unbreakable. He was released, but the torture had taken its physical toll, and Origen died around the year 254.

Origen's views caused considerable controversy during his lifetime. After his death, "Origenists" continued to promote his views, some taking them even further than Origen himself. Others, however, continued to accuse many of Origen's views of being unorthodox, even heretical. At the Second Council of Constantinople in 553, the order was given to destroy his written works, essentially declaring him to be a heretic. As a result, the vast majority of Origen's literary effort (which was vast) has been lost forever.

2. Ibid., 6.8.

Contribution

Origen's writing was greatly benefitted by a wealthy friend who converted to Christianity through Origen's influence, and then basically paid for a team of stenographers, scribes, and calligraphers to record what Origen dictated and turn it into publishable material. As a result of Origen's productive mind and this efficient means of writing, he became one of the most prolific writers of the ancient world, if not of all time. Eight hundred titles are connected to Origen, from shorter letters, essays, and sermons to lengthy volumes, including detailed commentaries on many books of the Bible. Origen was one of the first to write commentaries on the books of the Bible. He was a pioneer in the Christian study of the Old Testament, and he learned to read Hebrew in order to do so.

First and foremost, Origen wanted to be an *orthodox* and *biblical* theologian. He wanted his beliefs to be based upon apostolic tradition and the written Word of God. However, he was clearly influenced by philosophy as well. In his *Letter to Gregory*, Origen commended the use of philosophy and secular learning in general for understanding Scripture, and used the analogy of what the Hebrews did to the Egyptians leading up to the Exodus (Exodus 12:36). As a result, the phrase "despoiling of the Egyptians" came to apply to the use of secular ideas in Christian theology. As we will see, this had a profound effect on Origen's thinking and theology.

Origen's two most important works are *Against Celsus* and *On First Principles*. The former, which alone among Origen's writings survived in the original Greek, was probably the greatest Christian apologetic work to come from the early centuries. Celsus was a pagan philosopher who had attacked Christianity in a book entitled *On the True Doctrine*, the "true doctrine" being Greek philosophy. Origen's *Against Celsus*, more than any other previous apologetic work, made Christianity respectable, at least in an intellectual sense.

Origen's other great work, *On First Principles*, available only in Latin translations, was really the first systematic Christian theology. In it, Origen attempted to produce a comprehensive Christian philosophy or theology.

We will start with his view of Scripture, since he tried to base everything he believed on it, and he did quote liberally from the Bible throughout his writings. He clearly believed that it was the very Word of God inspired through the Holy Spirit. This is why he wrote so many commentaries on the books of the Bible.

However, from Clement, his predecessor in Alexandria, Origen adopted the idea that only "true Gnostic" Christians could get to the most important part of Scripture, and that was *not* the literal text—what it said on the surface. Rather, what is really important in Scripture is the "deeper meaning." Origen found this "deeper meaning" helpful in dealing with pagan critics, such as Celsus, who ridiculed some of what the Bible said for being illogical or ridiculous—for example, descriptions of God as having emotions, especially wrath. Origen also thought these to be illogical and ridiculous *on the surface*. But the real, deeper meaning intended by the Holy Spirit was under the surface. The exegetes' goal, then, was to search for the deeper, fuller, real meaning of the text. All of this was readily available in the Bible to all Christians if they would only look for it, but only a few ever find it.

How was this deeper meaning discovered? Origen's answer was through allegorical interpretation, an approach to literature that was common in his day. This method involved looking at every word in every biblical text, specifically narratives, in light of the use of that word in the rest of Scripture. That was what he did in his commentaries, and that was why his commentaries were so long! He believed that Scripture had three levels of meaning corresponding to humans as body, soul, and spirit. The literal or surface sense corresponds to the body. This is the least important. The moral or ethical sense corresponds to soul. This tells us how to live. And the doctrinal or theological sense corresponds to spirit. This tells us what to believe.[3]

---

3. For example, in a sermon on Genesis, Origen explained Lot's incestuous relationships with his daughters (Genesis 19:30–38) as follows: The literal sense is that this sin actually happened after the judgment of Sodom and Gomorrah. In a moral sense, Lot himself represents the human mind, his wife represents the human flesh inclined to pleasures, and his daughters to pride. In a doctrinal sense,

Allegorical interpretation is certainly valid. New Testament writers understood Old Testament things as pointing ahead to Jesus Christ (e.g., the tabernacle/temple, animal sacrifices, and the life of David as anticipating Jesus). The apostle Paul himself used allegorical interpretation in Galatians 4:21–31. However, the well-known weakness of using allegorical interpretation is how easy it becomes to import one's own ideas and beliefs into the biblical text. If something in Scripture does not seem to be appropriate to one's notion of God (e.g., God described as having emotions, something Greek philosophy denied), then it obviously means something else. But isn't this backward? Should not the Word of God shape our understanding of God and not the other way around, even when the other way around does not necessarily make sense to us? Origen's allegorization can especially be seen in his theology of God, as we will see next.

Appropriately, the "first principle" for Origen was God, but his notion of God was very much shaped by Platonic philosophy (although this was not at all what Origen intended consciously). This influence is clear in the following: "God, therefore, is not to be thought of as being either a body or as existing in a body, but as an *uncompounded intellectual nature*. . . . He is in all parts *Unity*, and, so to speak, *Oneness*, and is the *mind* and source from which all intellectual nature or mind takes its beginning." The divine nature is "simple and wholly intellectual" (*On First Principles*, 1.1.6, emphasis added). According to Origen, God is basically reason/mind and unity/oneness.

Origen also clearly believed in the Trinity, but with a catch: the Father, Son, and Spirit are equally God, but not all God equally. That probably needs some explanation! Origen recognized that Scripture taught the deity of Jesus Christ and of the Spirit. Thus, there are three persons who equally share the divine nature. However, this presented a problem for Origen, who, like Celsus and

---

Lot represents the Old Testament Law, his wife represents the rebellious Israelites, and his daughters represent Jerusalem and Samaria, the capitals of Israel and Judea. William W. Klein, Craig L. Blomber, and Robert L. Hubbard, Jr., *Introduction to Biblical Interpretation* (Dallas: Word, 1993), 34–35.

other Greek philosophers, emphasized the perfect unity or oneness of God. How could God who is one also be three? To solve this, he suggested (very much as Tertullian had) that the unity of God is to be found in God the *Father*, who is the divine source of all things, including the Son and the Spirit. This is not to suggest that there was a time when the Son and Spirit did not exist. To be God, they had to be eternal. Origen explained this through the doctrine of "eternal generation": The Father is eternal and *unbegotten*, whereas the Son is eternal and *begotten* or *generated*. After quoting John 1:1, Origen commented, "Let him, then, who assigns a beginning to the Word [*Logos*] or Wisdom of God [the Son], take care that he be not guilty of impiety against the *unbegotten* Father Himself, seeing he denies that He had *always* been a Father, and had [always] *generated the Word*. . . ." (*On First Principles*, 1.2.3, emphasis added). The same would be true of the Spirit. So God is *one* in that the Father is the single source of everything. And God is *three* in that the Son and Spirit share in the very same nature or essence of the Father as their eternal source.

The problem, however, (as with Tertullian) is that this essentially subordinates the Son and Spirit to the Father; there is inequality within the Trinity. For example, in his commentary on the Gospel of John, Origen wrote: "[Thus] we say that the Savior, and the Holy Spirit, transcend all the creatures, not by degree but by a transcendence beyond measure. But he [the Son, like the Holy Spirit] is transcended by the Father as much as, or even more than, he and the Holy Spirit transcend the other creatures, even the highest."[4] Even though elsewhere Origen seems to speak as if the Son and Spirit are completely equal to the Father (he was not consistent in this and other matters), he does seem to be guilty of generally subordinating the Son and Spirit to the Father—the Father, Son, and Spirit are equally God, but not all God equally. Ironically, Origen would be used to support opposite sides in the great theological controversies that were soon to come.

4. Michael A. G. Haykin, *Rediscovering the Church Fathers: Who They Were and How They Shaped the Church* (Wheaton: Crossway, 2011), 75.

A few other unique ideas from Origen, all of which reflect Greek thought, are these: He believed in the preexistence of souls, that is, God created them prior to their being united with a physical body. These preexistent souls reflect the rational nature of God and are essentially "minds" with free will. These minds eventually used that freedom (apparently being bored with adoring God!) to rebel against God and fell to various degrees—the greatest being that of Satan and demons, the least being that of holy angels, and humans being somewhere in between. The human soul of Jesus was one of these—however, one that stayed closest to God and did not rebel.

Salvation is the divine work of reversing this fall and bringing all things back into a final oneness with God, what the apostle Paul referred to when he wrote, "so that God may be all in all" (1 Corinthians 15:28; *On First Principles*, 3.6). This is Origen's distinctive doctrine of *apokatastasis* or final "reconciliation." Since everything came from one source—God—everything must return to that source. Origen was even accused of teaching that Satan could or would be a part of this ultimate reconciliation—Satan would be "saved"! Apparently Origen disputed that he believed this; however, he does seem to adopt a universalism otherwise, that *all* will eventually be reunited with God. So if he were consistent (which he wasn't), he should indeed believe in the ultimate salvation of Satan. Origen believed in the concept of hell but did not believe that it is eternal or ultimately punishment for sin. Rather, it is temporary and ultimately for purification from sin so that the soul can eventually be reunited with God. What about resurrection? This concept was repugnant to Greeks, who considered the body evil and a prison for the soul. Salvation for the Greeks was to be released from the physical body forever. Origen seemed to hedge by saying that there will be resurrection, but the resurrection body will be "spiritual," as Paul said in 1 Corinthians 15:44, and not material.

Furthermore, salvation involves turning away from lustful desires and becoming like God through the contemplation of God through Scripture. Since God is essentially intellect, according to Origen, salvation and sanctification, which are one and the same, are primarily intellectual—a lifelong process. As we have already seen, this is essentially the doctrine of *theosis* or divinization.

Conclusion

We can learn from Origen that brilliant people (which Origen was) don't always get it right. Therefore, all of us (especially those of us who aren't brilliant) need to be very humble as we seek to understand the Bible. We can also learn that commitment to believing only what Scripture says (which Origen did) does not guarantee that other factors will not influence our understanding of Scripture. There are cultural factors for all of us—for example, our own worldview and the influence of other worldviews—that affect how we interpret the Bible. Therefore, we need to be very dependent upon God's Spirit to overcome these factors and guide us into the truth of his Word. Third, we learn from Origen that commitment to being intellectual Christians is not mutually exclusive to being spiritual Christians. We are to use our minds to know God and his Word, but it should not stop there. What we know and believe from the Bible should affect how we live and who we are becoming. Origen demonstrated that through the way he lived and the way he died.

8

CYPRIAN OF CARTHAGE

Leadership in Persecution

Context

Thascius Cyprianus was born at the very beginning of the third century into a wealthy, upper-class, pagan family in Carthage, North Africa. He enjoyed the pleasures of wealth and privilege before converting to Christianity in his forties.[1] Very quickly he was ordained as a priest, and soon after that he became bishop of Carthage. He died as a martyr about ten years later, in 258, in the persecution of Emperor Valerian.

The context in which he wrote was the pastoral challenges he faced as bishop. For him, the issues were primarily practical, not intellectual. The most pressing problem was a new wave of persecution instigated by the emperor, Decius, beginning in 249 and ending several years later. As we saw in the previous chapter, this was initially directed at the leaders of the church, such as Origen. Cyprian was also threatened, but he fled into the North African

1. He explained his own conversion in his *Letter to Donatus*.

desert where he was protected. Some criticized Cyprian for fleeing the persecution, but others defended him, since, during this time in exile, he continued to give leadership to the church through a flurry of letters. Over eighty letters are a part of his legacy, most written by him but also some written to him.

Another aspect of the persecution was the requirement that all Christians were to offer sacrifices to the gods or be executed. Unfortunately, many yielded to this demand, and, at least by this action, renounced their faith in Christ. They were known as the *lapsi*, the "lapsed" or "fallen." The previous practice of the church had been to remove these people from the church and not allow them to rejoin. However, since so *many* of the fallen were seeking readmission to the church, the procedure had to be rethought.

The questions faced by Cyprian and other church leaders were these: First, how was this to be handled? Should the fallen be re-admitted at all, or immediately after they repented, or only after a more extended period of penance? Second, who should decide and then carry out the decision? Out of this situation came the two most important literary contributions of Cyprian.

Contribution

With regard to *how* the fallen were to be handled, Cyprian wrote *On the Lapsed*. His was the more moderate position—they could be readmitted to the church, but only after a period of penance, or acts of repentance. Not surprisingly, others wanted a stricter treatment—no readmission to the church at all. Yet others wanted a more lenient treatment—immediate forgiveness and restoration.

This raised the next question: *Who* should decide and carry out the decision; that is, who had the authority to grant forgiveness and restoration? Cyprian's answer is found in his second important book, *On the Unity of the Church*, where he argued that the deci-sion should be made and carried out by the *legitimate* authorities of the church, namely, the bishops. Others, however, argued that many of these bishops had themselves "lapsed" or fled persecution (as Cyprian himself had) and thus forfeited their authority. So those who had suffered persecution but had not yielded—called "confessors"—were the *new* legitimate authorities of the church, and they alone should have the power to declare the "fallen" forgiven and readmit them to the church.

Cyprian's position resulted in an authority structure in the church that would not be challenged until the Protestant Reformation in the sixteenth century. We have seen how Clement of Rome and Ignatius of Antioch emphasized the importance of bishops, who were to protect Christian truth and church unity because of "apostolic succession," that is, their authority is derived from the apostles who got it from Jesus. In the century or so that separated them from Cyprian, the office of bishop (*episkopos* or "overseer") had changed from a leader in a local church to a leader of many churches in an area ("see" or "diocese"). Cyprian wholeheartedly agreed with Clement and Ignatius and took this view a giant step forward. It became the basis for his answer to the question, Who has the right to forgive and restore fallen Christians? His answer was, Only those who have received spiritual authority through the generations of bishops going back to the apostles, and whose authority is recognized by the majority of other bishops. Most "confessors" could not claim that heritage or recognition, and therefore they had no right to forgive and restore anyone.

Cyprian took the concept of apostolic succession yet another step further: The church is essentially *identified* in the bishops, and the unity of the church is found in the unity of the bishops. After quoting Matthew 16:18–19, where Jesus tells Peter that he will build his church on "this rock," Cyprian wrote, "Thence, through the changes of times and successions, the ordering of bishops and the plan of the Church flow onwards; so that *the Church is founded upon the bishops*, and every act of the Church is controlled by these same rulers" (Epistle 26, *To the Lapsed*, 1, emphasis added). Therefore, according to Cyprian, churches founded and led by "confessors"—the "break-away" churches at that time—were not legitimate churches because they were not led by legitimate spiritual authorities.

The question of authority also extended to functions in the church, for example, the administration of the sacraments like baptism and the Lord's Supper. Who could perform these? Cyprian's answer: only the bishops and those ordained by the bishops, namely, priests. Those who had been baptized by someone other than a bishop or priest had not really been baptized at all. Cyprian's position contributed to and cemented in place what was already taking place: the elevation of bishops over priests and other church offices, who were elevated over the "laity." Thus was lost the New Testament idea of the "priesthood of the believer," that is, that *all* Christians are priests, not just some exclusive category of God's people, as in the Old Testament (1 Peter 2:9). This truth was eventually recaptured and reemphasized by the Protestant reformers.

Another dispute broke out between Cyprian and the bishop of Rome, Stephen. The latter argued vigorously for what others (like Clement of Rome) had only implied earlier—that the bishops of Rome, as successors of Peter, were superior to all other bishops. Cyprian's view was that all bishops were equal though also superior to all other clergy, and even more so, the laity. His view prevailed in the East and what would eventually become the Eastern Orthodox Church: The highest level of church leadership was the bishops acting together and in equality. Stephen's view would prevail in the West and what would eventually become the Roman Catholic Church: The highest level of church leadership was the pope, the bishop of Rome, the bishop of bishops. So even though Cyprian strongly believed that the bishops were vital for the very unity and existence of the church, he did not believe that one bishop was superior to any other bishops.[2]

Cyprian's views on the church spilled over into his views of salvation. He was really the first to clearly state that there is no salvation outside of the church (led, of course, by legitimate bishops

---

2. Interestingly, there are versions of Cyprian's works that do seem to argue *for* the superiority of the pope. Apparently his works have been "doctored," and both sides—those who support papal supremacy and those who do not—accuse the other side of this devious work (J. Patout Burns, "Cyprian of Carthage," in *Early Christian Thinkers*, Paul Foster, ed. (Downers Grove, IL: InterVarsity, 2010), 139–40.

in apostolic succession). For example, he wrote, "Whoever is separated from the Church and is joined to an adulteress is separated from the promises of the Church; nor can he who forsakes the Church of Christ attain to the rewards of Christ. He is a stranger; he is profane; he is an enemy. He can no longer have God for his Father, who has not the Church for his mother" (*On the Unity of the Church*, 6).[3]

Not only was there no salvation outside of the church, according to Cyprian, but salvation was a lifelong process that took place only within the church. It begins with baptism, particularly of infants. Infant baptism did not originate in the thinking of Cyprian; it was already firmly established in the practice of the church. However, in his letter *To Fidus, On Infant Baptism*, he *strongly* commended the practice and stated that it resulted in forgiveness for "original sin"—the belief that all people are born with guilt for Adam's sin.

According to Cyprian, baptism also resulted in being "born again" through the work of the Holy Spirit. He was one of the first to clearly state what came to be called the doctrine of "baptismal regeneration." His logic should sound familiar: Jesus gave Peter and the other apostles the authority to forgive sin (John 2:23). This authority is passed through the generation of their successor-bishops. Therefore, bishops and bishop-appointed priests had the authority to forgive sin, and that is exactly what they did as they performed the sacrament of baptism. In Cyprian's own words: "But it is manifest where and by whom remission of sins can be given; to wit, that which is given in baptism" (*To Jubaianus, On the Baptism of Heretics*, 7).

Furthermore, baptism is only the start of the lifelong process of salvation, which also includes participation in all of the sacraments of the church, such as doing penance when sin is committed. This "penitential system" came to characterize the Western Church for

3. In the context of the persecution at that time, he even went as far as to say, "Even if such men were slain in confession of the Name, that stain is not even washed away by blood: the inexpiable and grave fault of discord is not even purged by suffering. *He cannot be a martyr who is not in the Church*" (*Unity*, 14, emphasis added).

centuries to come. Cyprian himself believed that all of this was by the grace of God and not to the credit of the individual. Sinners cannot save themselves or even contribute to their own salvation through good works; it is *all* an act of God. However, Cyprian's emphasis on the importance of obeying Christ, participating in the sacrament, doing penance for sin, and so on did contribute to the acceptance of the concept of "works-righteousness," that is, that individuals do contribute to their own salvation and work along with God to assure that they will be accepted into God's presence at the end of their lives.

Conclusion

Cyprian is remembered as a very influential Christian leader at a very difficult time and in very difficult circumstances. His legacy came out of that historical setting and is primarily in the area of the church—specifically, the importance of its unity, that its unity is found in the bishops, and that apart from the church and the function of the bishops, there is no salvation. This legacy lasted for over a thousand years but would be challenged in a variety of ways during the Protestant Reformation.

9

ATHANASIUS

Arian Adversary

Context

To set the stage for our next influential Christian thinker, some important historical events must be noted, which we can summarize with the terms *Constantine, controversy,* and *council.*

First, Constantine became Roman Emperor in 312 and issued the Edict of Milan in 313, which declared that Christianity was to be tolerated by the empire. This quickly led to Christianity actually being favored over other religions and was a complete reversal of what the church had experienced to that point. Furthermore, Constantine wanted to unite the empire under the banner of Christianity (probably more for political than spiritual reasons), which meant uniting Christianity itself.

Second, a significant controversy developed in Alexandria, Egypt, that threatened the unity that Constantine so much desired. Arius, a priest in Alexandria, strongly reacted against a sermon on the Trinity that was preached by his bishop, Alexander.

Arius assumed, as did most theologians at that time, that God is one (unity), eternal ("unbegotten"), and perfect. Furthermore, God cannot change because what is perfect cannot change—any change would mean that perfection became imperfection, which is impossible. To Arius, the doctrine of the Trinity threatened the unity of God. So Arius reasoned that only the *Father* is *truly* God. He also reasoned that the idea of the *Son* being *fully* God threatened the perfect, unchanging nature of God. The Son became human through the incarnation, but it is impossible for God to change, specifically into a human. In addition, Arius *accepted* Origen's view that the Son was subordinate to the Father, but *denied* Origen's view that the Son was "*eternally* begotten" by the Father *out of his own divine nature or substance*. Origen's view would lead to the conclusion that the Son is fully God, which would really mean that there are two gods. So Arius reached the conclusion that the Son was less than *fully* divine because the Son was created *at a point in time* by the Father *out of nothing*, like the rest of creation. Arius supposedly said, "If the Father begat the Son, he that was begotten had a beginning of existence: and from this it is evident that there was a time when the Son was not. It therefore necessarily follows, that he had his substance from nothing."[1] So the Son is not eternal and only a creature but still very close to God, a "super-creature." Only this kind of Son, in Arius's thinking, could take on a *human* nature in addition to his *nearly* divine nature and be incarnated in the person of Jesus Christ. Arius also believed he had biblical support for this idea. For example, Jesus said, "The Father is greater than I" (John 14:28), Jesus called himself the "only begotten" Son of the Father (John 3:16, 18; cf. 1:14, 18, NASB), and Paul referred to Christ as the "firstborn over all creation" (Colossians 1:15).

Arius was a very persuasive personality, and he rallied many Christians in Alexandria to favor his position and oppose that of

---

1. Socrates, *Ecclesiastical History* in *Nicene and Post-Nicene Fathers*, second series, ed. Philip Schaff and Henry Wace (WORD*search* Database, 2006; Peabody, MA: Hendrickson, 1994), 1.5.

Bishop Alexander—that the Son was fully God. In response, Bishop Alexander convened a synod in Alexandria in 318 to examine Arius's views. The result was that Arius was condemned as a heretic and forced to leave Alexandria, but he continued to promote his views and convinced many others, including bishops and priests.

Third, this ongoing controversy was so disruptive to the unity of the church and empire that Emperor Constantine convened the first ecumenical[2] council in 325 in Nicea, near the capital of Constantinople. The outcome was that Arius's views were again condemned as heresy, and a creed was written—the Creed of Nicea—and signed by all but two of the bishops in attendance (although many signed under pressure or without being fully convinced of the substance of the creed, or even understanding the significance of the issues involved). The creed was worded so as to clearly reject Arianism, for example, "We believe in . . . one Lord Jesus Christ, the Son of God, begotten from the Father . . . begotten *not made*, of *one substance* with the Father . . ." (emphasis added).[3] But once again, this condemnation of Arianism did not solve the problem; Arianism did not go away. Historians and theologians have come to regard it as one of the biggest theological crises in the history of the church.

Alexander, the bishop of Alexandria whom Arius specifically attacked, attended the Council of Nicea to argue against Arianism, and he took with him his assistant, Athanasius. This young man was born near Alexandria, Egypt, around 298. He was in his late twenties when he accompanied Alexander to Nicea. He observed the proceedings of the council but could not participate because he was not a bishop. However, he very quickly became a bishop when Alexander died in 328 and Athanasius succeeded him—he was almost thirty. Athanasius served as bishop of Alexandria for

2. This term means that bishops from throughout the empire—East and West—who represented the church broadly and universally were invited to and did participate in the council.

3. The full text of the Creed of Nicea is included in the appendix. This is not the same as the more well-known Nicene Creed, which is an expanded version of the Creed of Nicea.

forty-five years, more or less. Due to political and religious intrigue, all related directly or indirectly to his uncompromising fight against Arianism, he was exiled five times in about seventeen years. Despite his exiles, the people in his diocese loyally supported him as their bishop. Athanasius died at the age of seventy-five in 373.

Contribution

Athanasius's main written works are *On the Incarnation of the Word* [*Logos*], his argument for the full deity of the Son, and *Against the Arians*, his refutation of Arius's view of the Son.

To his great credit, Athanasius started with Scripture rather than philosophy. Therefore, he rejected the philosophical assumption that the unity of God (which he believed in) means that God (the Father) could not share his substance or nature with another. Rather, the very nature of God is *community* in unity. How do we know that? That is how Scripture describes God. God has *always* been Father (which Arius denied), which means that the Son has *always* been God. Furthermore, *begotten*, which is indeed a biblical characteristic of the Son (e.g., John 3:16), does not mean "brought into existence" or "created at a point in time." This is why the Creed of Nicea stated, "begotten not made." "'Making' produces something of a *different* sort, while 'begetting' produces something of the *same* kind."[4] God makes humans, therefore they are only humans—a *different* sort; God the Father begets the Son, therefore he is fully God—the *same* kind.

The Creed of Nicea and Athanasius, in his defense of the creed, used the crucial Greek word *homoousios* to communicate this truth. It means "of the same nature, being, essence, or substance." The creed stated that the Son was "of one substance [*homoousios*] with the Father." This is exactly what Tertullian had argued for (in Latin) more than a century earlier: the Father and Son (and Spirit) shared *una substantia* (one substance). Arians rejected this word

4. Gerald McDermott, *The Great Theologians* (Downers Grove: InterVarsity, 2010), 40. Emphasis original.

and claimed that it was not biblical. Athanasius acknowledged that it was not a biblical *word* but a biblical *concept* (as is *Trinity*).

Athanasius also believed that God was unchanging by nature, but argued that the incarnation did not jeopardize this. Why? Because the Son's fully divine nature was not changed through the incarnation; rather, a human nature was added to his unchanging, divine nature. What about when Jesus said, "The Father is greater than I" (John 14:28), or when Jesus is described as hungry or tired? Athanasius said that those applied to his human nature, not his divine nature.

The primary reason that this was so crucial to Athanasius is because without the *full* deity of Jesus Christ, salvation is impossible. Why? Only God can save. Even a super-creature cannot provide salvation for other creatures because, after all, he is only a creature himself. Sin resulted in death. So true salvation requires (among many other things) the giving of life. Who can give life? Only the source of life, God himself. Along with others before him, Athanasius believed that salvation was a sharing in the divine nature— *theosis* or divinization, that is, the bringing together of humanity and deity, which sin had separated. Again, who can accomplish this? Only God, specifically, only the One in whom both deity and humanity had already been brought together—Jesus Christ. One of Athanasius's most famous statements was: "He [the *Logos*/Son] was made man that we might be made God" (*On the Incarnation of the Word*, 54.3). Athanasius did *not* mean that salvation results in humans becoming equal with God. He *did* mean what Peter meant: "[God's] divine power has given us everything we need for *life* and *godliness*. . . . Through these he has given us his very great and precious promises, so that through them *you may participate in the divine nature* . . ." (2 Peter 1:3–4). This was the goal that Jesus had in mind when he prayed, "That all [believers] may be one, Father, just as you are in me and I am in you. *May they also be in us* . . . I in them and you in me" (John 17:21–23). This is an amazing aspect of our salvation, but Athanasius clearly understood that without the incarnation—the uniting of true God and true human—this would be impossible; there could be no salvation for anyone!

Conclusion

Some have called Athanasius the theologian who saved Christianity. This, of course, does not overlook the fact that God is the one who *ultimately* safeguards Christianity. But it does highlight the incredible threat that Arianism was to the gospel and Christian truth, and how vital Athanasius's tenacious role in defending it was. More had to take place before his views became acknowledged as "orthodox" Christianity, but what would soon follow built on his work and brought it to completion.

10

BASIL, GREGORY, AND GREGORY

The Cappadocian Fathers

Context

The Creed of Nicea condemned it, the writings of Athanasius refuted it, but Arianism continued and spread. Athanasius's work was not in vain, however. It was picked up and advanced by three theologians from Cappadocia (in central modern-day Turkey): Basil of Caesarea; his brother, Gregory of Nyssa; and his friend, Gregory of Nazianzus. Together, these three are known as the Cappadocians, and are recognized as among the most influential theologians in the fourth century.

Basil (born around 330) and his brother, Gregory (born around 335), were from a wealthy Christian family. Basil was sent to Athens for his education, and it was there that he met Gregory from Nazianzus (also born around 330), who would become his closest friend. Basil quickly began to distinguish himself as a theologian, especially in support of Nicene theology and against Arian theology. In 370 he was made bishop of Caesarea, the major city of Cappadocia, giving him significant influence in the church. The emperor at that time, Valens, was an Arian who tried to limit Basil's influence. In response, Basil appointed allies to key positions. His good friend Gregory was appointed as bishop in a small town (and apparently he was not too thrilled with the idea). Basil also appointed his younger brother, Gregory, as a bishop. This Gregory had not followed his brother into the church. He was a secular teacher of rhetoric when Basil appointed him as bishop of Nyssa.

One of Basil's more important works is *On the Holy Spirit*, and much of his theology is revealed in over three hundred letters that he wrote. Basil died relatively young in 379. Due to his theological contributions as well as his significant successes as a bishop and church leader, he has come to be known as Basil the Great. After his death, the two Gregorys were able to step out of his considerable shadow and shine themselves.

Gregory of Nazianzus became famous for preaching his five *Theological Orations* in support of Nicene theology. He also produced many other orations and letters. In 380, largely due to the five *Orations*, he was made bishop of Constantinople, the most important city in the Eastern part of the empire. Again, Gregory did not want the position but accepted it nevertheless. He died about ten years later. He has come to be known as Gregory the Theologian, largely due to the impact of his *Theological Orations*.

The other Gregory, Basil's brother, carried Basil's anti-Arian work even further. Ironically, even though he was not trained as a theologian, he ended up overshadowing his brother and friend, who, unlike himself, had been trained in theology. He is recognized as the greatest thinker among them. In addition to his theological writings, he is also well-known for his works in philosophy and the spiritual life. He died in 394.

Contribution

The three Cappadocians were in constant communication, and their theological contributions showed it. So their theology is often examined together, and that is what we will do here.

With regard to the Arian threat, Basil began by making an important distinction between the general and the particular. For example, Tom, Dick, and Harry are three particulars of the general category of human. With regard to God, the Father, Son, and Spirit are three particulars of the general category of deity. The Greek word the Cappadocians used for the particular was *hypostasis*— "person"; the word they used for the general was *ousia*—"being," "substance," or "essence." This was helpful in the fight against Arians, because they thought in only one category. So to have two (or three) in the same category was implying that there were two (or three) gods—Father and Son (and Spirit)—in violation of monotheism. This is exactly what the Arians were accusing the Creed of Nicea of implying. Basil provided a way to say that the Trinity is not three *and* one of the same thing. Rather, the Trinity is three *of* one thing (the particular category) and one of something else (the general category). Monotheism is safeguarded in the general category.

However, this could still lead one to say that the Father and Son are two gods. After all, Tom and Dick are two humans in the category of humans, so wouldn't it be necessary to say that the Father and Son are two gods in the category of God? The Cappadocians pointed out that it is possible to distinguish between *humans* by characteristics such as gender, age, shape, etc. These are all different for each individual human. However, this is not the case with regard to the three persons of the Trinity, because the three persons of the Trinity share exactly the same characteristics.

So how are they to be distinguished? What makes them *different* persons if they share the *same* characteristics? The Cappadocians' answer was that it was their relationships to one another that distinguished them. In other words, the only thing that distinguishes the Father from the Son is that he is the Father and not the Son, and the only thing that distinguishes the Son from the Father is that he is the Son and not the Father. Another way of saying it is this: The Father alone is "unbegotten"; the Son alone is "begotten of the Father"; and the Spirit alone "proceeds from the Father."

This is how Basil stated it: "If you ask me to state shortly my own view, I shall state that *ousia* has the same relation to *hypostasis* as the general has to the particular. Every one of us both shares in existence by the common term of 'essence' (*ousia*) and by his own properties is such a one and such a one. In the same manner . . . the term *ousia* is common, like goodness, or Godhead, or any similar attribute; while *hypostasis* is contemplated in the special property of Fatherhood, Sonship, or the power to sanctify [the Spirit]" (*To Count Terentius*, Letter 214.4). This way of thinking was a major advancement in trinitarian theology.

But the Cappadocians were not only fighting Arians, who denied that the Son was fully God. They were also fighting a group known as the Macedonians or pneumatomachians, who affirmed that the Son was fully God but the Spirit was not; rather, the Spirit was either a created being or the impersonal power of God. Basil addressed this in one of his most important books, *On the Holy Spirit*. This was the first written work by a Christian devoted entirely to the subject of the Spirit of God. In this lengthy work, Basil argued convincingly for the deity of the Spirit and that he is to be as much an object of Christian worship as the Father and Son.

All of this came together in the Council of Constantinople. It was called in 381 by the emperor, Theodosius, who was Nicene in belief and wanted to do away with Arianism once and for all. The two Gregorys played a major role in the council. Although Basil had already died, his influence was also very much present through his friend and brother. The council also completed the work that Athanasius left incomplete when he died. The Council of Constantinople is the second ecumenical council and produced what is commonly called the Nicene Creed, one of the most important and widely used creeds in nearly all expressions and traditions of the church. The more accurate title is the Niceno-Constantinopolitan Creed, because it expanded on the Creed of Nicea and also clarified the deity of the Spirit.[1] Negatively, the council and creed placed

---

1. See the full text in the appendix. Another phrase (the *Filioque clause*) was added later. This will be discussed in chapter 14.

outside the bounds of orthodoxy two forms of belief that, in order to preserve the unity of God, denied the Trinity: modalism, which, even while claiming to believe in the Trinity, essentially denied it by concluding that the Father, Son, and Holy Spirit are three modes of operation rather than three persons; and Arianism, which denied the Trinity by claiming that the Son and Spirit were created beings, not fully God.[2] Positively, the council, through the creed, expressed in Greek what Tertullian had expressed in Latin about a century and a half previously—*tres personae, una substantia*: God is three persons (*hypostases*) in one essence (*ousia*): the Trinity.

One more important thing to note regarding the Cappadocians is that one of their arguments against Arianism (and many forms of heresy) is that it robbed God of his mystery; it made the Divine fit too easily into very small human minds; it dumbed down Deity. That is, it was arrogant. The Cappadocians were fighting to protect the majesty of God and insisted on the humility of humans as we try to understand God, but also in everything else.[3]

The majesty and mystery of God means that we never reach the goal of perfectly understanding him. One error is arrogance in thinking that we can, but another error, which unfortunately too many Christians would prefer, is to just give up—stop trying to understand God. The Cappadocians thought it should be just the opposite. Gregory of Nyssa expressed it beautifully: "This is truly the vision of God: never to be satisfied in our desire to see him. But by looking at what we do see, we must always rekindle our desire to see more. So there can be no limit interrupting our growth in ascending to God, because there is no limit to the Good [God], and our desire for the Good is not ended by being satisfied" (*The Life of Moses*, 2.239).[4] Amen! May the mystery of God certainly not repel us, but rather irresistibly attract us every day of our lives.

2. This does not mean that those forms of belief disappeared. Modalism is still present in the theology of Oneness Pentecostalism. Arianism is still present in the theology of the Jehovah's Witnesses.

3. See Basil's *Homily* 20, *On Humility*.

4. Quoted in Hill, *The History of Christian Thought*, 76.

Conclusion

The Cappadocians played a major role in what came to be the orthodox understanding of the Trinity. But for them, orthodoxy (right believing) and orthopraxy (right living) go together. That is why doctrine is so important and worth fighting for. If we do not believe what is true of God, we cannot live in a way that is pleasing to God.

11

THEODORE OF MOPSUESTIA

Antiochene Advocate

Context

The Council of Constantinople established orthodoxy with regard to the doctrine of the Trinity: the Father, Son, and Spirit are equally and fully God. However, controversy just shifted to another issue: If Jesus Christ is fully God, how can he also be fully human? The individual before us here can help us consider this question as well as another question that was being debated at that time: How is Scripture to be interpreted?

Theodore of Mopsuestia was born in Antioch (Syria) around 350. Another important Christian leader at this time, Chrysostom, convinced Theodore to pursue church ministry and theological studies. He was ordained as a priest in the church of Antioch, and in 394 became bishop of Mopsuestia (in present-day Turkey, not too far from Antioch). His reputation as a theologian and preacher was quickly established and spread throughout the Eastern church. He died in 428.

At this time, the important centers of Christian learning at Antioch, Syria, and Alexandria, Egypt, were theological rivals but also rivals for political and ecclesiastical power. They also represent two different approaches to the interpretation of Scripture. In the chapter on Origen, we were introduced to the approach practiced in Alexandria, namely, the allegorical method. This approach downplayed the literal meaning of the text and preferred to find its "deeper" or "spiritual" meaning. For example, the city of Jerusalem stood for the church or heaven. Adam stood for Christ. Generally speaking, those Christians who practiced this method saw Christ and the church in nearly everything, even in the Old Testament. A classic example is that the Song of Solomon is really about Christ's love for the church. They justified this by saying that even Paul practiced allegorical interpretation in Galatians 4:21–31. This method was also common in Greek philosophy, and the school of Alexandria—as we have seen in the persons of Clement and Origen—was very influenced by this philosophy.

Contribution

Theodore and others in the school of Antioch believed that the literal meaning was the important meaning, and Scripture was to be interpreted in its historical context first and foremost. They also tended to start doing theology with Scripture rather than philosophy. They did acknowledge that there was allegory and symbolism in the biblical text, but this was only recognized when the literal meaning fully justified a spiritual meaning as well. Theodore wrote many commentaries on Scripture using this method (as Origen did using the allegorical method). He was even somewhat unique at that time for understanding the Song of Solomon as a love poem that was not primarily about Christ's love for the church. In his commentary on Galatians, he addressed the Alexandrians' appeal to the example of Paul in that very epistle: "Countless students of Scripture have played tricks with the plain sense of the Bible and want to rob it of any meaning it contains. In fact, they make up inept fables and call their inanities 'allegories.' They so abuse the apostle's paradigm as to make the holy texts incomprehensible and meaningless. . . . [Paul] neither dismisses the historical narratives nor is he adding new things to an old story. Instead, Paul is talking about events as they happened, then submits the story of those events to his present understanding."[1]

Which method is to be preferred? Both are valid. The apostle Paul did indeed use allegorical interpretation, as noted above. Other New Testament writers understood Old Testament things as pointing ahead to Jesus Christ (e.g., the tabernacle and temple, animal sacrifices, and the life of David). But the weakness of this method is how easy it is to see what you want to see in Scripture (as Origen did). It is also too easy to go overboard when looking for allegories and find them where there are none.

A possible weakness in literal interpretation is to go to the opposite extreme and see little to no symbolism, allegory, or foreshadowing in Scripture. In fact, Theodore himself acknowledged only four psalms as messianic and denied that Isaiah 53 was a prophecy of the crucifixion of Christ.[2] So balance is the key, but the literal method seems the best one to begin with in order to guard against over-allegorization. The spiritual meaning should only be acknowledged when there is sufficient evidence from the literal, historical meaning of the biblical text. The allegorical method continued to be popular through the Middle Ages, but the literal, historical method did eventually become dominant, at least in Western Christianity.

These contrasting methods of interpretation also resulted in different ways of answering the question regarding Jesus Christ: If he is fully God, how can he also be fully human? In the same way that the Alexandrians looked past the literal meaning of Scripture to find its real significance, they also looked past Jesus' humanity and emphasized his deity as the real significance of his existence. On the other hand, the Antiochenes tended to emphasize the historical

1. Quoted in Joseph W. Trigg, *Biblical Interpretation* (Wilmington, DE: Glazier, 1988), 173.

2. Gregg R. Allison, *Historical Theology: An Introduction to Christian Doctrine* (Grand Rapids: Zondervan, 2011), 166, note 15.

meaning of Scripture and also the historical reality of Jesus—his humanity. With regard to the natures of Jesus—deity and humanity—in Alexandrian and Antiochene theology, the difference was one of emphasis, not denial. The denial of either Christ's humanity or deity had already been declared to be heretical.

The Alexandrian school tended toward "Logos-flesh" Christology. The humanity of Jesus was more of a means that was used by the Logos/Son after the incarnation to accomplish his work. Thus, Jesus' humanity was more human "flesh" than human existence and experience. Apollinarius (310–390), an Alexandrian theologian and bishop of Laodicea (in present-day Turkey), represents this perspective. According to Apollinarius, Jesus was "God-in-a-bod."[3] That is, Jesus Christ had a human body, but that was the extent of his humanity. The Logos replaced the human mind and spirit—the really important part of a human individual. Jesus' humanity was simply a physical shell for his deity. Jesus was flesh stuffed with deity. For Alexandrians such as Apollinarius, if Jesus had a human mind (and will), then he *could have* sinned (like every other human), and that was inconceivable because, they believed, it put at risk the very accomplishment of salvation. Also, for Apollinarius, the possibility of two natures in Christ seemed to threaten the unity of Christ, which was very important in Alexandrian theology due to the influence of Greek philosophy. So the Alexandrians tended to think in terms of *one* nature in Jesus Christ after the incarnation, not two. Apollinarius's Christology was actually declared to be heretical by the Council of Constantinople, largely due to the work of the two Gregory Cappadocians, because it denied the *full* humanity of Jesus Christ.

Theodore was a great defender of the Antiochene view of Jesus Christ, which can be called "Logos-Man" Christology. He reasoned that if Jesus was not fully human with a human body but also a human mind, will, consciousness, personality—*everything* that makes a human a human—then he did not *fully* identify with

3. As expressed by Roger Olson, *The Story of Christian Theology*, 207, not Apollinarius himself.

humanity, did not *fully* experience what humans experience, and therefore could not provide salvation for humans. So according to Theodore, Jesus Christ had both a fully divine nature (that was now orthodoxy) and a fully human nature—*two* complete natures. It is important to note that both Alexandrian and Antiochene Christologies are closely related to soteriology, the doctrine of salvation. Both were concerned that the other's view of Jesus Christ jeopardized his ability to be the Savior. This was not nitpicky wrangling about abstract theological ideas; both sides were fully convinced that salvation—the Gospel!—was at stake. That made it an important issue.

Conclusion

Even though the Council of Constantinople sided with Theodore's Christology, Alexandrian Christology continued to develop while acknowledging that Jesus' humanity was indeed complete. Theodore was highly respected by many of his contemporaries, but we should also note that he himself was eventually condemned as a heretic about one hundred years after he died. This came about through the efforts of those who preferred Alexandrian Christology and who exploited some unfortunate explanations of Theodore's view of Christ. Instead of saying that the Logos assumed a general human *nature*, Theodore said that the Logos assumed a specific human *being*. In his *On the Incarnation*, he speaks of the incarnation as "an indwelling in which he [the Logos] united the one [the man, a specific human being] who was being assumed wholly to himself and prepared him to share all the honor which he, the indweller, who is a son by nature shares. Thereby he [the Logos] constituted a single person by union with him [the man] and made him a partner in all his authority." The problem is that this makes the incarnation sound like a type of "possession."[4] In the same way that a demon can take control of a human, so the Logos

4. Harold O. J. Brown, *Heresies: Heresy and Orthodoxy in the History of the Church* (Peabody, MA: Hendrickson, 1988), 169.

took control of a man. This problem in Theodore's understanding of the incarnation takes us to the next stage of the controversy, specifically between one of Theodore's students, Nestorius, who took Theodore's views to the next step, and one who was more in line with Alexandrian Christology, Cyril of Alexandria. This next stage of the conflict resulted in the third ecumenical council of the church in Ephesus.

12

CYRIL OF ALEXANDRIA
Alexandrian Rival

Context

One word advanced the conflict between the Christian centers of
learning in Antioch and Alexandria and their rival Christologies
to another level—*Theotokos*. It means "God-bearer" and was used
regularly in the fifth century to refer to the Virgin Mary. The term
was a means of acknowledging the full deity of Jesus Christ by
saying that the baby born to Mary was none other than God himself. But to the shock of many, the bishop of Constantinople, in a
Christmas sermon (428) and later in an Easter letter (429), publicly
condemned the practice of referring to Mary in that way. His name
was Nestorius. He had been a student of Theodore of Mopsuestia and held to Theodore's Antiochene Christology. According to
Nestorius, Jesus Christ has two natures—deity and humanity—but
it was the human nature that Mary bore, not the divine nature.
Therefore it is wrong to refer to her as *Theotokos*. (*Christokos* was
better.) Furthermore, the term seemed to emphasize Christ's deity

and de-emphasize his humanity, which smacked of Apollinarianism and Alexandrian Christology.

Nestorius's personal and theological rival was Cyril, the bishop of Alexandria. Little is known about his life, but he became bishop in 412 and continued in that position until his death in 444. When Cyril heard about Nestorius's *Theotokos* proclamations, he immediately responded, anxious to defend Alexandrian theology and prestige (and seek a bit of revenge against an Antiochene). He first engaged Nestorius in correspondence, but Nestorius refused to change his views. Cyril then sought the support of the Patriarch in Rome and the emperor, which he received. The result was the third ecumenical Council of Ephesus in 431.

Both bishops were concerned that Christology must support soteriology, that Jesus Christ be who he needed to be in order to truly be Savior. But in addition to that valid concern, they both also certainly had political motives.[1]

Contribution

What Nestorius and Cyril had in common was the faith of Nicea: There is *one* Lord—Jesus Christ—who has *two* natures—a fully divine nature and a fully human nature. Both Nestorius and Cyril rejected the idea of Cyril's Alexandrian predecessor, Apollinarius, that Jesus had a divine mind instead of a human mind. They both agreed that Jesus was *fully* human. But what divided them was their answer to the question, How can "one" and "two" be true at the

1. By this time, the churches in cities such as Alexandria, Antioch, Constantinople, and Rome had become important centers of Christianity. The bishops of those important churches had risen in prominence above other bishops and more specifically bore the title "Patriarch." We are focusing on the theological rivalry between some of them, but there was also political rivalry—power and prestige in the church and empire—which is a part of the bigger story. This rivalry was especially strong between Antioch and Alexandria due to the humiliation of an Alexandrian, Apollinarius, after the Council of Constantinople resulting from the influence of Antioch. At this time, Cyril, the Patriarch of Alexandria, found himself in a place to challenge Nestorius, who, as an Antiochene theologian, was a *theological* rival, and, as the Patriarch of a rival diocese, Constantinople, was also an *ecclesiastical* rival—the perfect storm for controversy.

same time? As we saw in the previous chapter, the difference is one of emphasis, not denial. Nestorius tended to want to emphasize the "two." Cyril tended to want to emphasize the "one."

Nestorius's theology has been preserved in a few letters, sermons, quotes from him in the writings of his opponents, and one major work, *The Bazaar of Heraclides*, which he wrote near the end of his life (436) in order to defend himself and his views. Like his mentor, Theodore, Nestorius emphasized the two natures of Jesus Christ—divinity and humanity—but even more so than Theodore, Nestorius seemed to claim that the two natures were attached to two persons—Christ was the divine person and Jesus was the human person (the "possession" idea again). In response to the charges from his Alexandrian opponents that this destroyed the unity of Christ (which Nestorius claimed to believe), he tried to argue that the two natures/persons were brought together in the closest possible "conjunction." That is, they were united in every way while still remaining distinct. What he refused to do was acknowledge that the divine nature/person could be born (thus, no *Theotokos* language), be weak, suffer, or die (God cannot do those things; only humans can), and that the human nature/person could do miracles (humans cannot do those things; only God can). In other words, the divine nature cannot be passed to a human because it is divine, and a human nature cannot be passed to God because it is human. This is why Nestorius opposed Apollinarianism so strongly. It claimed that the divine mind had replaced the human mind of Jesus. This was impossible, according to Nestorius, because a human mind is a part of a human nature. If you don't have a human mind, you are not a human at all. So Nestorian Christology is basically two natures and two persons (although he would not have put it so explicitly); Jesus is the human nature/person and Christ is the divine nature/person.

In Cyril's Christology, it was not just that the divine Son was *added to* a human man, but rather that the divine Son *became* a human man. "Nestorius spoke of Jesus *and* God the Word, while Cyril believed that Jesus *was* the Word."[2] Therefore, Mary is truly

2. Tony Lane, *A Concise History of Christian Thought*, 54.

Theotokos, because baby Jesus *is* God.[3] Furthermore, Cyril wanted to preserve the unity of Christ, which was so central to Alexandrian Christology, and Nestorius's thought seemed to destroy that (even though Nestorius did not think it did). Cyril was consistently Alexandrian in understanding the incarnation as a divine nature and human nature being united in *one* nature, not two. The theological term attached to this is *hypostatic union*. The Greek word *hypostasis* means "person," so the term means a *union* of two natures in one *person*. Cyril would add that the one person had one nature, not two, after the union. As we will see, this ended up in yet another controversy, heresy, and council. Cyril believed that his Christology affirmed the incarnation—"the Word *became* flesh" (John 1:14)—whereas Nestorius's Christology actually denied it.

Once again, this is not a matter of theological word games (although there was some of that too). Both Nestorius and Cyril believed our very salvation was at stake. We can see Cyril's concern in the following: "If anyone does not confess that the Lord's flesh[4] is *life-giving* and that it pertains to the Word of God the Father as his very own, but pretends that it belongs to some other person [Jesus] who is united with him [Christ] only in honor and in whom the deity dwells, and if anyone will not confess that his flesh *gives life* because it is the flesh of the Word who *gives life* to all, let him be anathema" (*Anathema* 11, emphasis added). In other words, if Nestorius was right, it was only a human (Jesus) who suffered and died on the cross and not God (Christ). Therefore that death has no more saving value than the death of any other mere human. Only God can give salvation by giving spiritual life to spiritually dead sinners; no mere human can accomplish that.

The emperor Theodosius called the Council of Ephesus in 431 to resolve the matter between Nestorius and Cyril. The council convened before Nestorius and his Antiochene colleagues could

---

3. In contrast, one of Nestorius's more famous statements is, "I could not call a baby two or three months old God" (as recorded by Socrates, *Ecclesiastical History*, 7.34).

4. Notice the number of references to *flesh* in this statement, and remember the "Logos-flesh" Christology of Alexandria.

arrive, and Nestorius and his views were condemned. A few days later, the Antiochenes arrived, convened their council, and condemned Cyril. A few weeks later more bishops arrived from the Western part of the empire, agreed with the initial council, and Nestorianism was officially rejected as heresy.

Theodosius was still concerned about the tension between the Antiochenes and the Alexandrians, so he insisted on a compromise, called the Formula of Reunion (433). The Antiochenes agreed to send Nestorius into exile, and Cyril (sort of) agreed to acknowledge two natures, not one, in Jesus Christ after the incarnation, as long as it was recognized as a "distinction" rather than a "division" (semantics!).

Conclusion

The point, however, is that the issue—after the incarnation, was there one nature (the Alexandrian perspective) or two natures (the Antiochene perspective)?—was yet to be resolved. That happened in the fourth ecumenical Council of Chalcedon.

13

LEO THE GREAT

Chalcedonian Champion

Context

Jesus Christ is fully God; the Council of Nicea had declared
this to be orthodoxy and Arianism heresy.[1] Jesus Christ is fully
human; the Council of Constantinople had declared this to be
orthodoxy and Apollinarianism heresy.[2] Jesus Christ is not two
persons, but one person; the Council of Ephesus had declared
this to be orthodoxy and Nestorianism heresy.[3] But after the
incarnation, did Jesus Christ have just one nature (as Alexandrian theologians believed) or two (as the Antiochene theologians believed)?

1. *Arianism* claimed that Christ was not fully God, but rather a created being.
It is also known as *subordinationism*.
2. *Apollinarianism* claimed that Christ was not fully human. He had a human
body, but the rest was deity.
3. *Nestorianism* claimed that Christ was two persons: Jesus was the human
person and Christ was the divine person.

Eutyches was an elderly but highly respected monk in Constantinople who sided with the Alexandrian understanding of Christ. Little else is known about him other than the role he played in the next stage of the Christological controversies. He took Cyril's position another step and stated what Cyril had implied: Before the incarnation, there were two natures (deity and humanity), but after the incarnation, there was only one nature, a brand-new nature. The divine nature was no longer divine; the human nature was no longer human. Rather, the nature of Jesus Christ was a hybrid (just like sodium and chlorine, when combined, become salt). This alone was not really anything dramatically new, but Eutyches also took a giant step back toward Apollinarianism (and probably even beyond that to Docetism[4]) and stated that the new single nature of Jesus Christ was a whole lot of deity with just a pinch of humanity. As the Alexandrians jumped at the opportunity to condemn Nestorius and his fellow Antiochenes, now the Antiochenes jumped at the opportunity to condemn Eutyches and his fellow Alexandrians. Their concern was the same: If Jesus Christ was not truly and fully human (as well as truly and fully divine), how could he identify with and provide salvation for humans?

Eutyches was put on trial for heresy and condemned (448). The Patriarch of Alexandria, Dioscorus, came to his rescue and appealed to the emperor for a council, which took place in Ephesus (449). Dioscorus was able to throw his weight around; the result was that Eutyches was restored while some Antiochene bishops were deposed (what a soap opera!). These bishops then appealed to the Bishop of Rome, Leo I.

Leo became the bishop of Rome in 440 and came to be known as Leo the Great. His influential powers were demonstrated when he persuaded Attila the Hun not to attack Rome (452), and later (455) when he convinced the Vandals, after they had conquered Rome, not to slaughter the residents of the city as well.

---

4. *Docetism* claimed that Christ only appeared to be human but was really *only* divine.

Contribution

Leo is known for two things: his involvement in the Christological controversy and his teaching regarding the Roman papacy. Regarding the latter, we have already seen how bishops had been elevated over most other clergy and all laity; how the bishops of cities such as Rome, Constantinople, Antioch, and Alexandria were elevated even further as "patriarchs"; and how the patriarch of Rome was seen by some as the highest bishop of all. Leo was the first Roman bishop to overtly argue the case that the bishop of Rome was indeed the "unworthy heir,"[5] but heir nonetheless, of the apostle Peter on whom Jesus was building his church (based on Leo's interpretation of Matthew 16:18–19).

Leo's involvement in the Eutychian controversy was through his written work, *The Tome*, and through his ecclesiastical work in the fourth ecumenical council. In *The Tome*, also known as the *Letter* (28) *to Flavian* (the bishop of Constantinople and superior of Eutyches), Leo summarized orthodox Christology to that point: Jesus Christ had to be fully God and fully human in order to be Savior. If he were not fully human (as Eutyches was presently saying), then he could not have identified with humans and died in their place. If he were not fully God, his death would not be sufficient for many humans, and he could not forgive sins as a result of his death. Therefore, a hybrid nature in Jesus Christ, which was neither human nor divine, was insufficient for salvation. For example, he wrote,

> For not only is God believed to be both Almighty and the Father, but the Son is shown to be co-eternal with Him, differing in nothing from the Father because He is God from God, Almighty from Almighty, and being born from the Eternal one is co-eternal with Him; not later in point of time, not lower in power, not unlike in glory, not divided in essence: but at the same time the only begotten of the eternal Father was born eternal of the Holy Spirit and the Virgin Mary. And *this nativity which took place in time took*

5. *Sermon*, 3.3–4

nothing from, and added *nothing to* that divine and eternal birth, but expended itself wholly on the restoration of man who had been deceived in order that he might both vanquish death and overthrow by his strength, the Devil who possessed the power of death. For we should not now be able to overcome the author of sin and death *unless He took our nature on Him and made it His own,* whom neither sin could pollute nor death retain. (2, emphasis added)

Leo dubbed the council in Ephesus that restored Eutyches the "Robber Synod" and condemned it. But it was not until Marcian (who preferred Antiochene theology) became the new emperor that Leo was able to find a sympathetic ear and receive permission for yet another council. This was convened at Chalcedon, just across the Bosporus from Constantinople, in 451, and is recognized as the fourth ecumenical council of the church. Leo's *Tome* was read at the council and became a part of the official documentation of the council's conclusions, along with the Nicene Creed and the Formula of Reunion.[6] The Antiochene bishops who had been deposed at the Robber Synod were restored. Eutyches, who had previously been deposed and then restored at the Robber Synod, was now re-deposed, along with Dioscorus, his defender. (A scorekeeper would be helpful.)

The most significant product of this council is called the Chalcedonian Definition.[7] It was based on Leo's *Tome* but also reflects the thought of Cyril of Alexandria, specifically his letters to Nestorius and John of Antioch:

Following the holy fathers, we all agree that the one and only Son, our Lord Jesus Christ, is complete in Godhead and complete in manhood, truly God and truly man, consisting of a rational soul and body [**contrary to Apollinarius**]; of one substance (*homoousios*) with the Father with regard to his Godhead [**contrary to Arius**], and at the same time of one substance (*homoousios*) with us with regard to his humanity; like us in every way except sin [**contrary to**

6. See chapter 12.
7. It was called this in order to clarify that it was not a new *creed,* but rather a clarification and elaboration of the Nicene Creed.

Apollinarius]; with regard to his Godhead, begotten of the Father before the ages [contrary to Arius], but yet with regard to his humanity, begotten, for us humans and for our salvation, of the Virgin Mary, the God-bearer (*Theotokos*); one and the same Christ, Son, Lord, Only-begotten, recognized in two natures, without confusion, without change [these two terms are contrary to Eutyches], without division, without separation [these two terms are contrary to Nestorius]; the distinction of natures being in no way taken away by the union [contrary to Eutyches], but rather the characteristics of each nature being preserved and coming together to form one person and subsistence (*hypostasis*), not as parted or separated into two persons [contrary to Nestorius], but one and the same Son, Only-begotten, God the Word, Lord Jesus Christ, just as the prophets from earliest times spoke of him, and our Lord Jesus Christ himself taught us, and the creed of the fathers has handed down to us.

What is noteworthy about this statement is that it is primarily in negative terms in order to explicitly rule out the four Christological heresies (as I have noted in the text of the Definition above). But in another sense, the Definition allows the incarnation to remain somewhat of a mystery. In other words, it is easier to say what the incarnation is *not* as opposed to what it *is*. The Definition essentially said, "You cannot go beyond these boundaries in your thinking about Jesus Christ, but there is plenty of room within the boundaries for further reflection, thought, speculation—it is, after all, ultimately a mystery."

Conclusion

Leo the Great was the key person to bring together previous theological thought as well as to challenge the most recent threatening thoughts regarding the person of Jesus Christ. The result was "Chalcedonian Christology," which can be summarized in this way: the incarnation resulted in two natures—deity and humanity—in one person, Jesus Christ. Combining this with "Nicene Theology," it can be characterized as follows: God is three "whos" (persons) and one "what" (nature); Jesus Christ is one "who" (person) and two "whats" (natures). There were a few groups that did not accept the declarations of Chalcedon. Some churches in the area of Syria followed Nestorian theology. Some churches in Egypt followed Eutychian theology and came to be known as "monophysite" (one nature) churches. The present-day Coptic Church would be one such example. However, generally speaking, Chalcedonian Christology has been accepted as orthodoxy in the Western church and most of the Eastern church.

14

AUGUSTINE
Doctor of the Church

Context

Even as the Trinitarian and Christological controversies continued to rage, more controversies developed, for example, regarding the condition of humanity after the fall and the divine and human roles in salvation. The political-cultural times were also changing. The Roman Empire was declining and on the verge of falling; the "Early Ages" were giving way to the Middle Ages. The key transitional figure at that time weighed in on the continuing controversies and tackled the developing controversies as well. He is now recognized as one of the greatest theologians ever.

Aurelius Augustinus was born in Tagaste (in modern Algeria, North Africa) in 354. His father was an unbeliever, but his mother was a devoted Christian who saw to it that her son was educated in Christianity, which Augustine accepted (at least intellectually) as true. He continued his education in nearby Carthage, where he studied philosophy and, as a result, rejected Christianity. In its place he came to embrace Manichaeism, a philosophy/religion that assumed two eternal and equal principles of good and evil in constant struggle with one another.[1]

In 384 he moved to Italy and ended up in Milan teaching rhetoric. His mother had followed him to Milan and was desperately trying to persuade him to return to the Christian faith. In fact, Augustine had become disillusioned with Manichaeism and was again searching for truth in Neo-Platonic philosophy, but he also began reading Scripture again. The bishop of Milan, Ambrose, was well-known as a great preacher, and Augustine began listening to his sermons—more out of his interest in Ambrose's rhetorical skills than his biblical or theological beliefs. But Augustine also discovered that the allegorical interpretation practiced by Ambrose provided a way to reconcile the Old Testament with Greek philosophy.

Through all of this, Augustine was living in great sin—especially sexual—and struggling with guilt, uncertainty, and unhappiness. He described his own conversion in his *Confessions*: One day he went to a garden where he found himself weeping over his own miserable condition, when he heard a child's voice saying, "Take up and read. Take up and read." He randomly opened his Bible and read the first thing his eyes landed on: "Let us behave decently, as in the daytime, not in carousing and drunkenness, not in sexual immorality and debauchery, not in dissension and jealousy. Rather, clothe yourselves with the Lord Jesus Christ, and do not think about how to gratify the desires of the flesh" (Romans 13:13–14). In his own words, "No further would I read, nor did I need; for instantly, as the sentence ended, by a light, as it were, of confidence flooded into my heart, all the gloom of doubt vanished away" (*Confessions*, 8.12.29). Augustine repented, wholeheartedly

---

1. He would later write numerous works refuting Manichaeism in general, and specifically its view of evil as an eternal reality (for example, *Concerning the Nature of Good*). Augustine argued that evil is not something in and of itself but rather the absence of something. In the same way that darkness is not something in itself but rather the absence of light, evil is not something in itself but rather the absence of good and, more specifically, God. Evil came to be through the abuse of a good thing created by God—free will—on the part of both angelic beings and human beings.

embraced Christianity in 386, and was baptized the next Easter Sunday by Bishop Ambrose.

Augustine returned to Africa in 388, and three years later was (rather against his will) ordained as a priest in Hippo. In 396, at the age of forty-two, he was promoted to bishop of Hippo. He served in that role until his death in 430, even as the Vandal barbarians were besieging the city of Hippo and the Roman Empire itself was dying.

Contribution

Augustine was a prolific writer, second only to Origen in his literary legacy. After his ordination, he became devoted to studying and preaching the Word of God and left behind many of his sermons as well as essays on numerous theological and moral issues, commentaries on many of the books of the Bible, and over 250 letters. Augustine had a very high view of the authority and trustworthiness of the Bible. His writing was permeated with Scripture. On the other hand, Augustine relied upon a somewhat inaccurate Latin translation of the Bible (he did not know Greek), and he also practiced allegorical interpretation (although with careful limitations).

One of the first books written by him after he became bishop was his famous *Confessions*. It is essentially his life story—one of the first autobiographies to be written—in the form of a prayer, in which he was brutally honest about his own sinfulness. This book has had a profound impact. Not only have many people been able to relate to Augustine's experience, but *Confessions* also changed the way people think about themselves. At that time, people thought of themselves primarily in a corporate sense, as members of the human race, or, for Christians, as members of the church. But due to *Confessions*, in Western thought at least, people began to think of themselves primarily as individuals; Christianity also became more individualistic in emphasis.[2]

2. Hill, *The History of Christian Thought*, 83–84.

One of Augustine's major books was *On the Trinity*. He summarized the development of the doctrine to that point—God is one in essence and three in persons. However, Augustine, unlike almost all theologians preceding him, rejected the idea that the Father was the source of the divine nature of the Son and Spirit.[3] Rather, deity is a distinct nature that the Father, Son, and Spirit share in equally and eternally. Any distinctions between the persons of the Trinity can only be seen from a historical perspective—with regard to their work in the world—not an eternal perspective—before creation. It is only in this sense that Jesus could say, "The Father is greater than I" (John 14:28) and submit his will to the will of his Father. Therefore, Augustine rejected even a hint of subordinationism of the Son or Spirit to the Father, which had lurked in the theology of many of even the most orthodox theologians to that point.

It was exactly this line of thinking from Augustine that also led to the controversial *Filioque* clause in the Nicene Creed. The question was, did the Spirit proceed only from the Father (as the original Nicene Creed stated) or from the Father "and the Son"? From John 20:22, where Jesus breathed on his disciples and said, "Receive the Holy Spirit," Augustine argued that the Spirit proceeds from the Son as well as the Father. He does acknowledge that the Spirit comes from the Father *primarily* (John 15:26), but the Father gave the Spirit to the Son, and the Son gave the Spirit to his followers. None of this implies that one person of the Trinity is any greater than any other person; it just illustrates the relationships of the persons of the Trinity.

As a result of Augustine's influence, at the Council of Toledo in 589, the Western (Latin) church added to the end of the statement in the Nicene Creed, "We believe in the Holy Spirit, the Lord, the giver of life, who proceeds from the Father," the phrase, "and the Son." The Latin word for this addition is *filioque*, and it has come to be known as the *Filioque* clause. The Eastern (Greek) church

---

3. Remember that, to refute charges of tritheism, previous theologians argued for the *unity* of God on the basis that the *sole* source of divinity is the Father; God is *one* in that the Son and Spirit find their divine nature in the Father.

had a problem (to put it lightly) with this for two reasons: First, they were not consulted about adding the phrase—a snub to them. Second, they thought it demeaned the Holy Spirit by making him a junior member of the Trinity, inferior to the Father and Son—heresy to them. This became such a major issue that it was a part of what led to the split between the Western (Roman) Catholic Church and the Eastern (Orthodox) Church in 1054, known as the Great Schism.

Augustine is probably most well-known for his psychological analogies of the Trinity. His reasoning was that reflections of God's nature, specifically his trinitarian being, can be found in the highest level of his creation, those who bear his image—humans. So, for example, he saw the Trinity reflected in the aspects of human love—the lover, the object of love, and love itself—and in faculties of the human mind—memory, understanding, and will. Augustine has been criticized for his use of these analogies, but he also acknowledged that the Trinity is ultimately a mystery beyond human comprehension, and any analogy can only go so far.

Probably Augustine's most well-known book is *The City of God*. Rome had fallen to barbarians in 410, and Christianity received the blame. Christianity had been proclaimed as the official religion of the empire, and apparently the gods of Rome were angry. In response, Augustine wrote this great apology for Christianity. He traces two contrasting cities—of God (or, heavenly, the church) and of humanity (or, earthly, the state)—from creation to eternity. *The City of God* was immensely influential on Christian thought from that point on.

Augustine had to deal with two significant controversies, and from those came two important sets of his writings.

The first controversy came from a group of Christians known as the Donatists. Their roots go back to the persecution that caused many Christians, including clergy, to betray Christianity in one way or another. The questions were: How were these fallen Christians and clergy to be treated? Were they to be allowed back into the church? Some answered the latter question with a no and broke away from the orthodox catholic church in order to remain "pure" (as they understood it). Others answered the question with a yes, but with qualifications. Remember that Cyprian found himself in the middle of this issue and argued that schism or division of the church was always wrong and that fallen Christians could and should be forgiven and readmitted to the church.[4]

The Donatists were one of those sects that broke with the orthodox catholic church, claiming that it was illegitimate and that all that its clergy did was corrupt and worthless. By Augustine's time, the Donatists actually outnumbered the orthodox Christians in North Africa and were a profound threat to the catholic church, which it rejected. Like Cyprian, Augustine condemned the Donatists for the sin of destroying the unity of the church. Furthermore, in his response to this movement, Augustine laid out an understanding of the nature of the church and the practice of the sacraments that is still a part of Roman Catholic theology.

Augustine was the first to recognize that the catholic "visible" church contained some who were not true Christians even though they professed to be true Christians. He used Jesus' parables in Matthew 13 to show that the visible church is made up of saints and sinners (e.g., the parable of the wheat [saints] and the weeds [sinners]). He also developed the doctrine of the "invisible" church, which is made up only of those whom God (alone) knows to be true believers in Jesus Christ. All true believers are a part of the visible, catholic church (Augustine accepted Cyprian's doctrine that there is no salvation outside of the church), but not all members of the catholic church are true believers.

The Donatist controversy also prompted Augustine to address the functions of the church and its priests, specifically the sacraments, such as baptism and the Lord's Supper or Eucharist. The Donatists believed that unworthy priests could not perform the sacraments, and if they did, the sacraments were invalid. To the contrary, Augustine argued that the validity of the sacraments was not to be found in the human who administered them, but rather in the grace of Christ that flowed through them. In fact, it is really

4. See chapter 8.

Christ himself who is administering the sacrament through the priest.[5] The idea is expressed in the Latin phrase *ex opere operato*— "on account of the work itself." Only priests can administer the sacraments, and ideally those priests are worthy of that privilege, but even if they are not, the sacrament, by its very observance, accomplishes what God intended it to accomplish. This became the understanding of the Roman Catholic Church as well as most Reformers much later.

The second and maybe most important controversy faced by Augustine was prompted by Pelagius. This British monk came to the city of Rome and was stunned by its rampant immorality, much of it justified theologically—"I was born a sinner and therefore I really can't do anything about it." He was further upset when he became aware of Augustine's *Confessions*, specifically its most famous statements addressed to God: "Give [the grace to do] what You command, and command what You will" (*Confessions*, 10.29). To Pelagius, this seemed to make God a grand puppeteer of people and took away human responsibility for sin.[6]

In contrast, Pelagius reasoned that God would not have commanded us to "be holy because I am holy" (Leviticus 11:44–45; 1 Peter 1:15–16) if it were not possible for us to obey that command. Indeed it is possible, Pelagius said, because all of Adam's descendants are born in exactly the same way that Adam was created—without sin and able to be obedient to God; Pelagius fervently believed in the free will of all humans. Furthermore, Adam's sin did not affect anyone else, other than by providing a bad example. Pelagius went so far as to say that it was possible to live a *sinless* life without any help from God. This was highly unlikely due to the corruption of the world and the many bad examples around us, but it was *hypothetically* possible; for any individual, sin was *not* inevitable. So Pelagius taught that *we are sinners because* we *sin*—by the exercise of our own free will and not because of anything Adam did. If we do sin, baptism will wash that away, and

5. See, for example, Augustine's *On Baptism*.
6. Hill, *The History of Christian Thought*, 78.

then we can live sinlessly from then on. It seems that Pelagius did not dismiss the need for God's grace, but, in his mind, that came only in the form of creating humans with free will and then giving his laws to guide the will to make good decisions; God's grace is not any kind of internal spiritual or moral enablement for the will.

Augustine had already become convinced of very different things and therefore vigorously opposed the teachings of Pelagius while further refining his own views in a series of treatises such as *On Nature and Grace, On Grace and Free Will*, and *On the Grace of Christ and On Original Sin*. Augustine's views on these matters boiled down to two central ideas: First, humans are guilty sinners from birth and totally unable to do anything about it; second, God is totally sovereign and only his grace makes salvation of sinful humans possible.

Primarily from Paul's epistles, but also reflecting his own personal and intense struggle with sin, Augustine believed that, due to Adam's sin, all people are sinners and guilty of sin from birth (Romans 5:12–19); this is called the doctrine of original sin. Augustine believed that *we sin because we are sinners*—by nature, which comes from Adam (Ephesians 2:3). This means that sin is inevitable for everyone because all people are born with a predisposition to sin. Augustine did not deny free will but rather absolute free will. All people are born totally free to do what they *want* (to please themselves—sin) but not what they *ought* (to please God—obey). The famous Latin phrase is *non posse non peccare*—not possible not to sin. This is the polar opposite of Pelagius's view: *posse non peccare*—possible not to sin.

Augustine's doctrine of original sin necessarily leads to the absolute need of God's grace for salvation. In contrast to Pelagius's view of divine grace, Augustine understood it to refer to the inward work of God through his Holy Spirit to first turn our will so that we *want* to do what is good, and then to empower us so that we are *able* to do what we want to do—the good. Everything that we have is a gift of the grace of God (1 Corinthians 4:7), including saving faith, which is given, not to all, but only to the elect—those chosen by God for salvation. The Holy Spirit persuades—not coercively, but rather compellingly—the elect sinner to believe in the gospel—gladly and willingly. But God's grace does not end there; it continues to help the Christian to grow in faith and obedience. Christians are still unable, in themselves, to live as Christians; God's grace is necessary from beginning to end, from conversion to glorification. One of Augustine's favorite verses was John 15:5, where Jesus said, "Apart from me you can do nothing." Therefore, salvation is *not* a cooperative effort between God and the Christian—synergism—but rather entirely a work of God—monergism. This was a new idea that Augustine introduced into the flow of Christian thought; it would be continued in Reformation theology, as we will see.

Even though Pelagius's rather optimistic view of humans was condemned as heretical by the Council of Ephesus in 431, Augustine's rather pessimistic view was not accepted by all. Most theologians ended up somewhere in the middle. And so the story continues.

Conclusion

Not all agree with Augustine's theology, but all agree that he was one of the greatest and most influential theologians ever. His thought cannot be underestimated and should not be overlooked. It has profoundly influenced not just theology but political and psychological theory as well. "It is little exaggeration to say that the whole history of the Western Church for the last 1,500 years is the story of Augustine's influence."[7]

7. Ibid., 91.

15

GREGORY THE GREAT

Doctor of the Church Too

Context

After the death of Augustine and the fall of the Roman Empire, Christian thought stalled somewhat during what is known as the Dark Ages. Most theological interaction amounted to evaluating Augustine's theology—pro and con. Pelagius's view—*human* monergism[1]—was not an option after its condemnation in 431. But neither did Augustine's view—*divine* monergism—entirely catch on. Many tried to find some middle ground in syncrgism—some degree of *cooperation* between the human and God in the work of salvation.

Even though John Cassian (360–432) is most well-known for his promotion of Christian monasticism in the West, he also represented a view that has come to be known as semi-Pelagianism. This was the claim that salvation is by the grace of God, but that divine grace will only be extended when the sinful human takes the initiative to seek it by asking for God's help. For example, Cassian

1. Humans can live a holy life with no or little help from God.

wrote, "And when [God] sees in us *some beginnings of a good will*, He at once enlightens it and strengthens it and urges it on towards salvation, increasing that which He Himself implanted or which He sees to have arisen *from our own efforts*" (*Conference*, 13.8, emphasis added). He did go on to clarify that God's grace is necessary for salvation and that human effort or free will alone is insufficient. However, even the hint of human effort *prior to* divine grace struck the supporters of Augustine as Pelagianism.

This came to a head in 529 at the Synod of Orange (in present-day France), which condemned semi-Pelagianism and affirmed the absolute necessity of God's grace in salvation. This was basically a reaffirmation of Augustine's understanding *to an extent*: God's grace is prior to and the cause of human salvation and righteousness. However, the synod did not endorse Augustine's monergism, preferring instead a milder form of synergism, somewhere in between Augustinians and semi-Pelagians such as Cassian: Sinners are so affected by sin that they *cannot* take any initiative to seek God's help. So God *must* take the initiative (in contrast to semi-Pelagianism) and extend grace. Once that grace is received, then the human can cooperate with grace the rest of the way (in contrast to Augustinianism). This view is sometimes called semi-Augustinianism and is represented by one of the most important popes in Roman Catholicism.[2]

Gregory was born into a wealthy yet devoutly Christian family in Rome in 540. Like his father, he became a city administrator, but soon decided to devote himself to the monastic life. Monasticism suited him the best, but due to his administrative experience, the bishop of Rome—the pope[3]—sent him as his representative to

2. Up until now, I have referred to the church throughout the Roman Empire as the orthodox catholic church. At this time, however, the Eastern and Western parts of the church were beginning to diverge. The bishop of Rome oversaw the Western church, while the patriarch of Constantinople oversaw the Eastern church. The *official* division had not yet taken place (that would happen in 1054), but from this point on I will refer to the Western church as the Roman Catholic Church and the Eastern Church as the Eastern Orthodox Church.

3. The word comes from the Latin *papa*, which means "father." It was originally applied to all bishops, but beginning in the sixth century it came to be applied only to the bishop of Rome.

Constantinople, where he lived for five years. When he returned to Italy, he would have preferred to resume the life of study and asceticism, but, when the pope died in 590, Gregory was unanimously chosen to succeed him. After the fall of the empire, there was a power vacuum in Italy, and Gregory reluctantly stepped into that role. He was the Roman pope for only fourteen years and died in 604. Historically, he is known as Gregory the Great and is the last of the four great "doctors" of the Roman Catholic Church.[4]

Contribution

Gregory was a prolific letter-writer (around 850 are still around), and in them he expressed his views on a wide range of ecclesiastical, moral, and theological matters. He also wrote a number of homilies; his series on Ezekiel and the Gospels have survived. His longest written work is the *Book of Morals*, which is a commentary on the book of Job examined, as was typical at that time, in terms of the historical/literal meaning, the allegorical/typical meaning, and the moral/ethical meaning. The *Dialogues* was his narrative of the lives of "saints" who were living at that time, or who had recently died, to illustrate the possibility of holy living even in those difficult days. His most influential book was the *Pastoral Rule*, a set of guidelines for bishops, written during his first year as pope.

Gregory is best known for important ecclesiastical contributions. Not surprisingly, because of his own background and personal preference, Gregory was a great promoter of monasticism, especially the form established by Benedict of Nursia (whose story Gregory told in Book 2 of the *Dialogues*) and his famous Rule of St. Benedict. He was also responsible for initiating a great missionary effort to the pagans in the old Roman Empire. Finally, Gregory promoted many religious practices, such as observing a variety of feast days, veneration of saints and relics, and acts of penance.

4. The others are Ambrose, Jerome, and Augustine.

These would become commonplace in Roman Catholicism and also part of the reason for the Protestant Reformation about a thousand years later.

Gregory's primary theological contribution was in the ongoing debate over Augustinian theology. Oddly enough, Gregory claimed to support Augustine's theology but did so in a very synergistic way. When Gregory considered things from God's perspective, he was very Augustinian: God is sovereign and his grace is crucial and decisive. When he considered things from a human perspective, he sounded a bit Pelagian in the sense that he urged Christians to take moral living seriously. This was why Gregory heartily approved of practices such as prayer, penance, attending mass, participating in the sacraments, giving to the poor, and even asceticism; these were means of cooperating with divine grace. In fact, *apart from these human works, there was no assurance of salvation, but through such human works, one could be assured of one's election.* Due to this emphasis on what humans do (on which Gregory would always superimpose divine grace), Gregory opened himself to the charge of legalism. This ambivalent position regarding the divine and human aspects of salvation basically characterized the soteriology of the Roman Catholic Church in the Middle Ages. It was an Augustinian monk in the theological tradition of Gregory who reacted so strongly against this emphasis and launched the Reformation. His name was Martin Luther.[5]

Conclusion

Gregory represents much of what became general Roman Catholic thought and practice during much of the Middle Ages. Theologically he represents the middle ground between hardline Augustinianism and heretical Pelagianism—salvation is accomplished through a cooperative effort between God and the human, with a priority on God's grace to be sure, but still much emphasis on

5. See chapter 21.

human works as well. In popular practice, unfortunately, the grace aspect was overshadowed by the human aspect.

Gregory should be recognized for his stress on the importance of humility. This was true in the study of Scripture. In the words of Pope Benedict XVI, Gregory believed that "Intellectual humility is the primary rule for one who searches . . . the sacred book." Serious study was necessary, "but to ensure that the results are spiritually beneficial . . . humility remained indispensable."[6] Humility was also necessary for bishops and clergy. The very last section of Gregory's *Pastoral Rule* concerns humility. He wrote, "It is necessary that, when abundance of virtues flatter us, the eye of the soul should return to its own weaknesses, and profoundly humble itself; that it should look, not at the right things that it has done, but those that it has left undone; so that, while the heart is wounded by remembrance of frailty, it may be the more strongly confirmed in virtue before the author of humility" (Part 4).

It was this kind of humility that characterized Gregory himself. He explicitly rejected the title of "Universal Pope," claiming that such a label would only inflate one's ego. Rather, he insisted on being called "servant of the servants of God," a title that would be passed on to his successors. It makes me wonder if he himself would have wanted "the Great" tacked on to his name.

6. Pope Benedict XVI, *Great Christian Thinkers*, 145.

16

JOHN OF DAMASCUS

Last Greek Father

Context

The Western Roman Empire was falling apart in the fifth century due to barbarian invasions, but the Eastern Empire was unaffected and survived, becoming known as the Byzantine Empire.[1] This contributed to the ever-widening divergence between the Western church and the Eastern church. They had always been divided by language (Latin in the West and Greek in the East), and now they were divided politically as well. After the Council of Chalcedon in 451, the Eastern church itself was divided between those who believed in the two natures of Christ (Chalcedonian Christology) and those who believed in a single nature of Christ (monophysitism). In order to bring unity to the Eastern church, Emperor Justinian called for the fifth ecumenical council to meet at Constantinople in 553. Two of the outcomes of this council were these: the

1. Byzantium was the old name for the capital, Constantinople.

condemnation of Origen and his teachings, [2] and the affirmation of the Definition of Chalcedon in a way that might appease the monophysites (which it failed to do).

Yet another attempt to placate the monophysites was to suggest that Jesus had not one nature, but one *will*—the decision-making capability of a person—and that will was divine. This view is called *monotheletism*. An important figure in what came to be known as Eastern Orthodox or Byzantine theology was Maximus the Confessor. He vigorously opposed monotheletism, claiming that to deny that Jesus had a *human* will as well as a divine will was no different from denying Jesus' human nature entirely. Without a human will, it could not be a human nature. This would also amount to a denial of the incarnation and invalidate salvation through Jesus Christ. Maximus was given the title "Confessor" because he was tortured to death as a result of his opposition to monotheletism. All of this resulted in the sixth ecumenical council, once again in Constantinople (680–681), which condemned monotheletism and affirmed that Christ had a human will and a divine will, each as a necessary characteristic of their respective natures.

This brings us to our primary focus here, the theologian who is regarded by the Eastern Orthodox Church as the last of the great Greek church fathers and the culmination of Byzantine theology.

John Mansour was born in Damascus, Syria, sometime in the middle of the seventh century, and he died in the middle of the eighth century. He became a monk, but not much else is known about his life.

Contribution

John's written theological works are not original but rather a compilation and summary of the teachings of the church fathers and theologians to that point. His most famous book is *Fount of Knowledge*, which has three parts, the third being the most important:

2. This is rather ironic since, just as Augustine was the theological giant for Western Christianity, Origen was the theological giant for Eastern Christianity—despite his condemnation.

"An Exact Exposition of the Orthodox Faith," which focuses on Trinitarianism and Christology (including the two wills of Christ).

John of Damascus played a major role in a major aspect of orthodox Christianity—icons. This is actually a Greek word (*eikōn*), which means "image." Icons are paintings of Christ and saints that were used as a means of drawing the believer into worship and sometimes referred to as windows into the spiritual realm. Christ, of course, is the focus of the worship, but saints were regarded as intercessors—those who relay petitions to God. Icons are not idols. They are never to be worshiped but rather are an aid to worship. Unfortunately, this was not always understood by ordinary, everyday Eastern Christians.

In the eighth century, Byzantine churches were filled with icons to the extent that the emperor, Leo III, was concerned that their use was becoming excessive and ordered the destruction of icons. This resulted in the next great Byzantine showdown—the iconoclasm controversy—between those promoting the use of icons (iconodules, or icon respecters) and those opposed to them (iconoclasts, or icon smashers). The latter argued that icons were a form of idolatry and therefore should be prohibited.[3]

Into this fray stepped John of Damascus, who provided theological justification for the use of icons in his *Discourses Against the Iconoclasts*. Against the argument that icons violated the second commandment prohibiting idols (Exodus 20:4–5), John wrote, "In the old days [of the Old Testament], the incorporeal and shapeless God was never depicted. Now, however [after the incarnation], when God is seen clothed in flesh and conversing with humanity, I make an image of the God whom I see. I do not worship matter; I worship the God of matter, who became matter for my sake and was prepared to inhabit matter, who worked out my salvation

3. Using some rather sophisticated theology, they also argued that the use of icons amounted to the heresies of either Nestorianism (Jesus Christ is not one person with two natures but rather two persons, each having a distinct nature) or Eutychianism (Jesus Christ does not have two distinct natures, but rather one brand-new nature). Go figure! Another factor was likely the growing influence of Islam in the East, which prohibited all religious images.

through matter. I will not cease from honoring that matter which works my salvation. I venerate it, though not as God."[4]

Note a few crucial things in this quote. First, the word *veneration* is important in that it provides a distinction from *worship*. Icons are venerated (honored, respected); God alone is worshiped. Second, salvation is at stake as it was also in the previous Trinitarian and Christological controversies. Salvation could only happen through a genuine incarnation—eternal deity taking on a fully human nature. Icons were legitimate because God really became matter when Christ really became human. So in the same way that we paint pictures of humans to represent them, we can paint pictures of Jesus Christ to *represent* him. On the other hand, to deny icons is to deny the incarnation; the iconoclasts were really guilty of Docetism.[5] Once again, this is not nitpicky, esoteric theological one-upmanship; important issues were at stake.

The iconoclasm controversy led to the seventh ecumenical council in Nicea in 787, which exonerated the use of icons and condemned the iconoclasts. The *Definition of the Council of Nicea* (787) in part says, "The more men sees them [icons of Christ, Mary, angels and saints] in artistic representation, the more readily they will be aroused to remember the originals and to long after them. Images should receive due salutation and honorable reverence, but not the true worship of faith which is due to the divine nature alone. . . . For the honor paid to the image passes on to its original, and he who reveres the image reveres in it the person represented."[6]

Conclusion

John of Damascus is a helpful figure by which to summarize Eastern Orthodox Christianity. As previously mentioned, he is regarded

---

4. Quoted in Jonathan Hill, *The History of Christian Thought*, 110.
5. Docetism is the denial of the true humanity of Jesus. This is what the monothelites were earlier charged with—to deny the human will of Jesus is to deny his humanity.
6. Quoted in Tony Lane, *A Concise History of Christian Thought*, 78.

as the culmination of Eastern Orthodox or Byzantine theology. And he was the major theological influence in reestablishing the use of icons, which remains a vital aspect of orthodox worship. The seventh ecumenical council, which affirmed this, was the final church council to be recognized by the Eastern Orthodox Church. In fact, it is known as the "Church of the Seven Councils."[7] The declarations of these councils are an essential facet of orthodox theological tradition and are regarded as having equal if not greater authority than the Bible. "The Eastern Church became fiercely traditional. After the age of the Fathers [ending with John of Damascus], the overwhelming concern became the preservation of the orthodox tradition without the slightest variation. This applied both to dogma or belief and to liturgy or worship."[8] This is not to say that there were no more orthodox theologians; rather, orthodox theologians such as Gregory Palamas (d. 1359) simply restated or clarified traditional orthodox theology in and for their own times.

7. See the complete list in the appendix.
8. Lane, *A Concise History of Christian Thought*, 66.

17

ANSELM OF CANTERBURY

First Scholastic

Context

The old Roman Empire was a thing of the past, and the Roman Catholic Church stepped into the power void and brought a degree of unity to what was left of the empire in the West. Like Gregory the Great, the various popes became the effective civil, political, military, as well as religious leaders in the West. Even the kings that eventually arose were appointed and coronated by the pope, such as the French king, Charles, who was crowned by Pope Leo III in the year 800. He became known as Charles the Great, or Charlemagne, and with his coronation, what came to be known as the Holy Roman Empire began. The term *Holy* is significant because of the close association between church and state that characterized the Middle Ages in Europe.

The centers of education during the so-called Dark Ages were the monasteries. By about 1000 (roughly the end of the Dark Ages), Europe had been "Christianized" religiously and stabilized politically.

This set the stage for a revival of theological study—but under the influence (once again) of philosophy, or more specifically, reason or logic. As a result, medieval theology focused on the relationship between faith and reason—how can Christianity be shown to "make sense"? *Scholasticism*[1] is the term applied to this philosophical approach to theology at this time (until about the fifteenth century).

If one individual brought the Dark Ages to an end and launched Scholastic theology, that individual would be Anselm. He was born in Italy in 1033. From an early age he wanted to be a monk and eventually accomplished that at a monastery in Bec, Normandy (modern-day France), a well-known center of learning. Anselm devoted himself to studying the Bible and the church fathers and became known for his intellectual abilities, but also for his spiritual maturity and ascetic lifestyle. In 1078 he became the head (abbot) of the monastery. Due to his significant reputation, in 1093 Anselm was appointed archbishop of Canterbury, in England, but only after he was literally carried to the church where he was forced to accept the appointment. Apparently when he was given the bishop's staff as the symbol of his position, he refused to grasp it until his fingers were pressed around it by others. Much of his time in that office was spent in exile due to his clashes with several kings in England regarding political and ecclesiastical authority. He was allowed to return to Canterbury in 1106, and it was there that he died three years later.

Contribution

Anselm's most famous books are the *Monologion* (*Monologue*), the *Proslogion* (*Discourse*), and *Cur Deus Homo* (*Why God Became Man*). These are considered the very first books on "natural theology," or the philosophical study of God. Anselm was trying to defend and explain Christian beliefs by appealing to reason alone apart from Scripture. It was *not* his intent to ignore or

---

1. From the Latin word *schola* or "school."

eliminate Scripture from theological method. Rather, he was trying to strengthen Christian belief, which is derived from Scripture, by adding the evidence of reason to it. In fact, the original title of the *Proslogion* was *Faith Seeking Understanding*. He wrote, "I do not seek to understand in order to believe, but I believe in order that I may understand. For this I also believe: that unless I believe, I shall not understand" (1). Even though this is counterintuitive, it has been the contention of Christian theologians all along (clearly so in Augustine). Normally we would think that we come to an understanding of something first, and then we decide whether it is worthy of belief or not. But the things of God must first be accepted by faith, and only then can they be more fully understood through the use of human reason. In Anselm's thinking, reason or logic is the God-given link between our thoughts and his thoughts.

In the *Proslogion*, Anselm expressed his famous ontological[2] argument for the existence of God. He had been intrigued by what the psalmist said in Psalm 14:1, "The fool says in his heart, 'There is no God.'" Why was atheism inherently foolish? Supposedly, the answer came to him in the middle of the night (and it has probably been keeping people awake in the middle of the night ever since). His argument goes something like this: Even atheists had to be able to *imagine* a being called God in order to deny God's existence. Anselm believed that any atheist would agree that "God" could be defined as "a being than which nothing greater can be conceived," that is, the greatest of all beings that can be imagined. Furthermore, a being that exists in reality is greater than a being that exists only in the imagination. So if existence is greater than nonexistence, then a God who exists is greater than an imaginary God. And if God is the *greatest* of all beings imaginable, then God must really exist. According to Anselm, his argument shows that atheists are fools because atheism is irrational. Many have tried to refute the argument, but it is still around today.

Anselm's *Cur Deus Homo* is written in the form of a dialogue between himself and a monk named Boso. As the title indicates,

2. *Ontology* is the philosophical study of being or existence.

Anselm is trying to answer the question, Why did God become man? His answer, again based on reason primarily, was to solve the problem of sin. His view has come to be known as the "satisfaction" view of the atonement of Christ.

We should note first how Anselm's cultural setting—medieval feudalism—affected this view. After the collapse of the centralized power of the Roman Empire, the nation-state arose. In this structure, the king of the nation owned all of the lands he ruled. He would appoint overlords to supervise those lands, who in turn would appoint "underlords" to manage their lands, and so on down to the serfs, who actually worked the land. This hierarchy was based on sworn allegiance to one's lord, and to disobey one's lord was regarded as robbing him of his honor. In the case of such dishonor, the lord demanded "satisfaction," namely, reparation for the harm done plus something extra due to the personal disgrace. If this "reparation plus" could not be met, then there would be punishment.

In the same way, God is King, our sin dishonors him, and he demands satisfaction. However, sinful humans are unable to provide that because God's honor is infinite and only something "infinite plus" would be sufficient to provide satisfaction. Obviously, only God himself could provide something like that. Humans *ought* to provide satisfaction because it is they who sinned. But only God *can* provide it because only he is infinite. Conclusion? The God-man is necessary to provide satisfaction for God regarding human sin. Jesus Christ, being God, can offer his life, which is of infinite worth, and, being human, can pay the price for humans.

Remember that, in the feudal system, it was only if satisfaction—reparation plus—could *not* be made that punishment would follow. In the death of Jesus, satisfaction *was* made, so in Anselm's theory, Jesus was not *punished* for our sins; rather, he provided the "reparation plus."

There are several things that are right in this idea: First, our sin does dishonor God. Second, this view of Christ's atonement virtually replaced the prevailing view at that time, namely, that Christ's death was a ransom paid to Satan. Anselm could not stomach this view (rightly so) because it implies that Satan's power is equal to if not greater than God's. How can this possibly be if God is the greatest being imaginable? Third, Anselm seeks to make theology understandable to the people of his day whose existence was feudalism.

There are also several things that are wrong here: First, the Bible does say that Jesus died in our place as punishment for our sins (e.g., 2 Corinthians 5:21; Galatians 3:13; 1 Peter 3:18). Anselm seems to make sin more like a debt that needs to be paid than a crime that needs to be punished. God's honor is at stake, but so is his justice or righteousness (Romans 3:25–26). Second, when feudalism ceased, this way of explaining the death of Christ made less sense to Christians; it became a bit outdated.

Conclusion

Anselm is considered one of the greatest theologians of the Middle Ages. He gets much of the credit for jump-starting creative Christian thought after the Dark Ages. Furthermore, it was his view of the atonement that came to be assumed in most of medieval theology. The Reformers would build on it by emphasizing that Christ's death was also a substitutionary payment for our sins. As mentioned, his ontological argument for God's existence is still the matter of much thought and debate. To cap it off, "Anselm seems to have been one of the most thoroughly likable people of the Middle Ages."[3] Would that every theologian be thought of in such a way.

---

3. Hill, *The History of Christian Thought*, 131.

PETER ABELARD

Proud Provocateur

Context

Much is known about this twelfth-century thinker's life because, like Augustine, he wrote an autobiography (which was rare in those days) called *The Story of My Misfortunes*. Peter Abelard was born in 1079 in Brittany, France, and studied theology under a variety of well-known teachers. Abelard was every bit a nonconformist and had a tendency to disagree with his teachers, humiliate them in debate, set up rival lectures, and draw many of their students away from them and to himself. He eventually began teaching in Paris, and his reputation as a theological free spirit continued to attract many students.

Whereas the monasteries were the centers of learning in the Dark Ages, the great cathedrals that were being built throughout Europe after that period also included schools, which were eventually opened to laymen as well as aspiring clergy. Eventually great teachers at these cathedral schools would attract students from far and wide. This gave birth to what we now call "universities."

Peter Abelard was one of those magnetic schoolmasters, and the University of Paris was established largely due to his notoriety.

Abelard fell in love with Heloise, a teenage girl whom he was tutoring. As he described it in his autobiography (among other more steamy descriptions that would not be appropriate here), "Love drew our eyes to each other far more than the lesson drew them to the pages of our text." Their neglect of a lesson resulted in the birth of a baby. He secretly married Heloise to make the baby legitimate, but her uncle and guardian paid some thugs to assault Abelard and render him, shall we say, incapable of ever fathering another child. Eventually Heloise ended up in a convent, and Abelard ended up in a monastery. They corresponded but were never reunited, except in a common grave in Paris. Their correspondence made their love affair renowned at that time and ever since.

Abelard was eventually condemned at the Council of Sens in 1140, largely due to Bernard of Clairvaux, who vehemently disagreed with Abelard's theology and wrote a book entitled *The Errors of Peter Abelard*. Abelard died several years later. The title of his autobiography seems most appropriate.

Contribution

Abelard's major written work is *Sic et Non* (*Yes and No*), in which he recorded apparently conflicting texts in Scripture and the church fathers, and then tried to harmonize or explain them. Even though in many ways Abelard was a provocateur, in doing this he was not trying to discredit authoritative sources but rather to show the problems that needed to be addressed. He then attempted to solve the problems in a typically scholastic way—by reason. But whereas Anselm came to the Christian theology from the starting point of faith—"I believe in order that I may understand" (*Proslogion*, 1), Abelard came at it from the opposite direction—"By doubting we come to enquire and by enquiring we reach truth" (*Sic et Non*, preface). Both the method and the motive of Abelard in this book did not endear him to the established religious authorities, to say the least.

Even though Abelard considered himself a philosopher rather than a theologian, his most lasting contribution was in the area of theology and also something that he said relatively little about—the reason Jesus died. His ideas were primarily expressed in his *Exposition of Romans* and have come to be called the moral influence view of the atonement.

Abelard believed that sin is not the act in itself but rather the motive that led to the act. A sin is only that which is done contrary to one's conscience. He rejected the notion of original sin; we are sinners because *we* sin, not because of anything Adam did. The problem of sin, therefore, needs to be solved within the sinner.

Abelard rejected both the ransom-to-Satan view of the atonement as well as Anselm's satisfaction view. He reasoned that if salvation is a *free* gift of God, how could any kind of payment to God be required to get it? Furthermore, the honor or justice of God is not the issue, but rather the love of God. God loves sinners and wants to forgive them if they will only repent. He sent his Son to demonstrate his love for humans through his death.[1] When sinners come to grips with this great love, a responsive love is instilled in them, resulting in their repentance and God's forgiveness. This love also breaks the power of sin and produces obedience. As he put it, "Our redemption through Christ's suffering is that supreme love in us which not only frees us from slavery to sin, but also acquires for us the true liberty of sons of God" (*Commentary on Romans*).

There is something that is very innovative here. Up until Abelard, the atonement was viewed as *objective* in the sense that its primary effect was *outside* of the sinner. In the ransom to Satan theory, there was a transaction between God and Satan resulting in our salvation. In Anselm's satisfaction theory, the transaction was between the Son and the Father resulting in his satisfaction and our salvation. But in Abelard's theory, the atonement is understood for the first time as *subjective*, that is, it prompts a change *within* the sinner—love and obedience—resulting in salvation.

1. He quoted John 15:13: "Greater love has no one than this: to lay down one's life for one's friends."

Abelard's views were rejected in his day for a variety of valid reasons: First, God's overall character is misrepresented. Is God love? Absolutely (1 John 4:8). Does God love sinners? Absolutely (1 John 4:9–10). But God is also righteous, holy, and just. Since sinners have broken his laws, he is angry with them (Romans 1:18), and that anger needed to be propitiated.[2] Second, Abelard's view really makes Christ's death unnecessary. God *could have* shown his love for sinners in many other ways, and therefore Jesus did not really *have to* die. Third, this view implies that Jesus is not really our Savior, but rather the one who influences us to change our behavior, which results in salvation. In other words, we are saved because of what *we* do for God (love and obey him) rather than what Christ has done for us (died in our place). This leads to the fourth problem, and that is that Christ's death changes what we *do* (our behavior) but not who we *are* (our nature). These last two problems are why Abelard's view was accused of being Pelagian, that is, asserting that we have the innate ability to please God by how we live.

Some scholars argue that Abelard's view of the atonement and salvation includes more than described above, which may be true. However, the moral influence view of the atonement has come to characterize recent liberal Protestant theology, in which God's love is affirmed but his wrath is denied. God is love, and that is pretty much it. Salvation is accomplished if we just do our best to love and obey God.

Conclusion

If Anselm was one of the kindest men of his time, Abelard was somewhat of the opposite. He was rather brutal in his disagreements with others. He was a ruthless debater and anything but humble about his ability to out-think everyone else. His brilliance

---

2. This idea is found in connection with God's love in 1 John 4:10 (NASB, ESV). The word *propitiation* means "something that turns away wrath." The NIV's translation, "atoning sacrifice," does not quite capture this aspect of Christ's death.

(along with his infamous love affair) also made him somewhat of a celebrity, which also fed his pride. As has been observed, it is ironic that his relationship with Heloise was one of the greatest love stories of that time, and his idea of the atonement was centered on love, yet he did not seem to be a very loving or loveable person himself.[3] Nevertheless, Peter Abelard deserves his reputation as a great thinker, intellectual innovator, and brilliant theologian/philosopher.

3. Hill, *The History of Christian Thought*, 141.

19

THOMAS AQUINAS

Angelic Doctor

Context

If any philosophy affected Christianity (and it did), it was Platonism (as we have seen). This philosophy seemed to "fit" with Christianity due to its emphasis on "universals" or (in theological terms) the *spiritual* realm and reality. However, in the Middle Ages that began to change. Aristotle (Plato's student) and his philosophy had largely been rejected and forgotten in the Christian West due to his emphasis on the "particulars" of the *natural* realm. However, Aristotelian philosophy did flourish in the East, specifically in Islam, and it was through Islamic philosophers that it was reintroduced in the West (specifically Spain, which Muslims had conquered and occupied). Scholastic theology at this time focused on the integration of theology (revelation) and philosophy (reason), so it stands to reason (no pun intended) that the thought of Aristotle would attract attention. The application of Aristotelianism to Christianity reached its peak in one of the greatest theologians of all times.

Thomas Aquinas was born into an Italian aristocratic family in 1225, the youngest son of the Count of Aquino. His early education came from local Benedictine monks, but at the age of eleven, he was sent to the University of Naples, where he was introduced to Aristotle's philosophy and where he continued to show himself superior to his teachers. To the great displeasure of his parents, he became a Dominican friar and embraced the monastic life of poverty. On behalf of his family, two of his brothers kidnapped and imprisoned him. For two years they tried to persuade him to renounce his vows. At one point they even sent a prostitute to his room to seduce him but, in a way very unlike Peter Abelard, Thomas drove her from his room with a burning log from the fireplace. Rather than renounce his vows, Aquinas spent his time in captivity studying Scripture. Eventually he was released by his sisters, who lowered him in a basket from the tower of his castle-prison.

In 1245 Aquinas moved to Cologne, France, to study under the famous Dominican theologian-philosopher, Albert the Great. Due to his quiet personal demeanor and considerable physical dimensions, Aquinas's fellow students called him "the dumb ox." Albert, however, recognized the potential in Aquinas and said, "One day this dumb ox will make a bellowing that will be heard throughout the world."[1] Aquinas was ordained as a priest in 1250 and began his teaching career at the University of Paris in 1256.

Even though Aquinas was every bit the theologian, he also loved to pastor. While performing the Mass one day in 1273, Aquinas had what he characterized as an intense spiritual experience,[2] and from that point on he did not write another word, saying, "Compared to what I have seen, all that I have written seems like straw." He died the next year at the age of forty-nine.

1. Interestingly, eventually those who disagreed with Aquinas were considered stupid. One influential theologian who challenged Aquinas's thought was John Duns Scotus. From his name and due to his disagreement with Aquinas, the word *dunce* (a stupid person) came into being.

2. Others have suggested this was a stroke or a nervous breakdown.

Contribution

Aquinas produced an incredible number of written works, aided, very much as Origen had been, by a production team that recorded what he dictated. Apparently he was capable of dictating several different books *at the same time*! Like Aristotle, whom he simply referred to as "the Philosopher," Aquinas wrote on an amazingly wide variety of topics, but his two primary works are the *Summa*[3] *Against the Gentiles* and the *Summa Theologica*.[4]

Aquinas's first book was *Summa Against the Gentiles*. This was intended to be a systematic theology presented in such a way that even Jews and Muslims (the main religious rivals to Christianity in the Middle Ages) would be rationally convinced of the truth of Christianity.

Aquinas's most famous book is the *Summa Theologica*—a summary, exposition, and critique of Christian theology from the first century. It was written in the form of a series of 512 questions; followed by suggested answers from Scripture, previous theologians, and reason; followed by an in-depth critique of those answers; and ending with Aquinas's concluding answer and support for it. It is divided into three sections: The first deals with the Being of God, the Trinity, creation, and providence. The second deals with moral theology—ethics, virtues, and vices. The third deals with the person and work of Christ, sacraments, and the future.

In typical Scholastic manner, Aquinas had a high view of reason, but it did not eclipse revelation. Rather, Aquinas believed that some things could be understood only by special or supernatural revelation—e.g., the Trinity, the incarnation, matters of salvation—but some things could be understood through general or natural revelation by means of the senses and reason—e.g., the immortality of the soul, basic moral principles. Both divine revelation and human reason come from God and are never contradictory. Aquinas's work predominantly comes from natural

---

3. The term *summa* refers to a comprehensive summary of a particular discipline.
4. He died before he could complete the latter.

theology—using human reason to "process" what is observed in nature through the senses.

Like Anselm before him, Aquinas believed that reason alone could provide arguments for the existence of God, but he did reject Anselm's ontological argument for God's existence because, following Aristotle, one must start with what can be observed through the senses and reason from there. The ontological argument did not do that. So Aquinas offered five different arguments for God's existence in part 1, question 2 of his *Summa Theologica*. For example, any movement is caused by something else (cause and effect), but there must be an ultimate cause of all movement—the "unmoved mover," or God. Another argument is based on the apparent design of the universe. The parts of the universe seem to have a purpose and work in a certain way. Where did this come from? Aquinas answers, "Some intelligent being exists by whom all natural things are directed to their end; and this being we call God"—an "intelligent designer." Probably his most significant argument is known as the "cosmological argument": Something cannot come from nothing; therefore, the universe came from something—the "uncaused cause," or God. This idea of causation really runs through the rest: What causes motion or change, purpose or design, and indeed existence or being itself? The ultimate cause of all things that itself is not caused by anything—God.

So according to Aquinas, God's existence can be known by reason. What about God's attributes or characteristics? From the assumption that God is the Uncaused Cause, Aquinas reasoned that God does not just *have* existence like everything else; he *is* existence. His essence and existence are identical. As the Uncaused Cause, God must also be pure *Being* with no *becoming*. If God had potential to become something else, that becoming would be an effect, which would require a cause, meaning he was not the *Uncaused* Cause after all. Another way of saying this is that God is immutable, which, as we have seen previously, means God is impassible, unaffected by anything outside of himself, emotionless. On the reasoning goes, but the bottom line is that this understanding of God is really no different from previous theologians like Augustine and Anselm. It is known as classical Christian theism. The criticism is that the God who comes from natural theology and reason *alone* seems to be a rather impersonal Being. But what about the God of the Bible who loves, hates, grieves, cares, and so on? Aquinas does talk about God in these latter terms and did not believe God to be impersonal by any means.[5] But this does illustrate the limits of reason. It can only take us so far in thinking about God. From that point on, we are dependent upon what God tells us about himself in special revelation, the Word of God.

This brings us to Aquinas's famous view of analogical language (*Summa Theologica*, part 1, question 13). If God is the Uncaused Cause, pure Being, existence itself, unchanging, infinite, perfect, eternal, how can he really be known by creatures who are not *any* of these things, and how can he even be described in human language? Aquinas came back to God as the Uncaused Cause of everything else. Even unseen and unknown causes can be known *to a degree* by their effects. Causes are both like and unlike their effects. Therefore, God can be known and described by means of *analogy*, which is a term used to describe something that is both like and unlike that which it is describing.[6] Aquinas used the example of wisdom, which applies to both God and humans. Human wisdom is *similar* to God's wisdom, but they are also different. For example, we can cease to be wise (become a "dunce"), but God cannot cease to be wise. God does not just *have* wisdom like humans, he *is* wise. This use of analogical language to talk about God was very influential in the history of Christian theology, both Roman Catholic and Protestant.

As we have already noted, Aquinas did not believe that matters of salvation could be known apart from special revelation; reason fails to provide this knowledge. Like Augustine, who greatly influenced

5. A very practical question might be, If God does not and cannot change, then why pray? Aquinas would answer, If we are trying to get God to change, then prayer is useless. But the real purpose of prayer is to align our will with God's, not the other way around.

6. For example, God is a fortress (Psalm 18:2). God is like a fortress in some ways and different in other ways. That is, he is not *exactly* like a fortress.

Aquinas along with Aristotle, he did believe that humans are entirely dependent upon the grace of God for salvation, and even the faith by which this is received is a gift of God. These convictions come not just from Scripture, but as implications of Aquinas's view of God as the Uncaused Cause of all things. Like Augustine, Aquinas also had a very high view of divine providence (God is the ultimate cause of all things, although he sometimes works through secondary causes such as human choices freely made) and predestination (God has chosen those who will be saved and gives them the faith and grace necessary to accomplish that). The bottom line here is that God alone, as the Uncaused Cause, does the work of salvation—monergism.

Aquinas equated justification and sanctification. The former is more outward, in relationship to God's holiness, and the latter is more inward, in relationship to personal holiness, but they are inseparable, and both are incomplete until the end of life. Protestants have protested. They charge that this leads to works righteousness, at least partially, that is, that we must contribute to our own salvation by living a holy life (sanctification). Aquinas probably does open himself to such a charge, but it is probably not completely justified (again, no pun intended).[7] He does emphasize the importance of participation in the sacraments, but he also clearly states that those are merely channels of divine grace and not meritorious works that impress God in any way. The very choice and effort involved in participating in the sacraments are gracious gifts of God.

Aquinas also made rather definitive statements regarding some uniquely Roman Catholic doctrines such as the following:[8] 1) the immaculate conception of Mary: Jesus' mother was born sinless, that is, without original sin; 2) the Church as the mediator of salvation: Christ's death provides salvation, but the Church distributes that salvation, primarily through the sacraments; 3) the seven sacra-

---

7. Although a distinction between *justification* and *sanctification* seems to be biblically correct. They are closely related, but they are different concepts.

8. Although most of these views were already held in Roman Catholicism in Aquinas's day.

ments of the Church: In addition to baptism and the Lord's Supper (the Eucharist), these included penance (i.e., acts of contrition), ordination (holy orders), marriage, confirmation, and the last rites (extreme unction); 4) transubstantiation: When the priest consecrates the bread and wine at the Eucharist, they are transformed and actually become the body of Christ and the blood of Christ, respectively; and 5) purgatory: This is where Christians who have not lived faithfully while on earth are purged of sin before they are accepted into heaven.

With the exception of baptism and the Lord's Supper as sacraments, all of these would eventually be disputed and rejected by the theologians of the Protestant Reformation.

Conclusion

Thomas Aquinas's influence was immediate—although not always positive—and lasting. Some disagreed with and even condemned his views due to the influence of Aristotle. Nevertheless, Aquinas was canonized as a saint in 1323 and given the title "Angelic Doctor." The title "Universal Doctor of the Church" was added in 1567. In 1879, Pope Leo XIII made official what was already unofficial, declaring in an encyclical letter that Aquinas's theology was the standard for Roman Catholic theology. It is still the authoritative teaching of the Roman Catholic Church today. His philosophy and thought developed into a system known as "Thomism." His only real theological peer before and after his own lifetime was Augustine.

20

JULIAN OF NORWICH

Monastic Mystic

Context

Another line of Christian thought developed during the Middle Ages—it has come to be called spiritual or mystical theology. The roots of this go back to the Alexandrian School and their allegorical interpretation of Scripture. Early mystical theology can be found in some of the thinkers we have already considered—for example, Augustine, Anselm, and Aquinas—and many others—for example, Bernard of Clairvaux, Francis of Assisi, Bonaventure, Meister Eckhart, and Thomas à Kempis. Monasticism provided the context out of which came most of the mystical theology of the Middle Ages.

Mystical theology is hard to define but, generally speaking, it is more about knowing God experientially than knowing him intellectually. "Briefly and generally stated, mystical theology or Christian mysticism seeks to describe an experienced, direct, non-abstract, unmediated, loving knowing of God, a knowing or seeing so direct as to be called union with God."[1] Such an experience of God came through "contemplation"—observing an object (God, in this case) in an adoring and loving way such that one is drawn to and even into that object, thus the important idea of "union with God" in mystical theology. At its best, this was not apart from the intellect, but it certainly went beyond the intellect.

A biblical basis for this has been found in the vine and branches imagery of John 15:1–8, where Jesus spoke of "remaining in him," and Jesus' prayer in John 17, where Jesus asked for his disciples, "Father, just as you are in me and I am in you, may they also be in us" (v. 21). The doctrines of the incarnation and humanity of Christ are also central here: God became human so that he could unite humans with God.

The activities associated with Christian mysticism were many and varied: certainly the study of Scripture, but also prayer, meditation, and asceticism in many forms. These were all intended to purify one of sin (purgation) and draw one toward God (illumination) in order to be one with him (unification).

It is in this area of mystical theology that women began to make significant contributions. For example, Hildegard of Bingen (1098–1179) was a German nun who began to have visions at a very early age. In addition to mysticism, her writings include works on theology, science, music, poetry, philosophy, and many more subjects. Catherine of Siena (1347–1380) was an Italian nun who never learned to write but, through a secretary, "wrote" many letters and recorded a vision of and conversation with Christ, called the *Dialogue*.

Our focus here will be Julian of Norwich (around 1342–after 1416). Very little is known about her, even her name. She came to be known as "Julian [a man's name] of Norwich" because she lived in a small room built next to the wall of the Church of St. Julian in Norwich, England. The term *anchoress* would describe her—a

---

1. Dennis D. Martin, "Mysticism" in *Evangelical Dictionary of Theology* (Grand Rapids: Baker, 1984), 744. Much of my description of mystical theology here is based on this article.

woman who withdraws from the world to live in isolation and practices silence, study, prayer, and meditation. As in the case of Julian, this seclusion would often take place next to a parish church.

Contribution

Julian's sole contribution to mystical theology is entitled *Revelations of Divine Love*, the record of sixteen "shewings" or visions that she experienced on May 8, 1373, and her reflections on those revelations over the next twenty years. It has been described as "the most perfect fruit of later medieval mysticism in England"[2] and "one of the warmest, most optimistic and sensible works of medieval theology."[3]

Several themes are prominent in Julian's *Revelations*. The first is evident in the title—the love of God, specifically for his creation. This emphasis resulted in a very positive view of nature and humanity, somewhat the opposite of Augustine and his view of the effects of sin. "[Julian] represents the resurgence of a Christian optimism, a spirituality which is not dominated by sin and fallenness, but by grace and glory, a materialistic spirituality which rejoices in the goodness of nature. Nature is all good and fair in itself, says Julian, and grace was sent to save it."[4] This is not to imply that Julian denies evil and suffering—quite the opposite. But with regard to those awful realities, she offers profound comfort to her readers through the Lord's words to her repeated over and over in chapter 32: "all things will be well." Sin did have negative effects on nature and humans but, due to his love, God is at work "enfolding" all to himself.

In the very last chapter of her *Revelations*, she recorded God's own explanation of her visions fifteen years previously: "Would

2. John H. Morgan, *Catholic Spirituality: A Guide for Protestants* (Bristol, IN: Wyndham Hall, 1994), 39.

3. Hill, *The History of Christian Theology*, 168.

4. Kenneth Leech, *Experiencing God: Theology as Spirituality* (San Francisco: Harper & Row, 1985), 329.

you learn to see clearly your Lord's meaning in this thing? Learn it well: Love was his meaning. Who showed it to you? Love. What did he show you? Love. Why did he show it to you? For Love." She added, "Thus I was taught that Love was our Lord's meaning" (chapter 86).

God's love for and "enfolding" of his creation leads to a second theme in Julian's mysticism, which is referring to God (specifically the Son) as "Mother." There is feminine imagery used of God in the Bible (e.g., Deuteronomy 32:18; Isaiah 42:14; 49:15) and in many of the church fathers, but it is seen in Julian in "its strongest and most developed form."[5] The love of God and the mother imagery of God come together, for example, in the following: "In our Father, God Almighty, we have our being; in our merciful Mother [the Son], we are remade and restored. Our fragmented lives are knit together and made perfect man. And by giving ourselves through grace to the Holy Spirit, we are made whole" (chapter 58). Later she wrote, "The human mother will suckle her child with her own milk, but our beloved Mother Jesus feeds us with himself, and with the most tender courtesy does it by means of the Blessed Sacrament, the precious food of all life. . . . The human mother may put her child tenderly to her breast, but our tender Mother Jesus simply leads us into his blessed breast through his open side and thus reveals part of the Godhead and the joys of Heaven, with spiritual certainty of endless bliss" (chapter 60). The main point of the mother imagery is that God is the source of all things, especially humans' being, and therefore he cares for what he has brought into being in the most loving and nurturing way.

Conclusion

Protestants tend to be skeptical regarding mystical theology in general out of concerns that it is rooted in Neoplatonic philosophy or even pagan mystery religions, and that mystical experiences

5. Ibid., 363.

sometimes supersede biblical revelation. As a Protestant and evangelical, I would share these concerns; however, I also appreciate and applaud the intent of Christian mystics overall—to draw closer to God in experiential relationship. If Christian mysticism can be faulted for, at times, relying too much on experience, the opposite tendency is, at times, seen in Protestantism, namely, a rationalistic approach to theology and God. Getting one's theology straight seems to be the highest virtue. Christianity is reduced to reason rather than relationship. The best of Christian thought, however, works hard to understand God as much as possible with the mind, and then to be irresistibly drawn into a closer and more intimate relationship with him in order to more deeply experience his infinite glory, grace, and worth. May that be true of all of us.

21

MARTIN LUTHER

Founder of Protestantism

Context

The state of *popular* Roman Catholic theology in the sixteenth century can be summarized in this way: Salvation was accomplished through semi- (or nearly) Pelagian synergism. That is, divine grace was necessary to be saved, but that grace could be earned ("merited") or even bought through human means, such as living faithfully according to the practices of the Church (penance, sacraments) or purchasing "indulgences" (the elimination or reduction of temporal punishment for sin granted by the pope or his representatives). God was generally understood to be demanding payment for sins *from humans* and perfect holiness *within humans* before he would grant justification and salvation. Salvation was mediated through the Church, particularly through the sacraments. Authority in Roman Catholicism was to be found in Scripture *and* tradition, namely, what the Church taught Scripture to mean.[1] In practice, this boiled down to what the pope said. "Papal infallibility" was not official Roman doctrine, but it was unofficially held. What the pope said was what God said. All of this gave the Church hierarchy—especially the pope—considerable clout, and, as is too often the cause, this resulted in abuse of power and corruption. For example, the Church had become incredibly wealthy through the sale of tickets on the high-speed train to heaven (indulgences). All in all, the Roman Catholic Church was ripe for reform.

There were also other crucial cultural factors. One was the revival of classical learning and languages. The cliché was "back to the sources," which, in the case of theologians, were the Hebrew Old Testament, the Greek New Testament, and the writings of the church fathers. Another related factor was the invention of the printing press with moveable type in 1450 by Johann Gutenberg. This made possible the efficient propagation of old sources as well as new ideas.

The official beginning of the Protestant Reformation is October 31, 1517, when an Augustinian monk nailed ninety-five theses to the church door in Wittenberg, but reformation had really begun long before. For example, John Wycliffe (1320–1384) was an English theologian-pastor who boldly condemned the deficient theology and corrupt practices in the Roman Church. His views profoundly affected John Hus (1369–1415), a preacher in the city of Prague. Wycliffe was condemned as a heretic after his death by the Council of Constance in 1415. The same council condemned Hus to be burned at the stake. Their views did not die, however, but were carried on one hundred years later by men such as Martin Luther.

Luther was born in 1483 in Germany, the son of a successful businessman. He went to the University of Erfurt to study law, abiding by his father's wishes. However, after surviving a terrifying thunderstorm on his way home, Luther left his university studies and took the vows of an Augustinian monk.

1. The term *magisterium* is used in this sense. It refers to the right and power of the Roman Catholic Church to teach spiritual truth.

In the monastery, Luther was plagued by both his own sinfulness and by the prevailing notion of God as full of wrath—the perfect storm that caused Luther to fear and hate God. He was haunted by Romans 1:17: "For in the gospel a righteousness from God is revealed." As he had been taught, this divine righteousness meant that God was out to punish sin. He wrote, "I could not believe that he was placated by my satisfaction [acts of penance]. I did not love, yes, I hated the righteous God who punishes sinners. . . . I was angry with God" ("Preface to Complete Edition of Luther's Latin Writings"[2]).

Luther was eventually sent back to the University of Erfurt, but this time to study philosophy and theology. He was also sent to Rome. He found it not to be a place of spiritual fulfillment as he had expected, but rather full of immorality and indifference. In 1512 Luther completed his doctorate of theology at the University of Wittenberg and joined its faculty.

While preparing lectures on Paul's Epistle to the Romans, Luther's "tower experience" took place (around 1519). He described it as follows:

> At last, by the mercy of God, meditating day and night [on Romans 1:17], I gave heed to the context of the words, namely, "In [the gospel] the righteousness of God is revealed, as it is written, 'He who through faith is righteous shall live.'" There I began to understand that the righteousness of God is that by which the righteous live by a gift of God, namely by faith. . . . Here I felt that I was altogether born again and had entered paradise itself through open gates. There a totally other face of the entire Scripture showed itself to me.[3]

Luther's breakthrough was the realization that he need not fear that God would punish him for his own unrighteousness, but rather he should trust that God would provide God's own righteousness to him.

2. *Martin Luther: Selections from His Writings*, ed. John Dillenberger (Garden City, NY: Anchor Books, 1961), 11.
3. Ibid.

It was the posting and printing of Luther's ninety-five theses in 1517 that thrust him into the public spotlight, and the occasion of these was the selling of indulgences nearby. Indulgences were being sold not only to shorten one's own time in purgatory, but also that of a dearly departed loved one. The slogan was, "As soon as the coin in the coffer rings another soul from purgatory springs." The ninety-five theses were Luther's protest against this particular practice as well as many other practices and doctrines of the Church. Almost immediately Luther became a hero to his German countrymen as well as a heretic to the Church establishment. Eventually the pope excommunicated Luther in 1520, but Luther publicly burned the papal order in Wittenberg, much to the delight of those who observed. The next year Luther appeared before Emperor Charles V at the infamous Diet (court) of Worms (Germany). When asked if he would renounce his views, Luther's well-known response was, "My conscience is held captive by the Word of God. I cannot and will not recant, because it is neither safe nor right to go against conscience. Here I stand, I can do no other. God help me. Amen." The emperor condemned Luther as a heretic.

For a year afterward Luther was protected in a castle where he spent his time translating the Bible into German. The protest against the Church continued during this time, and the outcome was a new church—the Lutheran Church—something that Luther himself never intended nor desired. Nevertheless, after his year in hiding, Luther emerged to give leadership to the new Lutheran churches.

Luther married a former nun, Katharina, and had six children. He continued to preach, teach, write, and lead the reform movement. The stress of it all took its toll, and in 1546 Luther died of a heart attack as he was passing through the same town where he had been born sixty-two years previously.

Contribution

Martin Luther was not a systematic theologian, but rather wrote (extensively!) primarily in order to address a specific issue that was crucial at that time. His body of written work includes sermons, commentaries, treatises, pamphlets, and books.

Since Luther launched the Protestant Reformation, it is possible to summarize his emphases in terms of his "protests" against the prevailing Scholastic Roman Catholic theology in his day.

First, he rejected the very methodology of Scholastic natural theology, that is, knowing God through general revelation (how God has revealed himself in nature) and human reason. The problem with this, according to Luther, was the profound limitation of human reason, which is further complicated by the effects of sin. After all, with regard to general revelation, Paul said that all people "suppress the truth by their wickedness" (Romans 1:18). In addition, Luther believed that God *supremely* revealed himself, not through his works in nature, but through his Son's suffering on the cross. And that wonderful truth, according to Paul, was "foolishness" according to human reason (1 Corinthians 1:18ff.). What pleases God according to *human reason*? Crank out good works; be obedient to God; love others. . . . What pleases God according to *the "foolishness" of the gospel*? Be *desperately* dependent upon God for *everything*.

This leads to his second protest: Luther broke not only from prevailing doctrine regarding how God can be known, but also from the prevailing understanding of how salvation was accomplished. In essence, he recaptured what had been lost in Christian theology for over one thousand years. His "rediscovery" was that human merit plays no role *whatsoever* in salvation, but rather it is *completely* the gracious gift of God that is received by faith. Humans contribute nothing to their own salvation; God does it all. This is taken for granted by evangelicals today, but in Luther's day, this was radical!

Third, and related to the previous, Luther rejected the Scholastic optimism regarding the freedom of the human will to cooperate with God in the process of salvation. To Luther, that smacked of pride and ignorance of the doctrine of original sin. Therefore, it should not be surprising that Luther agreed with the founder of his monastic order, Augustine, regarding divine predestination and monergism. How could it be otherwise, if the human is completely sinful and the human will is a slave to that sin? The only hope for salvation is that God does everything necessary to secure it—from start to finish. These views were expressed in his famous book *The Bondage of the Will*.

Fourth, Luther differed from Augustine and rejected the Roman Catholic view of justification as equivalent to sanctification, both being progressive through life (and even beyond in purgatory). According to Augustine's view, individuals are not declared righteous (i.e., "just") until *all* of the sin has been purged from their life and they actually are righteous in *every* sense. Luther's view was that justification was immediate and complete when the sinner believes in the gospel of Jesus Christ. This does not mean that the sinner is righteous in the sense of sinless. Rather, the individual is now both at the same time—*simul justus et peccator* or "simultaneously righteous and a sinner." But how could a holy God declare an individual "righteous" when that person is still a sinner and still sins? Luther's answer was through the "sweet and wonderful exchange": When sinners believe the gospel, their sin is transferred (imputed) to Christ, and Christ's righteousness is transferred to the sinner (2 Corinthians 5:21). It is on the basis of Christ's righteousness (not the sinner's, because the sinner has no righteousness of his own) that God declares the sinner righteous. By Luther's own confession, the doctrine of justification by grace through faith alone was at the center of his theology and the center of theology, period. Everything else hangs on it.

The to-be-expected criticism of justification by grace through faith alone is that it will lead to "antinomianism," that is, lawlessness, because there will be no incentive for Christians to obey God; they are already forgiven. Luther's response was that obedience and other good works would naturally flow from the justified Christian, who is now a new creation in Christ (2 Corinthians 5:17). Those saved through faith and not works were "created in Christ Jesus to do good works" (Ephesians 2:8–10). So good works do not result in justification; it is the other way around—they flow from it as evidence of it. Luther's doctrine of justification and its implications are expressed, for example, in *The Freedom of a Christian*.

Fifth, Luther rejected the Roman Catholic view of authority, which was that, alongside Scripture, tradition was a valid source of authority for the Church, and it was the Church alone (the pope and bishops) that had the right to interpret both Scripture and tradition. So in practice, the Church ended up being the ultimate authority in spiritual matters. For Luther, the sole authority was the written Word of God. Anything that was not to be found in Scripture is not valid theology or practice for Christians, which brings us to the final "protests" of Luther.

Sixth, Luther rejected the elevation of the clergy, long a part of Roman Catholic doctrine and practice, and affirmed the priesthood of the believer. He believed that any Christian had the right to know, study, and teach the Word of God (this was why Luther was compelled to translate the Bible into German) and even perform the sacraments. Luther expresses this in *Appeal to the German Ruling Class*.

The seventh protest of Luther was with regard to the Roman Catholic doctrine of the sacraments. He rejected five of the Roman sacraments and accepted only baptism and the Lord's Supper as biblically qualified sacraments. He rejected the idea of *ex opere operato*[4] and believed that the sacrament was invalid without the faith of the person receiving the sacrament. He rejected the concept of transubstantiation and believed instead that the bread and wine remained bread and wine while also becoming the body and blood of Christ.[5] Luther's view of the sacraments can be found in *Babylonian Captivity of the Church*.

We can see from these protests and emphases in Luther's writings the famous principles of the Reformation: *sola scriptura* (Scripture alone), *sola gratia* (grace alone), *sola fide* (faith alone), and *solus Christus* (Christ alone).

4. The sacrament is valid and effective by the very fact that it is done. See chapter 14.

5. We will come back to his view on this matter in the next chapter.

Conclusion

We could probably fault Luther for some of his methods. He was rather caustic, belligerent, arrogant, tactless (and so on) with those who disagreed with him (to pretty much any degree), both Catholics and his fellow Protestants. He was the proverbial "bull in a china shop." Nevertheless, as one historical theologian expressed it, "Martin Luther was a giant of history, probably the most significant European figure of the second millennium. His ideas and actions changed not just the church but the world."[6] This seems to be verified by the fact that more books have been written about Luther than any other historical figure with the exception of Jesus Christ himself.

6. Hill, *The History of Christian Thought*, 181.

22

ULRICH ZWINGLI
Founder of Reformed Theology

Context

Several months after Martin Luther's birth, another future reformer was born in Switzerland—Ulrich[1] Zwingli—on January 1, 1484. After receiving his education at the universities of Vienna and Basel, he became the priest in several parishes, the third being the Great Cathedral Church in Zurich when he was thirty-five years old (1519). During his pastoral ministry, Zwingli was reading widely under the influence of the "back to the sources" movement and, independent of Luther, was coming to share many of the same reformation convictions that Luther had. He was also gaining a reputation as a writer and preacher, adopting the unusual practice (at that time) of preaching through entire books of the Bible.

In Zurich, Zwingli worked to bring reform in both the church and the government. During the 1520s, the Roman Catholic mass was abolished, statues were removed from churches, indulgences

---

1. Or, Ulricht, Ulrecht, Huldrych, Huldreich, or, if you like Latin, *Huldrychus*.

were banned, Mary and other saints were no longer to be venerated, and other Roman Catholic practices were eliminated.

All of this went even further in reform than Luther was willing to go in Germany, and even Luther regarded some of it as fanatical. On the other side, Roman Catholic authorities regarded Zwingli's reforms as outright rebellion. Amazingly, some of Zwingli's own followers wanted to go even further in reform and accused Zwingli of not being radical enough.[2] They were repressed and even persecuted by Zwingli and the Swiss civil leaders.

While the northern cantons (counties) of Switzerland were becoming reformed, the southern cantons remained staunchly Catholic, and war broke out between the two regions in 1529. Zwingli and other Reformed pastors accompanied the soldiers into battle, and Zwingli, at the age of forty-seven, was killed in battle in 1531.

Contribution

Like Luther and other reformers, Ulrich Zwingli was a prolific writer. His first publication was *The Clarity and Certainty of God's Word* (1522), in which he articulated the Reformation principle of *sola scriptura*, that the Bible is the final authority for Christians (not the Church), and that it is clear to all Christians (not just the clergy) through the help of the Holy Spirit. In 1525 Zwingli wrote *On True and False Religions*, which is considered to be the first Reformed systematic theology. In 1531 Zwingli produced two more significant works: *A Short and Clear Exposition of the Christian Faith* and *On the Providence of God*. In the latter, he treated the doctrine of the sovereignty of God as the primary organizing principle for all theology. This became typical of Reformed theology from that point on. For Zwingli, this included a strong belief in divine predestination and monergism.

Like Luther, Zwingli became involved in a number of controversies, some of them with Luther himself, specifically with regard to

2. These came to be known as the Radical Reformers, and we will take up their story in chapter 24.

the sacraments of baptism and the Lord's Supper. With regard to baptism, the controversy was with his own followers (as mentioned above) who wanted to abolish the practice of infant baptism and follow believer's baptism instead. In response, Zwingli wrote *Baptism, Rebaptism and the Baptism of Infants* (1525).[3] He defended the practice of infant baptism as the means of initiating babies into the New Covenant community of the Church, but (unlike Luther) rejected the Roman Catholic doctrine that baptism removed the guilt of original sin.

Zwingli's controversy with Luther had to do with the Lord's Supper. As noted briefly in the previous chapter, Luther rejected the Roman Catholic doctrine of transubstantiation or "actual presence"—the consecrated bread ceases to be bread and is transformed into the *actual* body of Christ, and the consecrated wine ceases to be wine and is transformed into the *actual* blood of Christ. Rather, Luther believed in what has come to be known as consubstantiation or "real presence"—the consecrated bread remains bread but also contains the *real* body of Christ, and the consecrated wine remains wine but also contains the *real* blood of Christ. After all, Jesus had said at the last supper, "This is my body given for you" (Luke 22:19) and previously, "I am the bread of life" (John 6:35, 48). As the Lutheran creeds put it, the body and blood of Christ are "in, with, and under" the bread and wine respectively.

Zwingli disputed both transubstantiation and consubstantiation. He believed that Luther was misunderstanding the metaphorical references in Luke 22 and John 6 and was taking them far too literally. He argued, for example, that just later in John 6, Jesus said, "The Spirit gives life; the flesh counts for nothing" (v. 63), the point being that physical things (such as bread and wine) cannot pass on spiritual things (such as eternal life and divine grace). This is also why Zwingli did not like the term *sacrament*, because it implied that the bread and wine do indeed channel the grace of God and

3. The term *rebaptism* was a reference to the practice of the Anabaptists (rebaptizers), a derogatory term for the Radical Reformers. Again, we will take this up further in chapter 24.

spiritual blessings to the believer. Furthermore, Zwingli charged both transubstantiation and consubstantiation with being a pagan practice (cannibalism). To that Luther replied, "I would eat dung if God demanded it."[4] Zwingli also disputed the actual or real presence idea, saying that the body of Jesus Christ is now in heaven, not on earth (in the bread and wine). Humans can only be at one place at one time, and this is true of Jesus as well in his *genuine* humanity. That is, Jesus Christ is not omnipresent *in his humanity.* To say anything else is to deny his true humanity—which is heresy.

Instead, Zwingli believed that the bread and wine were simply material/visible symbols that point to spiritual/invisible realities, the body and blood of Christ. The body of Christ *is* present in the Lord's Supper ceremony, not physically, but in the form of the gathered believers, the church, the Body of Christ. The Lord's Supper is important, not because God's grace is channeled through the elements, but rather because through those symbols Christians are reminded of what is fundamental to their faith—the sacrificial death of their Savior. Therefore, the Lord's Supper was to be observed as a memorial service done "in remembrance of" (Luke 22:19; 1 Corinthians 11:24–25) Christ and his sacrificial death on the cross. Zwingli put it this way in his *Confession of Faith* (1530):

> I believe that in the holy eucharist (that is, the supper of thanksgiving) the true body of Christ is present by the contemplation of faith [on the part of believers]. In other words, those who thank the Lord for the kindness conferred on us in his Son acknowledge that he assumed true flesh and in it truly suffered and truly washed away our sins by his own blood. Thus everything done by Christ becomes present to them by the contemplation of faith. But that the body of Christ, that is his natural body in essence and reality, is either present in the Supper or eaten with our mouth and teeth, as is asserted by the papists [Roman Catholics] and by some who long for the flesh pots of Egypt [Lutherans], we not only deny but firmly maintain to be an error opposed to God's Word.

4. Heiko A. Oberman, *Luther: Man Between God and the Devil*, trans. Eileen Walliser-Scharzbart (New York: Image Books, 1992), 244.

All of this came to a head in October 1529 at the Marburg (Germany) Colloquy, which was convened with the hope that this dispute between Zwingli and Luther could be settled. It was not. The two parties departed even more divided and bitter toward each other. Zwingli's view of the Lord's Supper did not prevail in Reformed theology generally (as we will see in the next chapter), but ironically it was adopted by the Radical Reformers/Anabaptists who bitterly opposed his view of baptism and vice versa.

Conclusion

Ulrich Zwingli is appropriately regarded as the founder of Reformed theology and tradition within Protestantism. He was largely overshadowed by a second-generation Reformer, John Calvin, whose name has come to be associated with Reformed theology— "Calvinism." "Zwinglianism" would be more fitting historically, but now that term normally refers exclusively to Zwingli's view of the Lord's Supper described above. Nevertheless, it was Zwingli who paved the way for what is now known as Reformed theology, and his view of the Lord's Supper is still held by many Protestant traditions today.

23

JOHN CALVIN

Second Generation in Geneva

Context

Reformation thought and "fever" spread quickly from Germany
and Switzerland. In France it captivated a young student at the
University of Paris. John Calvin was born in Noyon, France, in
1509. He initially intended to enter the legal profession, but his
interests turned to theology after he became sympathetic with
Protestantism, and specifically with French Protestants who were
being persecuted by the French king. Due to this same persecution, Calvin had to flee from Paris in 1534. He moved to Basel,
Switzerland, where he intended to live the quiet life of a scholar.
During this time, he published the first edition of his most well-
known publication, *Institutes of the Christian Religion* (1536, at
the age of twenty-five!), a relatively short explanation of Protestant
theology. It was very quickly recognized as a significant contribution to Reformation thought.

While on his way to Strasbourg, Calvin had to take a detour through the city of Geneva. During a brief stopover, Guillaume Farel, a disciple of Zwingli, tried to persuade Calvin to relocate to Geneva by saying that if he did not, he would be in disobedience to God and God would punish him. Calvin did not like that possibility, and so in 1537 he complied and began his work to further establish Protestantism in Geneva. However, his attempted reforms moved too quickly for some, causing division in the city and forcing Calvin to leave Geneva the very next year. He returned to Basel with the intention of resuming his life of scholarship, which was not to be. Another reformer, Martin Bucer, urged him to come to Strasbourg. Calvin resisted until Bucer told him (you guessed it) that if he did not, he would not be in God's will and God would punish him. Again, Calvin gave in and moved to Strasbourg, where he pastored French Protestants who also had to flee France. He married a widow during this time. By his own admission, this was the happiest period of his adult life and ministry.

In the meantime, the church in Geneva was falling apart, and the Genevan city council pleaded with Calvin to return and fix the mess. He adamantly refused at first, but then reluctantly agreed to return to Geneva in 1541. This time he stayed until his death in 1564 at the age of fifty-five. He had a profound impact on the entire city of Geneva, though it came with much difficulty and through many trials. His goal was basically to transform the city (not just the church) of Geneva into a theocracy. Calvin also established a Protestant training center in Geneva, which attracted students from throughout Europe who then returned to their homes to further the Reformation there. One of these was John Knox, who brought the Reformation to Scotland. He described the academy in Geneva as the "most perfect school of Christ" since the time of Christ.

Calvin lived a very simple yet demanding life. He ate very little. He worked very hard. As a result, he was constantly battling ill health. Nevertheless, his literary output was staggering. The Latin edition of his works fills fifty-nine volumes. Calvin considered himself a preacher more than a theologian. He preached an average of three times a week, around 160 sermons each year. His theology flowed from his sermon preparation. Calvin was committed to doing theology through the exposition of Scripture.

Contribution

Due to his commitment to preaching and exposition of God's Word, it is not surprising that Calvin wrote not only sermons but commentaries on nearly all the books of the Bible. In addition, he composed many letters, treatises, lectures, and books on a variety of topics. He continued to revise his *Institutes* throughout his life; there were five editions, the final one being published in 1559. Some consider this to be the most important work on Protestant theology ever to be written.

Little in Calvin's theology is unique or original. His thought reflected the first generation of reformers—Luther and Zwingli. Like Luther, he rejected the notion of natural theology and philosophy in general due to the debilitating effects of sin on the human mind. Rather, the sole authority and only trustworthy source for theology is God's Word—*sola scriptura.*

With regard to sin, Calvin agreed with Augustine and Luther that, due to Adam's sin, all are sinful and unable to do anything about it. Sin, in fact, has invaded every aspect of one's being: "Paul removed all doubt when he teaches that corruption subsists not in one part only, but that none of the soul remains pure or untouched by that mortal disease. . . . Here I only want to suggest briefly that the whole man is overwhelmed—as by a deluge—from head to foot, so that no part is immune from sin and all that proceeds from him is to be imputed to sin" (*Institutes*,[1] 2.1.9). This is the famous (infamous?) Calvinistic doctrine of "total depravity." Calvin and this doctrine do *not* mean that all people are as evil as they can possibly be; they *do* mean that the only good sinful people can do comes from the grace of God, and none of that impresses God or improves one's standing before him.

1. John Calvin, *Institutes of the Christian Religion*, ed. John T. McNeill, trans. Ford Lewis Battles (Philadelphia: Westminster, 1960).

Therefore, salvation can only come through the gracious work of God—*sola gratia*—received by faith—*sola fide*—based on the sacrificial work of Christ on the sinner's behalf—*solus Christus*. This is none other than Augustinian/Lutheran monergism, which brings us to what was sometimes thought to be the center of Calvin's thought and Calvinism in general—the doctrine of predestination.

Calvin does indeed have a strong view of divine predestination (he preferred the term *election*), but it is in reality a reflection of predecessors such as Augustine, quite a few medieval theologians, Luther, Zwingli, and most other reformers. Like them, Calvin had a high view of the sovereignty (he preferred the term *providence*) of God over *everything*—meticulous providence. *Nothing* happens apart from his sovereign will, and therefore a strong view of divine predestination necessarily follows. But predestination was not the *central* doctrine for Calvin. He doesn't even deal with it until about two-thirds of the way through the final edition of his *Institutes* (3.21 ff.), and then under the heading "God the Redeemer in Christ" (2) and the application of that redemption to us (3). What was the central doctrine for Calvin? It was justification, which he says "is the main hinge on which religion turns" (*Institutes*, 3.11.1). Calvin does indeed emphasize God's sovereignty and predestination, but primarily in connection with salvation, that is, as reflections of God's goodness and love. And being the pastor that he was, especially to people who were being persecuted for their faith, Calvin stressed that divine sovereignty and predestination should help the believer trust God, especially in difficult circumstances, as well as find great comfort and hope in those difficult times. It should also produce appropriate humility before such an awesome God: "How much the ignorance of this principle [election, specifically] detracts from God's glory, how much it takes away from true humility, is well known" (*Institutes*, 3.21.1).

Calvin was explicit that Christ's sacrificial work was a substitution that actually took the punishment for sin in the place of the sinner, somewhat in contrast to Anselm's idea of Christ's death as satisfaction, displacing the need for punishment. Calvin wrote, "Hence, when Christ is hanged upon the cross, he makes himself subject to the curse [of the law]. It had to happen this way in order that the whole curse—which on account of our sins awaited us, or rather lay upon us—might be lifted from us, while it was transferred to him" (*Institutes*, 2.16.6). This is clearly an objective view of the atonement,[2] but for Calvin this did not exclude a subjective aspect. Through God's work in salvation we are united with Christ (an important emphasis in Calvin's theology) through the work of the Holy Spirit (also important to Calvin), and though in one sense things stay the same, in another sense things profoundly change: "We experience such participation in [Christ] that, although . . . we are sinners, he is our righteousness; while we are unclean, he is our purity; while we are weak, while we are unarmed and exposed to Satan, yet ours is that power which has been given him in heaven and on earth . . . while we still bear about with us the body of death, he is yet our life" (*Institutes*, 3.15.5). The point is that, through union with Christ, Christ lives his life out through the believer who lives in utter dependence upon the power of the Holy Spirit.

Like Augustine and Luther, Calvin believed that the entire Christian life involved a struggle with sin: "There remains in a regenerate man a smoldering cinder of evil, from which desires continually leap forth to allure and spur him to commit sin" (*Institutes*, 3.3.10). Calvin admitted that, for him, that struggle was with anger, his "ferocious beast." But if we are united with Christ and the Spirit is dwelling within us, why is sin not thoroughly defeated in this life? Calvin would say because God is out to keep us humble and desperate for his grace. This lifelong, grace-dependent struggle with sin and longing for righteousness is known within Calvinistic theology as the "perseverance of the saints."

Regarding baptism, Calvin did diverge from both Luther and Zwingli. Although he did agree with them in rejecting the Roman Catholic notion of transubstantiation, he also rejected the Lutheran idea of consubstantiation or real presence, agreeing with Zwingli

2. As we saw in chapter 18, this means that the primary effect of Christ's death was outside of the sinner, in this case, appeasing God's wrath regarding sin and satisfying God's justice and holiness.

that Christ's human, physical body was now in heaven only and not in the elements of the Supper. However, he also rejected the Zwinglian concept that the Lord's Supper was merely a memorial service. Calvin mediated the two views by concluding that the body and blood of Christ was present in the elements, not physically, but spiritually: "Yet Christ's flesh itself in the mystery of the Supper is a thing no less spiritual than our eternal salvation" (*Institutes*, 4.17.33). He also believed that the elements were channels of divine grace that strengthened the believer's faith in and union with Jesus Christ through the Holy Spirit.

Conclusion

It seems right to say that Calvin himself would disagree with some of what is categorized today as "Calvinism." For example, a case can be made that Calvin himself did not hold to the "Calvinistic" doctrine of limited atonement, that is, that Christ died only for the benefit of the elect. On the other hand, Calvin (like Augustine, Luther, and many others) did believe in "double predestination," that is, that before time, God predestined some for salvation and others for condemnation.[3] Many later Calvinists softened this by saying that God predestined some for salvation and simply passed over the rest.

Calvinism and *Reformed theology* have become somewhat synonymous, although this is not entirely accurate.[4] Nevertheless, Calvin's impact on the Reformation in general and Reformed theology specifically is hard to overstate. His *Institutes* basically became the textbook for Reformed theology. His influence went far beyond theology to politics, economics, and ethics (e.g., the "Protestant work ethic").

3. He also acknowledged that this is beyond our comprehension (*Institutes*, 3.23.5) and "The decree is dreadful indeed, I confess" (3.23.7).
4. A recent attempt at correcting some of this is Kenneth J. Stewart, *Ten Myths About Calvinism: Recovering the Breadth of the Reformed Tradition* (Downers Grove, IL: InterVarsity, 2011).

In the last three chapters we have seen that the Protestant movement split into two primary divisions. The Lutheran branch became predominant in Germany and Scandinavia—Sweden, Denmark, and Norway. The Reformed branch spread from Switzerland (under Zwingli and Calvin) to France, Holland, England, Scotland, and eventually America through the Puritans. Together, these branches are known as the "Magisterial Reformation," in that they believed that the church and state (magistrates) should cooperate closely in the work of God on earth. As we have seen in this chapter, Calvin's Geneva was an excellent illustration of this conviction.

There is yet a third branch of the Reformation that needs to be noted—the "Radical Reformation"—which is the subject of the next chapter.

24

MENNO SIMONS

Radical Reformer

Context

During the Reformation period, there were some who did not think the traditional Reformers—Luther, Zwingli, Calvin—were going far enough; they wanted to reform the Reformation, or, if you prefer, they protested Protestantism, at least to a point. Specifically, this grew out of the followers of Zwingli and the Swiss Reformation. This group was broad and diverse, but there were primarily two areas in which they disagreed with the traditional Reformers, and these two areas are closely intertwined.

The first was with regard to church and state. The traditional Reformers continued the custom of the Roman Catholic Church through the Middle Ages of promoting a very close association between church and state, for example, what Calvin was doing in the city of Geneva. A current example is the Lutheran Church as the state church of Germany and the Scandinavian countries. The term *Magisterial Reformation* is applied in this sense. The traditional

Reformers wanted to cooperate with the civil "magistrates" in the work of the church in a certain geographical area.

In contrast, the Radical Reformation believed that there should be no association between the church and state, and that the local church should be free from any state control and completely autonomous in its decisions and programs. That is, they believed in the separation of church and state. The term *radical* comes from the Latin word for "root," the connotation here being "going back to the roots," namely, the New Testament. When these reformers did that, they could find no basis for a "state church." Rather, they found that the church should be made up only of those who have professed faith in Jesus Christ and voluntarily associated themselves with the church, as opposed to pretty much everyone who lived in a certain geographical location simply because that's where they live—including infants. Today that idea is pretty much taken for granted, but in the sixteenth century it was, well, radical. And this brings us to the second issue.

The Radical Reformers also rejected the practice of infant baptism and believed that baptism should be exclusively for those who personally profess faith in Jesus Christ—believer's baptism. The traditional Reformers denied the Catholic doctrine that infant baptism had anything to do with salvation; rather, they viewed it—along the lines of the Old Testament ritual of circumcision as practiced by the covenant community of Israel—as a means of including an infant in the covenant community of the church. The "radicals," on the other hand, believed that the church was made up of true believers (infants do not qualify as that) who voluntarily associate themselves with the church (infants cannot do that) and are serious about living out their faith. The derogatory term *Anabaptist*—rebaptizer—was applied to these radicals by the traditionalists. Of course, the Anabaptists did not think they were *re*baptizing at all, since infant baptism is the same as no baptism at all.

This movement grew and spread quickly, to the extent that it threatened the traditional Reformation. The traditionalists also understood that the state-church concept could not succeed apart from infant baptism. As a tragic result, the traditionalists (along with the Roman Catholic Church) ruthlessly persecuted the Anabaptists. In 1525 the city of Zurich ordered that Anabaptists be exiled, and a year later imposed the death sentence on Anabaptists, ironically by "prolonged immersion," that is, drowning. Many of the leaders of the movement were in fact executed.

One of the exceptions to that tragic fate was Menno Simons. He was born in Holland in 1496 and became a Roman Catholic priest. He had come to reject the Catholic doctrine of transubstantiation based upon his own study of Scripture. When he heard of the Anabaptist movement, he went back to Scripture and was convinced that there was no biblical basis for infant baptism. In 1536 he became convicted of his own hypocrisy in remaining a Roman Catholic, experienced his own personal conversion, aligned himself with the Anabaptist movement, and was baptized as a believer. For the next eighteen years he was constantly on the move due to persecution, but in 1554 he found a safe haven in Holstein, Germany, and there he stayed until his death in 1561.

Contribution

Unlike most other Anabaptist leaders who either died young or were constantly on the run, Simons lived to a relatively old age and had the opportunity to do extensive writing in relative safety. His complete works comprise over a thousand pages, including around twenty-five books as well as letters, sermons, and tracts.

Like the traditional Reformers, but unlike a minority among his fellow Anabaptists who believed in divine revelation through an "inner light," Simons believed that the Bible was the Christian's sole authority and tried to base his own beliefs exclusively on its teachings. This was exactly why he and other Anabaptists rejected infant baptism. He wrote, "Since, then, we do not find in all Scripture a single word by which Christ has ordained the baptism of infants, or that His apostles taught and practiced it, we say and confess rightly that infant baptism is but a human invention, an opinion of men, a perversion of the ordinance of Christ."[1]

For Simons, as well as most Anabaptists, what was of primary importance was not what you believed (even about baptism), but how you lived; a truly committed Christian life of holiness was more important than theology. For this very reason, Simons did not enthusiastically embrace the Reformation doctrine of justification as a legal declaration of righteousness by God because, he feared, it makes it easy to exclude a heart-felt commitment to an actual lifestyle of righteousness. Lest we think that, due to their title "Anabaptist," their view of baptism was central to the movement, Simons sets us right: "[Baptism] is the very least of all the commandments which [Christ] has given. It is a much greater commandment to love your enemies, to do good to those who do evil to you, to pray in spirit and in truth for those who persecute you, to subjugate the flesh under God's word, to tread under your feet all pride, covetousness, impurity, hate, envy and intemperance" and so on.[2] This reflects the true heart of the Anabaptist movement.

Simons did have a rather unusual take on the person of Jesus Christ, which he explained in *The Incarnation of Our Lord* (1554). In essence, he believed that the incarnation took place in heaven and that Mary did not contribute *her* human nature to her son, Jesus; rather, she was just the vehicle of his birth on earth. Apparently Simons saw this as the way to protect the sinlessness of Jesus since Mary's humanity was sinful (Roman Catholic doctrine notwithstanding), but Simons' critics accused him of denying the true humanity of Jesus. Regardless, the Anabaptist tradition did not adopt his view of the incarnation.

It was through Menno Simons' influence primarily that Anabaptists generally came to embrace pacifism, even when they are personally threatened. In his *Foundation of Christian Doctrine*, he unambiguously stated that the only sword a Christian should

---

1. William C. Placher, *Readings in the History of Christian Theology*, vol. 2 (Louisville: Westminster, 1988), 33.
    2. Ibid.

bear is the sword of the Spirit, the Word of God. Rather, it was the state's God-given responsibility to bear arms to punish what is evil and protect what is good. Thus, many Anabaptist churches today are "peace churches."

Conclusion

Not only was Menno Simons one of the few Anabaptists who lived long enough and had enough stability to produce much by way of written works, he was also one of the best organizers among the early leaders of the tradition. As William Anderson put it, "It was through the work and the example of Menno Simons that the best in the Anabaptist tradition was perpetuated and ultimately became very influential."[3] Menno Simons' followers became known as "Mennonites," and they are still thriving. More distant modern relatives of Anabaptism are Quakers, Baptists, Congregationalists, and "free" churches in general (i.e., free from the state). In a much broader sense, their views on believers' baptism and holy living are still alive and well in much of evangelicalism.

3. Anderson, *A Journey Through Christian Tradition*, 257.

BRIEF
INTERLUDE

MEANWHILE, BACK IN ROME

(or at least in Trent)

Context

In the previous four chapters we have been considering the Protestant Reformers and Reformation. But we also need to consider how the Roman Catholic Church responded to all of this, what is called the Catholic Counter-Reformation. No one theologian is associated with this, but it is a necessary part of the story of theology.

There were Roman Catholics who saw many of the same kinds of problems within the Church that the Reformers saw, and they wanted reform as well. For example, Desiderius Erasmus of Rotterdam (1466–1536) was the most highly regarded intellectual in Europe in his day. He was a Roman Catholic priest but also a free thinker. He desperately wanted to reform the Church, but just as desperately he wanted to keep it united. A few of his books became wildly popular due to their wit and insight, and in them he ridiculed things such as superstitions, pilgrimages, relics, the immorality of the clergy, and the secularization of the church hierarchy—they had become more concerned about matters of state than matters of church. For example, *The Praise of Folly* (1509) is a satirical tribute (praise) to the popular practices in Roman Catholicism (folly). Erasmus was influenced by and contributed to the "back to the sources" movement. He produced a Greek New Testament that took scholarship by storm in his day. All that had been available for centuries was a very flawed Latin Vulgate version of the Bible. Erasmus's desire was that ultimately everyone, not just the clergy elite, could read the Bible in their own language. The Protestants, of course, shared the same desire and used Erasmus' Greek New Testament to make that possible. Erasmus was actually sympathetic with the Protestants in a number of areas (not all), but he died profoundly disappointed that they ended up splitting the Church and that the Catholic Church remained unreformed.

Another example of a Roman Catholic who wanted reform was Gasparo Contarini (1483–1542), an Italian noble who came to Luther's convictions regarding justification by faith in Christ apart from good works even before Luther himself did. Late in life he became a cardinal and then a priest (yes, in that order), and he was involved in some efforts to reform abuses within the Catholic Church. He was also involved in dialogues with Protestants, specifically in the Regensburg Colloquy in 1541. There was surprising agreement on justification, but not much else.

Generally, with regard to Protestantism, the Catholic Church opted for condemnation rather than conciliation. Pope Paul III produced the *Index*, a list of prohibited books consisting of everything Protestants had written, including their translations of the Bible. He re-instituted the Inquisition to root out Protestant heresy. But most significantly he called for the nineteenth ecumenical council of the Church. It began meeting in Trent, Italy, in 1545, and after three lengthy sessions completed its work in 1563.

Contribution

The Council of Trent basically did two things: The first was to clarify what the Roman Catholic Church believed and taught in contrast to Protestantism. For example, the council defined the Church's authoritative sources—Scripture and tradition—and the Church (alone) was the authorized interpreter of those sources; it reasserted the Catholic doctrine of justification—which is progressive and essentially the same as sanctification; it restated its views on the sacraments—including the number of them being seven, *ex opere operato*, transubstantiation, holy ordination (specifically in contrast to the Protestant doctrine of the priesthood of all believers), and many (many, many) more.

The council also made official what had long been unofficial Roman doctrine, such as purgatory, indulgences, the place of relics and images, and so on. The Latin Vulgate Bible, including the apocryphal books, was made the official Catholic version of the Bible.

With regard to salvation, the Council of Trent clarified that human merit played a role in salvation. In the council's *Decree Concerning Justification* (1547), Canon 32 says, "If anyone says that the good works of a justified man are gifts of God to such an extent that they are not also the good merits of the justified man himself, or that . . . the justified man does not truly merit an increase of grace . . . and the attainment of life everlasting, and even an increase of glory: let him be anathema [cursed]." The idea is that, even though *eternal* payment for sins is remitted through the sacrament of confession, *temporal* payment for sins is necessary in the form of penance, indulgences, acts of love, and other "good works"—human merit. The council emphasized that even these were done by the grace of God; nevertheless, to the Protestants, this simply boiled down to work-righteousness, not Christ-righteousness. But then, the council also declared all Protestants to be heretics.

The second thing the Council of Trent did was to introduce significant reforms within the Roman Catholic Church itself. For example, the sale of indulgences *in order to raise money for the Church* was abolished (indulgences themselves were still offered). Decrees regarding the discipline of the clergy were enacted.[1] Generally, the council addressed and eradicated many areas of abuse and corruption within the Church and its clergy.

1. Ironically, the convening pope, Paul III, had four illegitimate children himself.

Conclusion

The accomplishments of the Council of Trent were enormous; it produced more church legislation than the previous eighteen councils combined.[2] It effectively widened and then set in concrete the divide between Catholicism and Protestantism. The result was a form of Catholicism known as "Tridentine Catholicism," which persisted for four centuries, until the Second Vatican Council, or Vatican II (1962–1965).

2. Lane, *A Concise History of Christian Thought*, 222.

25

RICHARD HOOKER

Architect of Anglicanism

Context

If the Lutheran, Reformed, and Anabaptist churches in continental Europe came about due to theological or ecclesiastical issues, the Church of England came about (at least in one sense) due to hormonal issues, namely, lust.[1] The story is rather infamous. King Henry VIII (1491–1547) was married to Catherine of Aragon, but she had not been able to bear Henry a male heir to succeed him. Meanwhile, Henry desired a lady of the court, Anne Boleyn. The complication was that the pope would not annul Henry's marriage to Catherine so that he could wed Anne. So (to make a long story short, as they say), Henry broke from the Church in Rome, established the Church of England, and declared himself to be the supreme head of that church. The Act of Supremacy (1534) stated, "The king's majesty justly and rightly is and ought to be and shall

1. There were, of course, previous influences setting the stage for the English Reformation, such as John Wycliffe and his followers, the Lollards.

be reputed the only supreme head in earth of the Church of England called *Anglicana Ecclesia.*" Thus, the Anglican Church came to be.

The only real change through all of this was that the reigning monarch in England replaced the pope as head of the Church in England. Essentially everything else stayed the same. In fact, King Henry despised and condemned the Reformation that was taking place across the English Channel. Henry did, however, appoint Thomas Cranmer, who *was* sympathetic to the Lutheran Reformation, as archbishop of Canterbury (the highest clerical position in England) in 1533.

Henry's young son, Edward VI, succeeded him on the throne in 1547, and during his six-year reign, Cranmer and Edward's advisors quickly moved the Church of England in a direction more sympathetic with the Protestant Reformation on the continent. In 1549 Cranmer produced a Protestant-leaning prayer book which, after its revision in 1552, took on the better-known title of the Book of Common Prayer. It has been revised numerous times since but still remains a central piece in Anglican corporate worship.

When Edward died in 1553, Mary, Catherine of Aragon's daughter (and Edward's older half-sister), succeeded him and reversed directions back toward Roman Catholicism. Hundreds of English Protestants, including Thomas Cranmer, were burned at the stake, resulting in her notorious title "Bloody Mary." To avoid execution and persecution, many others fled to the continent, for example, to Geneva, Switzerland, and were deeply influenced by Reformed theology.[2]

Mary died in 1558 and was succeeded by Elizabeth I (d. 1603), the daughter of Henry and Anne Boleyn (Mary's younger half-sister). Elizabeth was a Protestant (although not friendly toward Reformed theology specifically), but her problem was the counter-forces within the Church of England—Roman (those who thrived under Mary's reign) and Reformed (the Protestants who had fled during Mary's reign but had since returned to England). Her solution

---

2. Mary's reign of terror is the context in which the famous Foxe's *Book of Martyrs* was written.

was a compromise that, appropriately, came to be characterized as the *via media* or "middle way" between Catholicism and Protestantism. It is known as the Elizabethan Settlement (1559) and established the Anglican Church as theologically Protestant and ecclesiastically Catholic. The doctrinal statement that was imposed was the Thirty-Nine Articles of Religion, which was based on the Forty-Two Articles authored by Thomas Cranmer shortly before his martyrdom.

Even though Thomas Cranmer can be thought of as the father of the Protestant Church of England, the key early theologian and architect of Anglicanism was Richard Hooker (1554–1600). While studying at Oxford University, Hooker became committed to a very Roman Catholic–oriented Anglicanism. He became the lead clergy of the Temple in London in 1584. Ironically the associate minister was Walter Travers, who was an outspoken critic of Elizabethan Anglicanism and favored more Reformed influence in the Church of England. Hooker supported the current form of Anglicanism in the morning sermon, and Travers supported his more Reformed version of theology and the church in the afternoon. As others have put it, the church got Canterbury in the morning and Geneva in the afternoon. That must have made for a lot of confused church members.

Contribution

Hooker's main literary work was his eight-volume *Laws of Ecclesiastical Polity*, in which he basically promoted the Elizabethan Settlement and the form of the church that Queen Elizabeth desired, namely, a very Catholic-like liturgy focusing on the sacraments and a very Catholic-like hierarchical, episcopal church government[3] but whose theology was more in line with moderate continental Protestantism. That is, if one were to visit a typical Anglican

---

3. He did claim to embrace the Protestant principle of the priesthood of all believers, but this was not really reflected in his view of the Anglican priesthood and apostolic succession of bishops.

church at that time, the church service itself would feel very much like a Roman Catholic service. However, the doctrine believed and preached would reflect the basic principles of the Protestant Reformation, and like the Reformers, Hooker rejected the Catholic doctrines of transubstantiation, purgatory, indulgences, sacraments other than baptism, and the Eucharist.

Hooker was thoroughly in sync with Protestants with regard to justification by God's grace based upon the work of Christ alone through faith alone, as reflected in Article 11 of the Thirty-Nine Articles. On the other hand, in stark contrast to the Reformers, Hooker believed that even though Roman Catholics did not hold this principle theologically, they still could be saved by God's grace. Another twist on the typical Reformed doctrine of salvation was Hooker's belief that though salvation was an instantaneous and immediate declaration of righteousness—justification—it was also (somewhat inconsistently) a lifelong process of being brought into participation in the divine nature—the ancient and orthodox doctrine of deification or *theosis*.[4]

Even though he did affirm the Thirty-Nine Articles' expression of the ultimate authority of Scripture (Article 6), he also believed in lesser degrees of authority that ought to shape the lives and thought of Christians when the Bible was silent—authorities such as civil laws and personal reason and convictions. The following section from his *Laws of Ecclesiastical Polity* illustrates this specifically as well as his tendency to find the "middle way":

> Two opinions therefore there are concerning sufficiency of Holy Scripture, each extremely opposite unto the other, and both repugnant unto truth. The schools of Rome [the Roman Catholic Church] teach Scripture to be so unsufficient, as if, except traditions were added, it did not contain all revealed and supernatural truth, which absolutely is necessary for the children of men in this life to know that they may in the next be saved. Others justly condemning this opinion [Protestants who accept no authority other than Scripture] grow likewise unto a dangerous extremity, as if Scripture did not

4. See chapters 5, 7, and 8.

only contain all things in that kind necessary, but all things simply, and in such sort that to do any thing according to any other law were not only unnecessary but even opposite unto salvation, unlawful and sinful. Whatsoever is spoken of God or things appertaining to God otherwise than as the truth is, though it seem an honour, it is an injury. And as incredible praises given unto men do often abate and impair the credit of their deserved commendation; so we must likewise take great heed, lest in attributing unto Scripture more than it can have, the incredibility of that do cause even those things which indeed it hath most abundantly to be less reverently esteemed. I therefore leave it to themselves to consider, whether they have in this first point or not overshot themselves; which God doth know is quickly done, even when our meaning is most sincere, as I am verily persuaded theirs in this case was. (2.8.7)

One area in which Hooker seemed closer to medieval Catholicism than Reformation Protestantism was in his views regarding natural theology, which reflected the influence of Aristotle and Aquinas. This resulted in a view of original sin that was not nearly as pessimistic as the continental Reformers. Hooker believed that even fallen humans have the rational and moral abilities to respond positively even to general revelation and can cooperate with divine grace along with special revelation, resulting in a very synergistic form of salvation.

Conclusion

Hooker's version of Anglicanism has been carried on in Anglican (or, Episcopal) churches around the world. However, as we have already observed, there were other views within Anglicanism that were discontent with the Elizabethan Settlement and Hooker's views on belief and worship. We will take up these protests and reforms in chapters 28 and 29.

26

JAMES ARMINIUS
Calvinist Contrarian

Context

Not all Reformed theology was in lockstep. We have seen how the Reformers differed on the meaning of the sacraments—baptism and the Lord's Supper. They also differed on the nature of divine predestination and the practice of Christian living. In this chapter we will pursue the former in the form of Arminianism, and in the next chapter the latter, in the form of Pietism.

Jacob Arminius[1] was born in Holland around 1560. His studies were at the new University of Leiden in Holland and then at Geneva, where he studied under Theodore Beza, the successor of Calvin. In 1588 he began his pastoral ministry in the Dutch Reformed Church in Amsterdam. Soon Arminius began to question the more extreme form of Calvinism, particularly predestination, as taught by Beza. His views became public as he preached sermons based on Paul's

1. The alternative to his first name is James. His family name was Hermand-szoon. Arminius is the Latin name that he adopted.

epistle to the Romans, and controversy erupted. He was accused of heresy by many of his fellow Dutch Reformed colleagues, but the charges did not stick, and he was exonerated.

In 1603 he began teaching theology at the University of Leiden, but only after significant opposition from Francis Gomarus, a fervent Calvinist, also on the faculty at Leiden. Even though Gomarus failed to keep Arminius from the faculty appointment, he continued to accuse Arminius of a variety of misdeeds, such as being a "closet Catholic," most of which were completely false. Arminius tried to defend himself, but to no avail. Controversy continued to swirl around him and his beliefs until he died in 1609.

Contribution

The works of Arminius that relate to the controversy within Reformed theology are as follows: *Examination of Dr. Perkins's Pamphlet on Predestination* (1602); *Declaration of Sentiments* (1608); *A Letter Addressed to Hippolytus A Collibus* (1608); and *Certain Articles to Be Diligently Examined and Weighed* (date unknown).[2] These are included in *The Works of James Arminius*.[3]

Despite suggestions to the contrary, Arminius clearly considered himself to be in agreement with mainline Protestantism. He affirmed *sola scriptura*—the Word of God and it alone was the final, written authority for all believers. He also affirmed the doctrine of justification *sola gratia*, *solus Christus*, and *sola fide*—by God's grace alone based upon the work of Christ alone received by our faith alone. In his *Declaration of Sentiments* he wrote, "I am not conscious to myself, of having taught or entertained any other sentiments concerning the justification of man before God, than those which are held unanimously by the Reformed and Protestant churches, and which are in complete agreement with their expressed opinions."[4]

2. According to Olson, *The Story of Christian Theology*, 464.
3. *The Works of James Arminius*, London Edition, 3 vols., trans. James Nichols and William Nichols (Grand Rapids: Baker, 1983).
4. As quoted by Olson, 465, from *The Works of James Arminius*, 1:695.

What Arminius primarily rebelled against in Reformed theology was the view of predestination, which asserted that *everything* is caused by God's decisions or decrees, including the fall of humanity into sin, the choice of both the righteous for eternal blessing and the unrighteous for eternal punishment (double predestination), and the monergistic view of salvation of those chosen for righteousness. He rejected these primarily because he believed them to be contrary to Scripture, but also because, in his assessment, they essentially make God the "author of evil." According to Arminius, the implications of the strong Calvinistic doctrine of predestination were "that God really sins . . . that God is the only sinner . . . that sin is not sin."[5] In other words, if the fall and sin are according to God's plan and purposes in the first place, is not he the one who is ultimately responsible for them? And if so, "sin is not sin" because all that God does is good. How did the fall come about, then? Arminius believed that it was not that God determined it, but rather that God permitted it, necessarily so, since God created humans with genuine free will. God foreknew that the fall would take place, but he did not foreordain that it would take place.

He also rejected a monergistic view of salvation, that is, that God alone accomplishes it with no human involvement. His Calvinistic objectors claimed that any other view—synergism, or cooperation between God and sinners—makes it possible for saved sinners to take credit, at least in part, for their own salvation, thus robbing God of his glory. On the contrary, Arminius would respond, it is the Calvinistic view that robs God of his glory and is contradictory to his love and goodness.

Arminius's synergistic view of salvation was certainly not based on any optimistic view of the abilities of sinful humans. In his *Declaration* he wrote,

> In his lapsed and sinful state, man is not capable, of and by himself, either to think or to will or to do that which is really good. But it is necessary for him to be regenerated and renewed . . . by God in

5. Ibid., 467; from *Works*, 1:630.

Christ through the Holy Spirit, that he may . . . perform whatever is truly good. When he is made a partaker of this regeneration or renovation, I consider that, since he is delivered from sin, he is capable of thinking, willing and doing that which is good, but *yet not without the continued aids of Divine Grace* (III. The Free Will of Man, emphasis added).

In Arminian theology, this necessary "Divine Grace" is called "prevenient grace,"[6] that is, grace that precedes or comes before. This kind of grace is given to everyone (not just the elect), enabling them to do what they are unable to do on their own in their fallen, sinful state: accept by faith the free gift of salvation through Jesus Christ. Even though Arminius's doctrine of salvation was synergistic, he in no way believed that saved people could take any credit for their salvation; it was *entirely* due to the grace of God, but with that grace the sinner *freely* chose to cooperate (and also the grace that the sinner could freely choose to reject—it was *not* irresistible).

Strong Calvinists tended to consider God's decree to predestine some to salvation and the rest to damnation to be his first and primary determination out of which flowed all of his other decrees. In contrast, in his *Declaration of Sentiments*, Arminius ordered God's decrees as follows: 1) God appointed his Son, Jesus Christ, to be the Redeemer and Savior; 2) God determined to receive and forgive those who repent and believe in Christ and persevere in that faith until the end, and to leave the rest in their sin and under divine wrath and ultimate damnation; 3) God chose to provide the sufficient and effective means necessary to bring about saving faith and repentance, that is, his grace; and 4) God chose to save those whom he foreknew would cooperate with his grace and believe in Christ.

So Arminius did indeed believe in divine predestination, but not the variety that, at least in his assessment, tended to deny genuine human freedom and responsibility. For Arminius, divine predestination was primarily corporate, not individual. As he understood

---

6. The older term is *preventing grace,* which, to us today, sounds just the opposite of what it really means.

Romans 9, God chose two categories: believers and unbelievers. This kind of predestination could be called "unconditional" in that God determined to bless those in the believer category and curse those in the unbeliever category. But at the individual level, God's choice of those who would be saved was based only upon his foreknowledge, that is, his ability to look into the future and know who would eventually believe in Jesus as Savior. As Paul wrote in Romans 8:29, "For those God foreknew he also predestined. . . ."[7] This has come to be known as *conditional election*, the condition being the foreknown, eventual, saving faith of the individual.

Conclusion

The year after Arminius died, forty-six Dutch pastors who had come to accept his views, known as Remonstrants (Protesters), produced the *Remonstrance*, which made five points: 1) God chose to provide salvation by his grace through Jesus Christ to all who would have faith in Christ and persevere in that faith; 2) Christ's death on the cross was for all people, but only those who believed in him would realize its benefit; 3) Fallen humans cannot do any good apart from regeneration and the work of the Holy Spirit; 4) God's grace is necessary to do any good, but that grace can be resisted; and 5) True believers by grace can persevere in their faith, but that perseverance is not certain.

The *Remonstrance* prompted the Synod of Dort, Holland (1618–19), which was essentially a heresy trial of Arminianism and Arminian pastors. One of the outcomes was that Arminian Dutch pastors were excommunicated and exiled. Another outcome of Dort was the famous (infamous?) five points of Calvinism, which were none other than counterpoints to the five points of the Remonstrants. The Calvinistic doctrine of *total depravity* is very similar to point 3

7. Calvinists argue that "foreknowledge" means more than God's ability to know what is going to happen before it actually happens; rather, it refers to God's knowledge of the future because the future is simply what God has determined to be. He knows it because he planned it.

above. *Unconditional election* is in contrast to point 1—*conditional election. Limited atonement* is in contrast to point 2—*unlimited atonement. Irresistible grace* is in contrast to point 4—*resistible grace*. And *perseverance of the saints* is somewhat in contrast to point 5, which at least seems to imply that saints may not persevere and thus would lose their salvation in the end. And so the stage was set for the debate between Calvinism and Arminianism for the last four centuries.

As was true in the case of Calvin, so many of Arminius's followers took his theology further than he had. And as was true for Calvinism, Arminianism is often misunderstood and misrepresented.[8] Arminius and his views have been labeled as "Pelagian" or "Semi-Pelagian," both of which Arminius himself would deny. Let the debate between these two systems of theology continue, because the issues at stake are important and deserve thoughtful attention, but let us do so in such a way that *fairly* represents the opposing viewpoints and *graciously* makes the case both for and against the viewpoints.

8. A recent attempt to address this is Roger E. Olson, *Arminian Theology: Myths and Realities* (Downers Grove, IL: InterVarsity, 2006).

27

PHILIPP SPENER

Founder of Pietism

Context

Post-Reformation Protestant theologians seemed to quickly slip back into the type of medieval Roman Catholic scholasticism from which Luther and Calvin had departed, that is, adopting philosophy and logic—a type of rationalism—to the doing of theology that resulted in a "hardening of the arteries" of theology. Their goal was to produce an all-inclusive Protestant theology that would stand up against the assaults of both Roman Catholicism and religious skeptics, but in doing so, they resorted to the methodology of Aquinas. Sawyer put it this way: "Theology now focused on systematization and propositions, and attempted to extend theological knowledge into fine details, but in the process, *the intimate relationship of theology to life was again obscured.* This was the era of Protestant scholasticism."[1]

1. M. James Sawyer, *The Survivor's Guide to Theology* (Grand Rapids: Zondervan, 2006), 314, emphasis added.

This scholasticism affected Calvinism and was at least partially responsible for the reaction of Arminius and others, as we saw in the previous chapter. It also affected Lutheranism and prompted a different kind of reaction—Pietism.

By the middle of the seventeenth century, to be born in a "Lutheran" nation was to be born a Christian, at least after infant baptism, according to Lutheran theology at that time. Therefore, there was little concern about actually living like a Christian. Why bother? It was all a done deal. Generally speaking, Pietists had come to believe that Lutheranism had gone to the head and left the heart behind.

Philipp Jacob Spener is generally regarded as the founder of Pietism. He was born in Alsace, between Germany and France, in 1635. He was raised in a very religious environment and read the works of Johann Arndt, which could be regarded as the roots of pietistic thought. Spener was trained at the Universities of Strasbourg and Basel. While pastoring a Lutheran church in Frankfurt, Spener was particularly appalled by the spiritual conditions of "Christians" there and began to call for humble repentance and serious discipleship. His criticisms of the church and state as well as his preaching and practices resulted not only in significant opposition, but also the beginning of a movement that was sympathetic to his views. In 1686 he became the court chaplain at Dresden, and in 1692 he took his last pastoral position in Berlin. Throughout his ministry he taught Pietism, trained pietistic leaders, and nurtured the pietistic movement until his death in 1705.

Contribution

Spener's written contribution to the Pietist movement was *Heartfelt Desire for a God-Pleasing Reform of the True Evangelical Church, Together with Several Simple Christian Proposals Looking Toward this End*, which, thankfully, is better known as the *Pia Desideria* or "Pious Desires" (1675). It is essentially the handbook for Pietism.

Spener (and Pietists in general) were in full agreement with their fellow Lutherans in the following ways: Generally, Spener agreed with the central doctrines of the Protestant Reformation. However, he also believed that theological correctness should not be the uppermost concern of Christians. Pietists were concerned with what they called the "dead orthodoxy" of Lutheranism in their day—theological correctness without spiritual life. To his fellow Lutheran pastors, Spener said, "What does it help if our hearers are free from all papal, Reformed,[2] Socinian,[3] etc., errors, and yet with it have a dead faith through which they are more severely condemned than all those grievously heterodox better lives?"[4]

Specifically, Spener fully affirmed Luther's beloved doctrine of justification by God's grace based on the work of Jesus Christ received through faith alone. However, even though he agreed with this theologically, he did not tend to emphasize it, since, in his assessment, that was what led to Christians living lives that did not look very "Christian" at all. Spener also affirmed infant baptism, believing that it did result in salvation for the baby. However, he also believed that God's grace received at baptism was all-too-often lost out of neglect later in life.

Spener (and Pietists in general) departed from most of their fellow Lutherans and Reformers in the following ways: He emphasized the necessity of both conversion and sanctification in order to be a "heart Christian," as he put it. As just stated, even though he believed in infant baptism, he also strongly believed that the individual must eventually make a conscious choice to trust and follow Jesus Christ. This included genuine repentance, that is, a significant sense of one's own sinfulness and utter need for God's grace. This then should lead to regeneration—becoming a "new man"—and the beginning of lifelong sanctification—the inner transformation of the individual through the work of the Holy Spirit—which would express itself in growing holiness of lifestyle.

2. That is, Reformed theology that differed from Lutheran theology.
3. Socinianism was a thoroughgoing heresy that denied the Trinity, the deity of Christ, and other central Christian doctrines.
4. As quoted in Olson, *The Story of Christian Theology*, 477.

Luther himself believed in this type of sanctification, but, according to Pietists, he did not stress it nearly enough. The bottom line is Lutheran orthodoxy stressed the objective, external aspects of salvation (justification) and infant baptism as one's assurance of salvation; Pietists stressed the subjective, internal aspects of salvation (conversion, repentance, sanctification) and an increasingly holy life as one's assurance of salvation. For Pietists, Christianity was not real if it was not felt; it was not authentic if it was not experienced.

Spener was rather innovative in several ways. He stressed the importance of a personal devotional life, including meditation, prayer, and especially Bible study. Individual knowledge and understanding of Scripture was crucial for "heart Christianity." Spener called for a "more extensive use of the Word of God" because "the more at home the Word of God is among us, the more we shall bring about faith and its fruits." This needed to be more than what came from sermons that, even over the course of many years, covered only a small part of the Bible. He recommended three things: First, the Bible should be read among families: "It would not be difficult for every housefather to keep a Bible, or at least a New Testament, handy and read from it every day." Second, "where the practice can be introduced, the books of the Bible be read one after another, at specified times in the public service, without further comment" for the benefit of those who cannot read or who do not have access to a Bible. Third, "reintroduce the ancient and apostolic kind of church meetings [he cites 1 Corinthians 14:26–40]. . . . One person would not rise to preach, but others who have been blessed with gifts and knowledge would also speak and present their pious opinions on the proposed subject to the judgment of the rest. . . ."[5]

This led to another of Spener's innovations, what he called *collegia pietatis*, or "pious gatherings," that is, small groups of Christians who would meet regularly to pray, study the Bible, discuss

---

5. *Pia Desideria*, T. G. Taggert, ed. and trans. (Philadelphia: Fortress Press, 1964), 87–88. As quoted in Alister E. McGrath, ed. *The Christian Theology Reader*, 3rd ed. (Oxford: Blackwell, 1996, 2001, 2007), 118–119.

various topics, and generally hold one another accountable. Today that is rather taken for granted in church settings, but in Spener's day it was unheard of.

Conclusion

Two other influential Pietists were directly connected to Spener. August Hermann Francke was a convert of Spener and leader of the movement after Spener's death, and Count Nicholas Ludwig von Zinzendorf was Spener's godson. From the latter arose the Moravian Brethren Church, which reflected Zinzendorf's evangelistic spirit, and the Moravians in turn launched the first real Protestant missionary effort. It was through the influence of Moravian missionaries that John Wesley was set on the course that led to his conversion.[6]

Unfortunately, today the term *Pietist* often has some baggage in the sense that it implies a person who is not allowed to have any fun and is to withdraw as completely as possible from society. These caricatures, however, are not true of the original Pietists, who wanted to truly transform society through completely reformed saints. In fact, the concept and practice of "revivals" is largely founded in the pietistic spirit.

Strangely, in its homeland of Germany, Pietism remained on the fringes of the Lutheran Church, but it was exported to North America where it not only flourished but dominated church life. It is beyond dispute that Pietism has profoundly impacted nearly every American Protestant denomination in general and specifically evangelicalism and evangelical churches. There are pietistic elements in American Lutheranism, Methodism, Baptist churches and denominations, the Evangelical Free Church, the Church of the Nazarene, and Assemblies of God. Thankfully, it brought the heart back into Christianity.

6. See chapter 29.

28

JONATHAN EDWARDS

Last Puritan

Context

In chapter 25 we considered the English Reformation and the establishment of the Church of England, or the Anglican Church. Typical Anglicanism was the "middle way" initiated by the Elizabethan Settlement and established by Richard Hooker. But as noted, there were dissenters who wanted the Church of England to be more Reformed theologically—Calvinistic rather than some "muddled" middle way—and ecclesiastically—presbyterian or congregational rather than episcopalian. One such individual was Walter Travis, the associate minister under Richard Hooker, who preached "Geneva theology" in the afternoon after Hooker had preached "Canterbury theology" in the morning. Travis and those like him came to be known as "Puritans," since they wanted to purify the Church of England from its "Romish" or "popish" elements—bishops, altars, statues, high church liturgy, and the like—which they thought were all too dominant. They also rejected the Book of Common Prayer, which they also viewed as far too Catholic.

A faction of the Puritans thought that the Anglican Church was beyond reform and therefore established their own "separatist" churches. Their radical views resulted in persecution in the 1620s and 1630s, which forced them to flee to the continent or, for many, New England. We know them today as the Pilgrims. However, the Puritans who remained in England eventually gained the upper hand, first militarily and a bit later politically, under Oliver Cromwell. King Charles I was executed (1649), briefly ending the monarchy, and before the reestablishment of the monarchy in 1660, the Westminster Assembly (1643–1649) produced one of the most important Calvinist/Puritan doctrinal statements, namely, the Westminster Confession of Faith, which was intended to replace the Anglican Thirty-Nine Articles of Religion.

One of the greatest representatives of the Puritans, sometimes called the "Prince of the Puritans," was Jonathan Edwards. His life is sometimes used to mark the end of the Puritan period, thus, the "last Puritan." Edwards was born in East Windsor, Connecticut, on October 5, 1703. He entered Yale College at the age of thirteen, already having knowledge of Hebrew, Greek, and Latin. After a brief pastorate and returning to Yale to complete a master's degree and act as a tutor, in 1724 Edwards began serving as associate minister under his grandfather, Solomon Stoddard, one of the leading Puritans at that time and the pastor of the Congregational Church in Northampton, Massachusetts. When Stoddard died in 1729, Edwards succeeded him as pastor.

As a result of his ministry in Northampton, revival broke out in the mid-1730s, a part of the larger event known as the First Great Awakening (1725–1760). His most famous sermon, "Sinners in the Hands of an Angry God," was preached during this time:

> The God that holds you over the pit of hell, much as one holds a spider or some loathsome insect over the fire, abhors you and is dreadfully provoked. His wrath towards you burns like fire: he looks upon you as unworthy of nothing else, but to be cast into the fire;

he is of purer eyes than to bear to have you in his sight; you are ten thousand times more abominable in his eyes than the most hateful venomous serpent is in ours. You have offended him infinitely more than ever a stubborn rebel did his prince—and yet it is nothing but his hand that holds you from falling into the fire every moment.

This hard-hitting rhetoric has come to characterize Edwards' preaching, but unfairly so. Apparently Edwards was not an excessively expressive preacher. His style was more calm and reasonable rather than emotional and manipulative.

In 1750 he was dismissed as pastor of the church in Northampton due in part to his attempt to make the requirements for church membership and participation in the Lord's Supper more demanding. He then moved to Stockbridge, Massachusetts, a small frontier town, where he pastored a church and became involved in missionary work among the Indians. It was during this period, from 1752–1757, that he produced four of his most important literary works, which we will survey below.

In 1757 he reluctantly accepted the position of president of the College of New Jersey (today, Princeton University), but died in 1758, one month after his inauguration, as a result of a tainted smallpox vaccination.

Contribution

Since Edwards was first and foremost a pastor, it is not surprising that many hundreds of his sermons are available today. He also made significant literary contributions in ethics, psychology, and even science.[1] Being typically Puritan, his works reflect a consistent

1. Gerald McDermott notes, "One measure of [Edwards'] greatness is Yale University Press's critical edition of his works [*Works of Jonathan Edwards*], which has twenty-six volumes—but even that represents only half of his written products" (*The Great Theologians* [Downers Grove, IL: InterVarsity, 2010], 113). His writings are also available in other forms and anthologies, such as *A Jonathan Edwards Reader* (1995), *The Sermons of Jonathan Edwards: A Reader* (1999), both also published by Yale University Press, and *Jonathan Edwards: Representative Selections* (New York: Hill and Wang, 1962).

Calvinism in their emphasis on God. "No theologian in the history of Christianity held a higher or stronger view of God's majesty, sovereignty, glory and power than Jonathan Edwards." [2] He also reflects the influence of Pietism, specifically in a careful balance between head and heart—biblical truth was crucial to know and believe, but it should always result in pure worship and holy living.

Edwards' theology was not just the product of a powerful intellect reflecting on Scripture, but was also intensely personal. In his *Personal Narrative*, he describes what happened as he was walking in the woods for a time of "divine contemplation and prayer":

> I had a view, that for me was extraordinary, of the glory of the Son of God; as mediator between God and man; and his wonderful, great, full, pure and sweet grace and love, and meek and gentle condescension. This grace, that appeared to me so calm and sweet, appeared great above the heavens. The person of Christ appeared ineffably excellent, with an excellency great enough to swallow up all thought and conception. Which continued, near as I can judge, about an hour; which kept me, the bigger part of the time, in a flood of tears, and weeping aloud.

One way to summarize his writings is with regard to the theological challenges that he addressed. One of Edwards' primary concerns was the growth of Enlightenment rationalism, that is, a profound confidence in the intellect to bring humans to truth (including "religious" truth) as well as ethical decisions and action.[3] This perspective produced significant criticism of the revivals in the 1730s–1740s, namely, that they were based on emotionalism and even irrationalism. Edwards responded in one of his more famous works, *Treatise Concerning Religious Affections* (1746). Here he introduced an approach that was rather novel and revolutionary, namely, that what is most crucial in thought and action is not the mind alone (contrary to the rationalists) but rather the "affections." In fact, he argued, it is from the affections that all thoughts, emo-

---

2. Olson, *The Story of Christian Theology*, 506.
3. See chapter 30 for more on the historical background of the Enlightenment.

tions, decisions, and actions flow. The term as Edwards used it refers to the individual's deepest longings or desires. As he himself put it, "The affections are no other than the more vigorous and sensible exercises of the inclination and will of the soul . . . that by which the soul does not merely perceive and view things, but is some way inclined with respect to the things it views or considers; either is inclined *to* them, or is disinclined and averse *from* them." In other words, affections refer to what we most love (or detest), and therefore what we really crave (or loathe). It is closely related to what Scripture refers to as the "heart," which is not just the center of emotions but the center of our very being, including the physical, mental, and moral aspects in addition to the emotional.

So *true* religion, according to Edwards, is not just head knowledge, that is, information to know, nor is it mere emotionalism, that is, feelings to experience; rather, it is both and more. Head and heart go together. So over against the rationalists, he affirmed the appropriate place of emotions flowing from true affections in Christianity. But he also recognized that not all emotions flow from *true* affections, that is, God-honoring affections, and thus condemned mere emotionalism in revivals. According to John Piper, Edwards' *Religious Affections* "is probably one of the most penetrating and heart-searching Biblical treatments ever written of the way God works in saving and sanctifying the human heart."[4] Roger Olson adds, "Modern psychology has by and large vindicated Edwards's insights into human personality if not his theological interpretations, which included that God is the ultimate cause of all affections—both good and evil."[5]

In addition to Enlightenment rationalism, another of Edwards' concerns was the growth of Arminianism in the New England colonies. It was this concern that produced the first of his four great books written during his Stockbridge ministry, *Freedom of the Will* (1754), which is generally regarded as his greatest literary

4. *God's Passion for His Glory: Living the Vision of Jonathan Edwards* (Wheaton: Crossway, 1998), 59.
5. *The Story of Christian Theology*, 509.

accomplishment and that which established his credentials as one of the greatest American theologian-philosophers. He affirmed a freedom of the will, but not the kind of freedom characteristic of Arminian theology—*complete* freedom (or, self-determining freedom), even to the extent of being able to choose *contrary* to our nature and desires. This, Edwards reasoned, was totally contrary to the complete sovereignty of God, which determines everything. Rather, in harmony with Augustine and Calvinism in general, Edwards argued that we are free to choose *according* to our desires, that is, our "affections"—that which we *most* love and desire. Tragically, however, due to our sinful nature, our affections are all wrong and therefore so is our will, which brings us to another of Edwards' Stockbridge works.

The Christian Doctrine of Original Sin Defended was Edwards' response to one of the effects of Enlightenment thinking on Christian thought, namely, the denial that the human mind (rationalism) and will (Arminianism) are distorted by sin. Edwards demonstrated from Scripture that the effects of sin on all people were universal and pervasive, including most notably our affections. We long for bad things—anything and everything other than God himself. *True* affections, then, are for God in all of his glory and beauty in the person of Jesus Christ. And it is only through a gracious act of God that anyone can have these God-centered affections. The Bible speaks of this in terms of blinded eyes being made to see and deaf ears being made to hear (e.g., Isaiah 35:5; Luke 4:18). When God accomplishes this spiritual healing through Jesus Christ, salvation is the certain result. So this is more than just *knowing* that God is the greatest treasure; it is more than just *believing* that God is the greatest treasure; it is more than just *longing* for God as the greatest treasure; it is, through conversion, actually *experiencing* God as the greatest treasure through Jesus Christ *and* wanting him all the more. Edwards expanded on this theme in *The Nature of True Virtue*, where he states that, for the *true* Christian, *true* virtue flows from *true* affections, which long for God over everything else and therefore delight to do the will of God rather than anything else and to bring others into this same delight and satisfaction in God alone.

Another aspect of the Enlightenment that alarmed Edwards was Deism, the belief that the universe was created by God to operate on its own, much like a machine. In response, he wrote *The End for Which God Created the World*.⁶ Edwards argued, contrary to Deism, that the universe, created by God, operates second-by-second and at every level through the sustaining and directing power of God. Interestingly, in this way Edwards "anticipated post-Newtonian physics, in which all matter is ultimately seen in terms of interacting fields of energy, with every part dependent on every other part, and the forces governing these rather mysterious."⁷ But more significantly, Edwards' primary thesis is this: "The great end of God's works, which is so variously expressed in Scripture, is indeed but one; and this one end is most properly and comprehensively called, the glory of God." But God's glory is not just for himself; it is for the benefit of humans: "God's respect to the creature's good, and his respect to himself [his own glory], is not a divided respect; but both are united in one, as the happiness of the creature aimed at, is happiness in union with himself." Piper summarizes the idea in this way: "That end [for which God created the world], Edwards says, is, first, that the glory of God might be magnified in the universe, and second, that Christ's ransomed people from all times and all nations would rejoice in God above all things."⁸

In summary, over and against both Enlightenment rationalism and New England Arminianism, Edwards argued that God was *supremely* sovereign over his *entire* creation and intimately involved with it at *every* level, and, in fact, was the immediate cause of *everything* that happened. Through all of his writings, Edwards emphasized (to put it mildly) the God-centeredness of everything, and that it is only in God through Jesus Christ that anyone can receive what we all most long for—full happiness and complete satisfaction—all for the ultimate glory of God.

6. He composed this in the mid-1750s, but it was not published until after his death, a decade later.
7. McDermott, *The Great Theologians*, 119.
8. *God's Passion for His Glory*, 31.

Conclusion

Most scholars are in agreement that Jonathan Edwards is the greatest American theologian and one of the greatest theologians of all time. He is also considered one of the greatest American philosophers. Interest in Edwards was sparked by Perry Miller's *Jonathan Edwards,* in which he said, "He speaks with an insight into science and psychology so much ahead of his time that our own can hardly be said to have caught up with him."[9] Since then, "Edwards' scholarship has exploded, with the number of dissertations on his work doubling every decade. The most prestigious university presses and journals have published hundreds of books and articles on his thought and influence."[10]

Edwards' prose is challenging, but his concern is pastoral. He powerfully established the life-transforming truth that God's desire for his glory and the individual's desire to be happy are not contradictory, but rather are one and the same—it is *only* in God through Jesus Christ that we can find what we all *most* long for. Or, as Piper puts it: "God is most glorified in us when we are most satisfied in him."[11]

9. (Westport, CT: Greenwood Press, 1949), xiii.

10. McDermott, *The Great Theologians,* 114.

11. *God's Passion for His Glory,* 47. Also, see Piper's helpful implications of this great truth, 33–47.

29

JOHN WESLEY

First Methodist

Context

A few months before Jonathan Edwards was born in New England, John Wesley was born in England (June 17, 1703). Edwards was the consummate Calvinist, whereas Wesley became one of the main historical proponents of Arminianism. Both had a profound impact on present-day evangelicalism.

John Wesley was the fifteenth child born to Samuel and Susanna Wesley (there were more to come!), both from Puritan backgrounds. Samuel was an Anglican rector in Epworth, England. It was Susanna, however, who provided the spiritual training for her many children. At the age of five, John was rescued from a fire that destroyed their house. From that time on he considered himself as "a burning stick snatched from the fire" (Zechariah 3:2)—chosen by God for something special.

Wesley received his education at Oxford University, joined the faculty in 1726, and was ordained as an Anglican priest several years later. While at Oxford, John, along with his younger brother

Charles (1707–1788), formed a society—the "Holy Club"—for the enhancement of their spiritual lives. The derogatory term *Methodist* was eventually applied to them due to their methodical and rigorous routines of prayer, meditation, Bible study, and mutual exhortation. One of the Oxford students who joined the society was George Whitefield (1714–1770), who became a good friend and close associate of the Wesley brothers.

In 1735, both John and Charles journeyed to the colony of Georgia to engage in missions and pastoral work. During the journey there, John was impressed by a group of German Moravians[1] who exhibited an impressive calm during frightening storms, in stark contrast to his own terror in the face of death. Their brief ministry in Georgia was generally a failure, by John's own assessment, and he returned to England in 1738, well aware of his own sinfulness and weakness. He wrote in his journal, "I went to America to convert the Indians, but, oh, who shall convert me."

He recorded the now-famous account of his own spiritual turnaround in his journal: "In the evening I went very unwillingly to a [Moravian] society in Aldersgate Street, where one was reading Luther's preface to the Epistle to the Romans. About a quarter before nine, while he was describing the change which God works in the heart through faith in Christ, I felt my heart strangely warmed. I felt I did trust in Christ, Christ alone, for salvation. And an assurance was given me that he had taken away my sins, even mine, and saved me from the law of sin and death."[2] Some consider this his actual conversion, while others see it as the first time that he was assured of his salvation. Whichever it was, it was a major turning point in his life.

Charles Wesley[3] and George Whitefield[4] had also experienced recent "conversions" similar to John's, and all three immediately began

1. See chapter 27.
2. *Journal*, May 24, 1738.
3. Charles Wesley is remembered most for musical abilities and composition of thousands of hymns, many of them still popular today.
4. Whitefield is regarded as one of the greatest evangelistic preachers and later played an important role in the First Great Awakening in the colonies. He became a good friend of Jonathan Edwards.

preaching the gospel of salvation by faith in Jesus Christ wherever they could. But such good news was no longer welcome in the Church of England, which was in a period of spiritual decay. The same kind of Enlightenment thinking that Jonathan Edwards was opposing in New England had largely affected the Anglican Church in England. The influence of Puritan Pietism was lost and replaced by an Arminian rationalism that deteriorated into mere moralism, that is, preaching that only emphasized living a good life as best you could.

When Wesley lost the opportunity to preach in Anglican churches, he took to preaching outdoors to whoever would listen. He travelled thousands of miles every year, composed tens of thousands of sermons (many on horseback), and preached four to five times daily. This style of itinerant ministry, if not at the same grueling pace, was continued by Wesley until shortly before his death in 1791 at the age of eighty-seven.

He and other evangelical preachers faced significant opposition from the established Church of England, but they also enjoyed considerable success, especially among the poor. Through their ministry, England experienced a much-needed renewal—the English version of the Great Awakening. "Societies"[5] were formed in order to disciple and encourage their many converts to live holy lives. Originally, these were intended to operate alongside the established churches, but due to the ongoing opposition of the Church of England, these societies eventually broke away and became independent Methodist churches—but only after Wesley's death; he remained a loyal Anglican all of his life. The revival in England did also have a healthy impact within the Church of England as well as in other nonconformist churches, such as Baptists, Congregationalists, and Presbyterians.

Contribution

Even though he did not write a theological text, strictly speaking, Wesley's views are clear from his many sermons, along with his

---

5. These were very much like the "pious gatherings" among the Pietists (see chapter 27).

commentaries, treatises, and journal.[6] His theology was consistently Arminian. In fact, he had a later falling-out with George Whitefield, who was just as committed to Calvinism as Wesley was to Arminianism. He was even outspoken in his opposition to Calvinism, claiming that its doctrines of predestination, election, and monergism violated the very character of God.[7] Like Arminius and other Protestants, Wesley was completely committed to the doctrine of justification by God's grace alone through faith alone in Christ alone. Through the influence of pietistic Moravians as described above, he was also convinced of the importance of "heart Christianity."

Wesley's unique contributions to theology are in the areas of religious authority and personal sanctification. First, with regard to authority, Wesley firmly upheld the Protestant principle of *sola scriptura*—Scripture as the highest written authority for Christians; it is supreme over any other source. However, he also believed that there was an appropriate place for reason, tradition, and experience. "Wesley derived the strong emphasis on reason and tradition from Anglican theologian Richard Hooker, and from Pietism the stress on experience."[8] These four formed what has come to be called the "Wesleyan quadrilateral." Reason is not a source for knowledge but rather is useful for analyzing knowledge—specifically biblical knowledge—and for showing that Scripture, properly interpreted and understood, was reasonable; it is reasonable and believable. Tradition is not independent from Scripture but rather is based on Scripture, and is useful for explaining it and showing that what Christians have generally believed and taught through the centuries is consistent with Scripture; it is timeless and universal truth. Experience also is not independent from Scripture but rather confirms Scripture and is useful for showing how Scripture fits with life; it is applicable and relevant. Reason, experience, and tradition, then, are not equal with Scripture in authority but rather

6. Most of Wesley's works are readily available online.
7. Of course, Calvinists opposed Wesley's Arminianism for the same reasons.
8. Olson, *The Story of Christian Theology*, 513.

are helpful and necessary tools to properly understand and apply Scripture. One scholar calls Wesley's quadrilateral "his greatest contribution to theology."[9]

Wesley's second unique contribution is in the area of personal sanctification, specifically what he called "entire sanctification" or "perfection" in his treatise A Plain Account of Christian Perfection. While Luther and most other Protestant Reformers believed that Christians were completely justified yet continued to sin throughout life (simul justus et peccator), Wesley posited the idea that a form of complete sanctification was possible in this life. Aware of possible misunderstanding, Wesley tried to clarify his thinking by adding an appendix to his Plain Account:

> Some thoughts occurred to my mind this morning concerning Christian perfection, and the manner and time of receiving it, which I believe may be useful to set down: 1. By perfection I mean the humble, gentle, patient love of God and our neighbor, ruling our tempers, words and actions. I do not include an impossibility of falling from it, either in part or in whole. . . . I do not contend for the term sinless, though I do not object against it. 2. As to the manner, I believe this perfection is always wrought in the soul by a simple act of faith; consequently in an instant. But I believe in a gradual work both preceding and following that instant. 3. As to the time, I believe this instant generally is the instant of death, the moment before the soul leaves the body. But I believe it may be ten, twenty, or forty years before. I believe it is usually many years after justification; but that it may be within five years or five months after it, I know no conclusive argument to the contrary.

Note from this quotation that Wesley did not accept any idea of sinless perfection in this life. Rather the "perfection" that was possible was accomplished by the grace of God through the Holy Spirit, it was to be received by faith, it usually happened in a crisis experience subsequent to justification (a second work of grace), and it resulted in "the pure love of God and man, the loving God with all our heart and soul, and our neighbor as ourselves. It is love

9. Sawyer, The Survivor's Guide to Theology, 366.

213

governing the heart and life, running through all our tempers, words and actions."[10] What he seems to have in mind is an instantaneous breakthrough experience (much like his Aldersgate experience) in which the Christian, like never before, becomes motivated by love for God and empowered by the Holy Spirit. It is a *giant* step forward spiritually, but it is not *perfect* perfection; Wesley's notion of entire sanctification was one that could be advanced throughout one's life.

Conclusion

Not only was John Wesley a powerful and prolific preacher, he was also a gifted organizer. The Methodist societies and (later) churches proliferated throughout England, America, and eventually the world. When he died, "he left behind 79,000 followers in England and 40,000 in North America. If we judge greatness by influence he was among the greats of his time."[11] Today there are over 15 million Methodists worldwide. Wesley's influence is also seen in Wesleyan churches, Pentecostalism, the holiness movement, revivalism, and the evangelical movement in general.

10. *A Plain Account of Christian Perfection*, as quoted in Sawyer, *The Survivor's Guide to Theology*, 354.

11. Bruce L. Shelley, *Church History in Plain Language*, updated 2nd ed. (Dallas: Word, 1995), 340.

30

FRIEDRICH SCHLEIERMACHER
Father of Protestant Liberalism

Context

Jonathan Edwards was fighting its effects in New England. John Wesley was dealing with its impact on the Church of England. It *profoundly* changed how many people thought. It was the Enlightenment. From the first century through the periods of reformation and revival, the main question was "What is true Christianity?" The answers were varied: "It is Catholic," or "Lutheran," or "Reformed," and so on. However, Enlightenment thinkers changed the question to "Is Christianity true?" and mainly answered "No," at least as historically understood.

The Enlightenment, also known as the Age of Reason, was an intellectual movement during the seventeenth and eighteenth centuries in Europe. It had philosophical roots. For example, René Descartes (1596–1650)[1] and others began to argue that human reason was capable *on its own* of coming to truth. This was a significant

1. Many consider him the "father of the Enlightenment."

departure from the centuries-old Christian consensus that human reason was distorted by sin, and only by the grace of God could it operate in any helpful way, especially in the realm of spiritual truth. The Enlightenment also had scientific roots that amounted to the combination of human reason and observation of the natural realm. For example, Isaac Newton (1642–1727) and others demonstrated that the universe operated according to natural laws. It was like a vast machine that worked in a very predictable way.

With regard to Christianity, Enlightenment thinking essentially resulted in the rejection of divine revelation and religious authority, and in their place put human reason and individual autonomy. To the Church, the "enlightened" individual declared, "Don't tell me what I ought to believe or do; I've got a brain." Immanuel Kant (1724–1804), a German philosopher and important Enlightenment thinker, summarized the mentality in the title of his book *Religion Within the Limits of Reason Alone* (1793). The assumption of St. Anselm, "I believe in order that I may understand,"[2] was flipped on its head: "I understand in order that I may believe."

The religion of the Enlightenment was Deism or natural religion.[3] The God of Deism created the universe to operate according to natural laws and does *not* intervene through supernatural means such as "miracles." Deists ignored or rejected the doctrines of the Trinity and the deity of Jesus Christ as irrational. They basically stripped historic Christianity of everything supernatural. What was left was an all-purpose, minimalist religion that included a generic, rather detached God rather than the sovereign, intimately involved God of the Bible, and was more interested in showing the way to moral action than spiritual salvation.

Deism was the religion observed in Unitarian churches, founded in England and America in the late eighteenth century. Even though Unitarianism may consider itself "Christian," it rejected pretty much everything that had made Christianity distinctive,

2. See chapter 17.
3. This is related to *natural theology*, which, as previously discussed, is theology done apart from divine revelation using the human mind and senses alone.

for example, the Nicene Creed and the other historic creeds and confessions of Christianity.

A middle road between historic, orthodox theology and Unitarian, deistic theology was what is now called "liberal Protestant theology." It did not go to the extreme of *rejecting* historic Christian beliefs that were not considered acceptable to Enlightenment thinking. Rather, liberal theology *reinterpreted* these doctrines so as to make them acceptable to the "modern," enlightened mind. Liberals were not out to destroy Christianity; they were intent on preserving it in the modern period.[4]

Friedrich Daniel Ernst Schleiermacher is generally regarded as the founder of liberal Protestant theology. He was born in Breslau, Prussia (present-day Poland), in 1768. In keeping with his family background, his upbringing and early education was in the pietistic tradition. However, along the way he began to have significant doubts about what he was being taught and was becoming increasingly uncomfortable with some historic Christian doctrines. This continued during his university studies at Halle, where Schleiermacher was introduced to the Enlightenment way of thinking. He pastored several churches and also served on the theology faculties of the University of Halle and the University of Berlin (which he helped found). He died in 1834.

Contribution

His written work is massive, but two of his most important books are *On Religion: Speeches to its Cultured Despisers* (1799)[5] and *The Christian Faith* (1821, revised in 1830).[6] In the former, he addressed the attacks on religion from Enlightenment thinkers—the "cultured despisers." In doing so, he introduced a totally new concept of religion in general. This book became very popular and made

4. The Enlightenment is often regarded as the beginning of the "modern period" historically.

5. Richard Crouter, trans. and ed. (Cambridge: Cambridge University Press, 1996).

6. H. R. Mackintosh and J. S. Stewart, eds. (Edinburgh: T & T Clark, 1986).

Schleiermacher very famous. In the latter book, he explained his more mature views on theology and the essence of Christianity specifically. "It is this work that establishes beyond all doubt Schleiermacher's place in the theological pantheon: it is the model for all systematic theologies since. In it he attempts nothing less than the total revision of the whole of Christian doctrine, to re-present it in a new, contemporary way."[7]

In *Speeches* he explains his views on religion in general over against the attacks of the Enlightenment. From his pietistic background came his conviction that religion was more than just knowledge—believing the right things (theology)—and more than just action—doing the right things (ethics); it involved feelings as well—"heart Christianity." But where Schleiermacher radically departed from Pietism and historic Christianity was in reducing the essence of religion to "feelings" *only*. These are not mere emotions. Rather, the term, as Schleiermacher used it, refers to an inner sense of absolute dependence on something outside—the Infinite. Schleiermacher also called this "God-consciousness." This is a *universal* human attribute and the basis for all human emotions as well as knowledge and action, that is, all human experience. Thus, all religion is first and foremost *experiential*. The breakthrough here is this: If religion is primarily experiential rather than doctrinal or ethical, it is safe from the attacks of the Enlightenment because it is outside of the realm of reason and science. So what if the "doctrines" of any particular religion strike rationalists as irrational. They are not the core of religion. Religion can do what science and reason cannot—address the sense of neediness and dependence that everyone everywhere experiences every day, even the "enlightened."

He applies this to Christianity specifically in *The Christian Faith*, where he stated, "The piety which forms the basis of all ecclesiastical communions is, considered purely in itself, neither a knowing [theology] or a doing [ethics], but a modification of feeling, or of immediate self-consciousness," and even more specifically, "the consciousness of being absolutely dependent or, which is the same thing,

7. Hill, *The History of Christian Thought*, 231.

of being in relation with God."[8] That's it! The heart of Christianity is the sense of one's dependence upon God—God-consciousness.

Theology and ethics *are* part of religion, but in a *secondary* sense. Christian theology, for Schleiermacher, was not the necessary content of belief but rather the "accounts of the Christian religious affections [feelings, experiences] set forth in speech."[9] Similarly, the Bible is not revelation from God that must be accepted but rather the record of human religious experience that we learn from. But if historically accepted doctrines are no longer helpful in relation to one's "feelings" or conscious experience of God, they can be discarded and replaced by more helpful doctrines. Personal experience, not biblical truth, is decisive—the standard or norm by which everything is evaluated. In fact, anyone can experience divine revelation in their personal lives when they relate their experiences in life to their own dependence upon God. Basically, Schleiermacher reversed the basis of Christian theology from objective divine revelation to subjective human experience.

While all religions are about this self-conscious God-dependence, Christianity is unique, according to Schleiermacher, in that "everything is related to the redemption accomplished by Jesus of Nazareth."[10] What makes Jesus unique is not that he was God incarnate, but rather that he was a perfect example of God-consciousness. Jesus was human in that he shared in our dependence upon God; he was "divine" in that his consciousness of this dependence was perfect. This boils down to Jesus being more a very elevated human than the God-man.

"Redemption" comes not from trusting in Jesus as our substitutionary sacrifice, but rather in following his model of God-consciousness. The problem of sin is simply that we have an inadequate sense of our dependence on God. Jesus is "savior" in that he not only provides a perfect example but actually imparts his perfect God-consciousness to believers.

8. *The Christian Faith,* 12.
9. Ibid., 76.
10. Ibid., 52.

Since "*everything* is related to the redemption accomplished by Jesus of Nazareth,"[11] Schleiermacher examines every Christian doctrine in relation to Jesus. He concludes that doctrines such as the Trinity (which he dealt with in an appendix), the virgin birth of Jesus, his deity, resurrection, ascension, and second coming are not essential to Christianity since they are irrelevant to an individual's self-conscious dependence upon God through Christ. Similarly, the attributes of God are not objective facts about the Being of God, but rather descriptions of how we can experience God.[12]

Conclusion

There are significant problems with Schleiermacher's radically new ideas. For example, he claimed that *all* people have a self-conscious sense of weakness and dependence on God, but is this really true? Furthermore, if all doctrines flow from subjective personal experience, then can there be any objective truth in Christianity? If individuals experience God in different ways, then doesn't he basically amount to a different God for each individual? "This novel approach changes our view of God into a bigger view of ourselves."[13] That is, Schleiermacher changed theology from being God-centered to human-centered.

Later theologians criticized these weaknesses; nevertheless, Schleiermacher did effectively change the direction of much of Protestant thought. He pioneered the standard liberal theological response to Enlightenment thinking—give up those orthodox doctrines that seem (at least to liberals) to be less than rational. And in this reinterpretation, much of what is distinctive and crucial to Christianity is drained away, as we will continue to see in the next chapter.

11. Ibid. Emphasis added.
12. Ibid., 194.
13. McDermott, *The Great Theologians*, 145.

31

ALBRECHT RITSCHL

Framer of Protestant Liberalism

Context

Friedrich Schleiermacher is known as the Father of Protestant Liberalism, but his successor, Albrecht Ritschl, is closely associated with the actual structuring and establishment of classical liberal theology. Whereas Schleiermacher pioneered a new way of thinking for Protestants in light of the Enlightenment, Ritschl adopted that new way of thinking and gave it a more specific form and content. In fact, in the late nineteenth and early twentieth centuries, classical Protestant liberal theology was known as "Ritschlianism."

Albrecht Ritschl was born in Berlin in 1822, the son of a Lutheran pastor and bishop. He studied theology at the Universities of Tübingen, Halle, and Bonn, and began teaching at the latter. In 1864 he became professor of theology at the University of Göttingen, where he stayed until his death in 1889.

Contribution

His most important written work was the three-volume *The Christian Doctrine of Justification and Reconciliation* (1870–74).[1] Central to Ritschl's theological method was the idea that theological statements or "judgments" (to use his term) should not be considered statements of fact (as, for example, would be scientific statements), but rather of value. Statements of fact can be objectively proven but demand no personal or moral commitment on the part of the individual. On the other hand, statements of value are beyond objective verification and necessarily demand a personal and moral commitment. "[F]or Ritschl scientific knowledge can only be about the way things are, whereas religious knowledge is always also about the way things ought to be."[2] The "beauty" of this is that it protected religion—or more specifically, Christianity—from the "threat" of being shown irrelevant by modern science. Science deals exclusively with the natural, physical realm; religion or theology deals exclusively with the ethical, moral realm—thus, no potential conflict. The heart of Christianity, according to Ritschl, was a certain set of these value statements—the important things that affect how Christians ought to live.

An implication of this methodology was that God in his being—*facts* about God—can never be the object of theological study. Rather, theology can only know God in terms of how he works among people—his *value* in human experience. In doing this, he is following in the footsteps of Schleiermacher in practicing a human-centered theology rather than a God-centered theology. For example, even though Ritschl did not explicitly reject the doctrine of the Trinity, he said little about it since it had to do with the being of God, which is beyond theological knowledge. Similarly, God's attributes of being (e.g., omniscience, omnipotence, sovereignty)

1. Albrecht Ritschl, *The Christian Doctrine of Justification and Reconciliation*, trans. H. R. Mackintosh and A. B. Macaulay (Edinburgh: T & T Clark, 1900).
2. Stanley J. Grenz and Roger E. Olson, *20th Century Theology: God and the World in a Transitional Age* (Downers Grove, IL: InterVarsity, 1992), 54.

are unknowable, whereas the love of God—the primary affirmation about God from Ritschl's perspective—*can* be known in its effect upon people.

Another important emphasis in Ritschl's theology flows from this: the kingdom of God. This he understood to be all of humanity united by love and morality. It is the highest value for both God and humans. Christianity should best exemplify this in the community of the church, where the ideals of the kingdom of God are lived and promoted. The Christian life is basically living a good life and following the "golden rule" by treating others in love. When one lives according to these value statements, the kingdom of God is further established on earth. Basically, Christianity is stripped of anything supernatural or miraculous and reduced to only what is moral and practical. Christianity is not about the "sweet by and by," but rather the here and now. The highest good of the Christian is not preparing for the afterlife in heaven in the future, but rather promoting the kingdom of God on earth in the present.

Ritschl based this on the teachings of Jesus as recorded in the Gospels. But who was Jesus? According to Ritschl, Christians can affirm the "deity" of Jesus—He is "God"—but only as a statement of value, not fact. This basically means that Jesus is *not* God in fact; rather, he is merely a human who perfectly lived out the values of the kingdom of God during his life on earth. Ritschl speaks of this as the "vocation" that God gave to Jesus, which he perfectly fulfilled. Jesus Christ did not exist before his birth—other than in the mind of God—and he was certainly not born of a virgin. He did not work miracles, but he did teach important "values." And the only sense in which "Jesus is alive today" is that his teachings have had a lasting impact until today. In other words, according to Ritschl, Jesus is *not* the God-man; he is only the good man, who provided the teachings and the model that the rest of us humans should follow in order to establish the kingdom of God on earth.[3]

3. This is essentially a very early Christological heresy known as *adoptionism*, the idea that Jesus was *only* a human that God chose to use in a very special way.

From an orthodox point of view, "Ritschl's Jesus . . . is a rather insipid, watered-down version of the real thing."[4]

What about sin? According to Ritschl, sin is anything contrary to the highest good—the kingdom of God. Sin basically is selfishness, the opposite of love for others. He believed that sin is pervasive because all people tend to be self-centered, not because of any concept of original sin or an inherited sin nature. This universal sinfulness can only be remedied by God's gracious work of turning people into those who love others more than themselves.

The concept of salvation through Jesus Christ was important to Ritschl, but Jesus was not the savior in the sense of the one who died in the place of sinners and for the penalty of sin. Rather, he accomplished salvation through his perfect fulfillment of the "vocation" given to him by God—embodying and exemplifying the kingdom of God, which in turn became a powerful influence for world transformation.[5] As the title of Ritschl's three-volume work indicates, justification and reconciliation are central to Christian doctrine. Justification is when God forgives sinners who commit themselves to follow the example of Jesus. Reconciliation is what forgiven sinners are called to in the fulfillment of the ideals of the kingdom of God—love and unity.

Conclusion

Albrecht Ritschl has been considered the most influential liberal theologian of the nineteenth century. His influence can be seen in nearly an entire generation of Protestant pastors and scholars trained in German universities, and through these pastors and scholars, Protestant liberalism came to America. His theology of the kingdom of God stimulated what has come to be known in America as the "social gospel," that is, the task of Christianity to transform not just individuals but the whole of society through justice, morality, and love.[6]

4. Hill, *The History of Christian Thought*, 251.
5. This is essentially the moral influence theory of Peter Abelard. See chapter 18.
6. A major proponent of the social gospel was Walter Rauschenbusch, an American Baptist theologian. His major literary contribution was *A Theology*

Ritschl continued what Schleiermacher began, and in the theologies of these two, we can see some themes that came to characterize classical Protestant liberal theology.[7] First, liberal theology adopted Enlightenment thinking in order to make Christianity relevant in the modern age. For example, a scientific mind-set meant that anything miraculous or supernatural in this world had to be ruled out (e.g., virgins do not have babies and dead people do not come back from the grave). This also implied the rejection of classical sources of authority, specifically the Bible as understood to be supernatural, divine revelation, and a variety of orthodox doctrines, such as the inspiration and inerrancy of the Bible, the Trinitarian nature of God (one essence-three persons), and the dual natures of Jesus Christ (one person-two essences). These, they thought, were simply too much for the modern mind to accept. As we have seen in this chapter and the previous one, they might use the same term (e.g., the "deity" of Jesus Christ or the "inspiration" of Scripture) but mean something entirely different from the traditional understanding of the term. Apart from doing this, they feared Christianity would simply fade away in the same manner as countless other ancient religions.

Second, God was to be understood primarily through human experience of him and his work in this world. The God of liberal theology became very human-oriented, and the Christ of liberal theology became merely a human—although the ideal role-model for the rest of us. This can be seen in Ritschl's focus on the kingdom of God being simply all of humanity living in utopia here on earth. An implication of this is that humanity was no longer seen as in a different category from God (God is the Creator; humans are creatures); rather, God and humans were in the same category but at different levels within the category.

Third, the essence of Christianity was morality. Jesus was seen as the great example of moral living. The kingdom of God was everybody living moral lives and treating one another with love and

for the Social Gospel (New York: Macmillan, 1918), which reflects Ritschlian thought.

7. Adapted from Olson, The Story of Christian Theology, 549–551.

respect. Salvation was a matter of doing your best and following the Golden Rule. Closely connected to this was a belief in universalism—everybody would eventually be saved. Sin was not seen as that big of a problem. God was not seen as being angry with sin and intent on judgment; rather, he was a loving Father who would forgive all of his children and bless them—eventually, at least.

"Ritschlianism" dominated theology in the latter nineteenth and early twentieth centuries, but then came to be challenged, both by orthodox theologians who had never bought into liberal thinking—the movement that came to be known as "fundamentalism"—as well as from within liberalism itself by those who came to see its weaknesses and failings—this came to be known as "neoorthodoxy." We now turn to the stories of representatives of these movements. In anticipation, H. Richard Niebuhr's critical description of liberal theology in general has become a classic: "A God without wrath brought men without sin into a kingdom without judgment through the ministration of a Christ without a cross."[8]

8. *The Kingdom of God in America* (New York: Harper and Row, 1959), 193.

32

J. GRESHAM MACHEN

Defender of the Fundamentals

Context

Protestant liberal theology was thoroughly entrenched in German universities in the nineteenth century. It entered the North American scene as the "New Theology" through pastors and scholars who received their graduate theological training in these European universities. As noted in the previous chapter, the "social gospel" developed as a uniquely American application of liberal theology in the context of urbanization and industrialization—sin and salvation were seen as issues, not just of individuals, but of society collectively,[1] based on Ritschl's concept of the kingdom of God.

From the perspective of orthodox Christianity, liberal theology had not only turned away from essential doctrines of historic, biblical Christianity, it also went overboard in the direction of concern

---

1. For example, American capitalism was often regarded as a societal sin due to what was seen as its repression of the poor and the workers.

for society as a whole at the expense of concern for individual salvation and redemption. Furthermore, what concern for individuals there was seemed to be more in terms of physical needs than spiritual needs. Whereas liberal theology saw itself as trying to preserve Christianity in the modern age, conservative Christians saw it as threatening the very existence of *true* historic Christianity.

So in the early twentieth century, many conservative Christians reacted against liberalism and the social gospel; some even went to the opposite extreme—withdrawing from any engagement with or concern for the transformation of society and focusing totally on proclaiming the gospel in order to save individuals. Their concern was for the spiritual needs of individuals, often being negligent of physical needs, and their focus was preparing for the future, not transforming the present. This movement has come to be known as *fundamentalism*, due to the fact that it reemphasized the fundamentals of the faith—the historic, traditional, orthodox doctrines of Christianity.[2] An all-out "war" developed between this and liberal theology, known as the "modernist[3]-fundamentalist controversy." Historically, then, fundamentalism is not only defined as its defense of historic Christian theology, but also its militant rejection of and attack on liberal, Protestant theology.

A leading theologian of early fundamentalism was J. Gresham Machen (1881–1937). He studied theology at Princeton Theological Seminary, where he was taught by Benjamin B. Warfield, who was already waging a war against the encroachment of liberal theology, especially in its watered-down view of the Bible.[4] Machen was also directly exposed to liberal theology as he continued his studies at the German universities of Marburg and Göttingen. He began his teaching career in New Testament at Princeton Seminary in 1906, and when Warfield died in 1921, Machen stepped into his shoes as one of the leading defenders of orthodoxy over liberalism.

2. The term is also derived from a series of pamphlets called *The Fundamentals* that were published between 1910 and 1915.
3. *Modernist* refers to anyone holding to "modernism," that is, liberal theology.
4. See, for example, his classic work *The Inspiration and Authority of the Bible* (Philadelphia: Presbyterian and Reformed, 1948).

He did not merely demonstrate his opposition to liberalism in his teaching and writing, but also in his associations and actions. When Princeton Seminary was being reorganized with a liberal orientation, Machen resigned in 1929 and founded Westminster Theological Seminary in Philadelphia. He served as its first president and professor of New Testament until his death in 1937. In 1935 he was put on trial for insubordination by the general assembly of the Presbyterian Church in the USA (again, due to his opposition to liberalism as it crept into the denomination), found guilty, and suspended from ministry. As a result, he helped found the Orthodox Presbyterian Church in 1936.

Contribution

Machen's writings were primarily focused on this battle with liberalism. For example, in the introduction to his *What is Faith?*,[5] he mentions Schleiermacher and Ritschl in connection with the "intellectual decadence of the day,"[6] which, among other things, does not like to define terms. "Men discourse very eloquently today upon such subjects as God, religion, Christianity, atonement, redemption, faith; but are greatly incensed when they are asked to tell in simple language what they mean by these terms."[7] As we have already seen, liberal theology speaks in terms common to historic Christianity (e.g., *deity, inspiration, sin*) and even claims to believe in the concepts, but the terms mean very different things to them. Thus, the need to ask the question in the title of Machen's book, "What is faith?" He writes, "A more 'practical' question could hardly be conceived. The preacher says: 'Believe on the Lord Jesus Christ, and thou shall be saved.' But how can a man possibly act on that suggestion, unless he knows what it is to believe. . . . These [liberal] preachers speak about faith, but they do not tell what faith is."[8]

5. *What is Faith?* (Grand Rapids, MI: Eerdmans, 1925).
6. Ibid., 15.
7. Ibid., 14.
8. Ibid., 43.

Machen goes on to answer the question according to the teachings of the New Testament as historically understood.

In *The Origin of Paul's Religion*,[9] Machen takes on the liberal theological understanding of Jesus and Paul in relation to Christianity. He summarizes the liberal perspective as follows:

> Jesus of Nazareth, according to the liberal view, was the greatest of the children of men [merely a great human]. His greatness centered in His consciousness of standing toward God in the relation of son to Father. That consciousness of sonship, at least in its purity, Jesus discovered, was not shared by others. . . . He urged men, not to take Him as the *object* of their faith, but only to take Him as an *example* of their faith; not to have faith in Him, but to have faith in God like His faith.[10]

It was the *disciples* of Jesus who began "to attribute to His person a kind of religious importance which He had never claimed. They began to make Him not only an example for faith but also the object of faith . . . and to ascribe to Him divine attributes."[11] Paul's theology, then, "was the outer and perishable shell for the precious kernel. His *theology* was the product of his time, and may now be abandoned; his *religion* was derived from Jesus of Nazareth and is a permanent possession of the human race."[12] The bottom line is that, according to liberal theology, historic Christianity is based on Paul's over-embellishment of the person and significance of Jesus. Therefore, it is legitimate and timely to shed the "perishable shell" of Paul's way of putting it—"his *theology*"—and get back to the "precious kernel" of who Jesus really was and what he really taught—"[Paul's] *religion*." In the rest of the book, Machen demonstrates what Christians have historically believed, and that is: The origin of Paul's religion is Jesus himself. Paul got it right in his epistles; Christians have been justified all along in believing that the gospel of Jesus and the gospel of Paul are one and the same.

9. *The Origin of Paul's Religion* (Grand Rapids, MI: Eerdmans, 1925).
10. Ibid., 25, emphasis added.
11. Ibid.
12. Ibid., 26, emphasis added.

Machen's most straightforward confrontation of liberal theology was *Christianity and Liberalism*,[13] in which he tries to demonstrate that the Christianity of liberal Protestant theology is not Christianity at all:

> We shall be interested in showing that despite the liberal use of traditional phraseology modern liberalism not only is a different religion from Christianity but belongs in a totally different class of religions. . . . [I]t is not the Christianity of the New Testament which is in conflict with science, but the supposed Christianity of the modern liberal Church. . . . [T]he liberal attempt at reconciling Christianity with modern science has really relinquished everything distinctive of Christianity, so that what remains is in essential only that same indefinite type of religious aspiration which was in the world before Christianity came upon the scene.[14]

Through books and arguments such as these, Machen was recognized as a thoughtful and articulate defender of orthodox Christianity and spokesperson for the fundamentalist movement.

Conclusion

Central to Machen's concern, and that of fundamentalism generally, was liberal theology's rejection of belief in the Bible as the very written Word of God, including its divine inspiration, inerrancy, infallibility, and authority. In its place—and in keeping with Enlightenment thought—liberalism put the human mind and modern science. But with the rejection of a high view of Scripture, other beliefs were quickly rejected or redefined: the Trinity, the deity of Jesus Christ, the virgin birth of Jesus Christ, the death of Jesus Christ as a substitutionary atonement, the bodily resurrection of Jesus Christ, the return of Jesus Christ, miracles, original sin, and so on. These issues became the battleground in the modernist-fundamentalist controversy.

13. *Christianity and Liberalism* (Grand Rapids, MI: Eerdmans, 1923).
14. Ibid., 7.

The likes of J. Gresham Machen and the fundamentalist movement can be commended for upholding conservative, orthodox, historic Christian theology against the onslaught of Enlightenment thinking and its offspring, liberal Protestant theology. The modern evangelical movement is basically the continuation of early fundamentalism (as characterized by a high view of Scripture); commitment to the historic "fundamentals of the faith"; belief in the need for personal conversion through faith in Jesus Christ—the God-man—who died in the sinner's place; and that all of this should result in love and good deeds, which further result in social transformation—being "salt and light"—at least to a degree.

While J. Gresham Machen and others criticized liberal theology from the outside, others eventually began to criticize it from the inside (initially), and that is the story of the next chapter.

33

KARL BARTH

Founder of Neo-Orthodoxy

Context

European liberal Protestant theology, reflecting its Enlightenment roots, had turned away from traditional religious authority, specifically the Bible as divine revelation, and instead trusted modern science and human reason. They wanted to preserve Christianity for the modern world, but ended up with a very human-oriented God that could only be known through human experience. Liberalism also reflected the Enlightenment's great optimism about the future, finding great hope for a better tomorrow through science, reason, and education. Humanity was evolving into something really good. "Every day in every way, things were getting better and better."

Fundamentalism's reaction to liberal theology attempted to preserve historic, orthodox Christianity and its fundamental doctrines—specifically its high view of Scripture as divinely inspired, without error, and supremely authoritative—but also beliefs such as the Trinity, the deity of Jesus Christ, his virgin birth, and so on.

In the first half of the twentieth century, a handful of theologians who had studied in European universities and had been trained in liberalism also began to react against it and reject it. Their essential difference with both liberal theology and fundamentalist theology was in their view of divine revelation and the Bible, as we will see. Ironically, this movement eventually was seen by liberals as fundamentalism in disguise and by fundamentalists as liberalism in disguise. It has come to be called "neo-orthodoxy" because it was a corrective movement from within liberalism back toward orthodoxy. However, it did not come all of the way back to orthodoxy—it was a "new orthodoxy."

The founder of neo-orthodoxy is widely recognized as Karl Barth.[1] He was born in Basel, Switzerland, in 1886. His father was a pastor in the Reformed Church of Switzerland, as had been both of his grandfathers. Barth actually began his theological studies under his father, who continued to hold to a comparatively conservative theology and, by then, was teaching at the University of Bern. Barth continued his studies at the universities of Marburg, Berlin, and Tübingen. In each of these institutions he was trained by leading liberal theologians of the time, and he adopted their theological perspective (over against that of his own father). In 1909 he completed his studies, was ordained, and began pastoral ministry.

Barth pastored a small Reformed church in Safenwil, Switzerland, from 1911–1921. As he prepared for his weekly preaching responsibilities, he discovered that liberal theology had left him with nothing to offer to his people in wartime Europe,[2] and he turned back to the Bible. He discovered things there that he had never encountered in liberalism. He later wrote,

> It is not the right human thoughts about God which form the content of the Bible, but the right thoughts about men. The Bible tells us not

1. Although Barth rejected the term "neo-orthodoxy" as applied to his theology.
2. The two world wars were a part of what brought into question the optimism of liberal theology. Those devastating conflicts seemed to demonstrate that humanity was not getting better and better after all.

how we should talk with God but what he says to us; not how we find the way to him, but how he has sought and found the way to us; not the right relation in which we must place ourselves to him, but the covenant which he has made with all who are Abraham's spiritual children, and which he has sealed once and for all in Jesus Christ. It is this, which is within the Bible. The world of God is within the Bible.[3]

Barth began his teaching career at the University of Göttingen, Germany, in 1921, and also held faculty positions at the universities of Münster and Bonn. When Hitler rose to power, Barth joined those few who opposed him and Nazism. As a result, he lost his faculty position in Germany, returned to Switzerland, and in 1935 he began teaching theology at the University of Basel. He remained there until his retirement in 1962 and continued to write and lecture until his death in 1968.

Contribution

Karl Barth's first significant publication was his commentary on Romans in 1919,[4] while he was still a pastor. This book demonstrated that Barth had already adopted a more traditional understanding of Scripture than that held by liberal Protestantism. But Barth's theology was still in transition. By the time the second edition was published in 1922, the transition was complete. Barth had left behind most of the tenets of liberalism in which he had been trained, and returned to his roots in Augustinian-Calvinist Reformed theology. His Romans commentary particularly demonstrated this in his view of God. In stark contrast to the liberal understanding of God as nearly human and virtually trapped in his own creation, Barth recaptured and emphasized the absolute sovereignty and transcendence of God as "wholly other." As he

3. Karl Barth, *Credo* (London: Hodder & Stoughton, 1935), 43; as quoted in Sawyer, *The Survivor's Guide to Theology*, 424.

4. Karl Barth, *The Epistle to the Romans*, trans. Edwyn C. Hoskyns (London: Oxford University Press, 1933).

famously put it, you don't say "God" by saying "man" in a loud voice. One early reviewer wrote that Barth's commentary "landed like a bombshell on the playground of the theologians."[5]

In 1927 he published *Christian Dogmatics in Outline* and demonstrated in another way his break with liberalism. He stated his conviction that theology was not to be based on human feelings, experience, or rationality, as liberal theology presupposed, but rather on the Word of God alone.

Without question, Barth's *magnum opus* was his *Church Dogmatics*.[6] He came to believe that his *Christian Dogmatics in Outline* had been too heavily influenced by existential philosophy, contrary to his own convictions that theology should be based on the Word of God and nothing else. So in 1932 he began from scratch, determined to be truly consistent with that belief. He continued writing *Church Dogmatics* until his death in 1968, leaving his massive work (thirteen volumes, over six million words) incomplete.

In *Church Dogmatics*, Barth continued to present an understanding of God that was very different from the God of liberal theology. Whereas the doctrine of the Trinity had largely been abandoned in liberalism, Barth made it central to his doctrine of God.[7] "Under Barth's influence theology has returned to serious consideration of the Trinity."[8] His definition of God was "He who loves in freedom."[9] Overall, Barth's doctrine of God was very much like that of John Calvin and Jonathan Edwards, along with his other predecessors in Reformed theology.

Furthermore, Barth continued to argue for the radical transcendence of God, that is, the "infinite qualitative distinction" between God on the one hand, and humanity and all of creation on the other. Liberal theology had emphasized a "connectedness" between

---

5. Lane, *A Concise History of Christian Thought*, 273.

6. Karl Barth, *Church Dogmatics*, 13 vols. (Edinburgh: T & T Clark, 1957–1988).

7. For example, he began his *Church Dogmatics* with a discussion of the Trinity, whereas Friedrich Schleiermacher buried it in an appendix.

8. Stanley J. Grenz and Roger E. Olson, *20th Century Theology* (Downers Grove, IL: InterVarsity, 1992), 77.

9. *Church Dogmatics*, vol. II, part 1, *The Doctrine of God*, part 1.

God and humanity to the extent that God could hardly disconnect himself from humanity. Barth went to the other extreme: There is a vast separation between God and humanity. So according to Barth, knowing God is not a matter of looking up ahead on some kind of continuum that included both God and humans. In fact, knowing anything about God is totally impossible *unless* . . . Which brings us to one of Barth's most revolutionary tenets, which is central to neo-orthodoxy in general: his doctrine of divine revelation.

How has God revealed himself? How can he be known? As we have already seen, liberal theology generally answered the question in terms of human experience and reason. God can be known through nature (as understood by modern science) and how he has worked in all of human history.[10] On the other hand, fundamentalism, while acknowledging that God can be known somewhat through nature and history, adamantly believed that God had revealed himself primarily through the written Word of God, the Bible. Barth rejected both of these and steered a middle course. Since God is "wholly other" and completely distinct from humanity, humans *cannot* know God *at all* unless God allows it. And thankfully God, in his love and freedom, *did* allow it by taking the initiative to make himself known. This is divine revelation for Barth: God's *act* of revealing himself. The climax and epitome of this was the person of Jesus Christ. Jesus Christ *is* the ultimate, perfect divine revelation—THE Word of God.

What is the Bible, then? According to Barth, it is not the Word of God *per se*, contrary to historic orthodoxy and fundamentalism. Barth rejected the idea of divine revelation as propositional—written statements in human language. Rather, the Bible is a *witness* to the Word of God, who is Jesus Christ, or, stated another way, the Bible is *not equal* to divine revelation, but rather the *record* of divine revelation. However, Barth went on to say that the Bible

---

10. Barth vehemently rejected any possibility of natural theology, that is, discovering anything about God from human reason and nature alone. In fact, Barth had a famous and bitter falling-out with Emil Brunner, a friend and theological ally (otherwise), over this issue. Brunner's position embraced both revelation through Jesus Christ *and* nature. Barth's written response was simply entitled *Nein! (No!)*.

can *become* the Word of God (in a secondary sense) when God *acts* to reveal himself through the Bible to the reader. "The Bible is God's Word so far as God lets it be His Word, so far as God speaks through it. . . . 'The Bible is God's Word' is a confession of faith, a statement made by the faith that hears God Himself speak in the human word of the Bible."[11] So the Word of God is not an object to be possessed (like a big leather-bound book on a shelf), but an event to be experienced (like a personal relationship with someone who profoundly loves you).

Barth rejected the ideas of the verbal inspiration and inerrancy of Scripture; he believed the Bible to be a fallible, human book. This is not an overwhelming problem, however, because God has worked through other fallible, human "witnesses" to reveal himself (e.g., prophets). So he can do the same through the Bible. All of this may lead us to think that Barth was rather demeaning of the Bible, but in reality the Bible was very important to him, since it is the only witness to Jesus Christ that we have now, and it is the only written book through which God chooses to reveal himself. Therefore, he *treated* the Bible as though it *were* verbally inspired, inerrant, and divinely authoritative, even though theologically he denied these doctrines.[12]

Based on what we have just observed, it should not be a surprise to note that Barth's theology was radically Christ-centered. God revealed himself primarily through Jesus Christ. God works with humanity primarily through Jesus Christ. Therefore, all Christian doctrine must be related to Jesus Christ. In contrast to liberal theology's conception of Jesus as the ideal human, Barth's was consistent with orthodoxy and the ancient Christological formulations, such as the Chalcedonian Creed.

---

11. *Church Dogmatics*, vol. I, part 1, *The Doctrine of the Word of God*, part 1, 123.

12. Barth also regarded the church's proclamation of the gospel and Scripture as another secondary form of divine revelation when God chooses to reveal Jesus Christ through it. So according to Barth, there are three forms of divine revelation: the *revealed* Word of God—Jesus Christ (primary), the *written* Word of God—the Bible (secondary), and the *proclaimed* Word of God—preaching (secondary).

However, his radical Christ-centeredness led him to some rather unique conclusions. In keeping with Reformed theology, Barth had a very strong doctrine of election. But unlike classical Reformed theology, which asserted that the elect included humans who would be redeemed through the work of Christ, Barth's doctrine of election included *only* Christ—He *alone* is the elect *one*. This is a rather unique and revolutionary perspective, but he takes it even further.

Not only is Christ the only elect one, he is also the only "reprobate" one, that is, the only individual who will experience God's wrath for sin. "In this one man Jesus, God puts at the head and in the place of *all other men*. . . . [So] the rejection which *all men* incurred, the wrath of God under which *all men* lie, the death which *all men* must die, God in His love for [*all*] *men* transfers from all eternity to *Him* in whom He loves and elects them [*all men*], and whom He elects at their head and in their place."[13]

Backing up a step, we need to note that Barth rearticulated the seriousness of sin, God's intent to punish sin, and God's gracious work of pouring out his wrath upon Jesus Christ as he died on the cross—all of this in contrast to liberal theology and in keeping with orthodoxy. But, in contrast to orthodoxy, God apparently *only* poured out his wrath on Jesus, who died in the place of *all* people who will eventually be found "in Christ," the elect one and only. "[O]n the basis of God's decree, the *only truly rejected man* is His own Son . . . so that [God's rejection] can no longer fall on other men or be their concern."[14] This sounds very much like universalism, which had indeed become a feature of liberal theology. Did Barth really believe that *all* people will eventually be saved in Christ? Barth was certainly criticized for implying just that. Whether he really did or not is somewhat unclear; his responses to that criticism were rather ambiguous. But it seems that, to be consistent with his stated convictions, the possibility of salvation for absolutely everyone must be left open; after all, God is "He who loves in freedom."

13. *Church Dogmatics*, vol. II, part 2, *The Doctrine of God*, 123, emphasis added.

14. Ibid., 319, emphasis added.

Conclusion

Karl Barth is generally regarded as one of the greatest theologians—if not *the* greatest theologian of the twentieth century, and among the greatest theologians of *all* time. After him, the neo-orthodox movement became a theological force to be reckoned with, by both liberal and conservative theology. Other very influential theologians who, at least to some degree, were influenced by Karl Barth and/or a part of neo-orthodoxy were Emil Brunner, Rudolph Bultmann, brothers Reinhold Niebuhr and H. Richard Niebuhr, Dietrich Bonhoeffer,[15] and among Catholics, Hans Küng.

Barth does indeed deserve credit for important accomplishments. He reestablished that theology needs to be done "from above," based on divine self-revelation, rather than "from below," based on human reason and experience. Closely connected to this, Barth re-established, more by his practice than his doctrine, the role of Scripture in doing theology and preaching. On the other hand, his doctrine of revelation is troublesome in its denial of general revelation, which the Bible itself recognizes (e.g., Psalm 19:1–2; Romans 1:19–20), and in its assertion that the Bible is not the Word of God until it "becomes" the Word of God when God chooses to encounter the reader through it. Conservative theology acknowledges that God does indeed encounter the reader through the Bible, but calls this event "illumination," not "revelation"; nevertheless, the Bible should still be considered the Word of God (*primary* revelation) even when this "divine encounter" does not happen, even when it is sitting on a shelf.

Another of Barth's noteworthy accomplishments, which is based on what he found in Scripture, is the reestablishment of the Godness of God—his Trinitarian being, his complete sovereignty and radical transcendence. On the other hand, he may have gone too far and "sacrificed too much on the human side of the God-world relationship."[16] His doctrines of election and (apparent)

15. See chapter 35.
16. Grenz and Olson, *20th Century Theology*, 77.

universalism seem to remove the necessity of individual, human faith for salvation and overrule the freely chosen rejection of the gospel on the part of unbelievers.

Barth's massive intellect and immense literary production are nearly impossible to summarize in a few words. Nevertheless, Barth himself tried. During his only trip to the United States, he was asked to do just that. His response was, "Jesus loves me this I know, for the Bible tells me so."[17] Well said! His theological magnitude also did not go to his head. He is reported to have said, "When once the day comes when I have to appear before my Lord, then I will not come with my deeds, with the volumes of my *Dogmatics* in the basket upon my back. All the angels would have to laugh. But then I shall also not say, 'I have always meant well; I had good faith!' No, then I will only say one thing: 'Lord, be merciful to me, a poor sinner!'"[18]

17. Olson, *The Story of Theology*, 579.
18. Lane, *A Concise History of Christian Thought*, 278.

34

Paul Tillich

Foremost New Liberal

Context

The neo-orthodoxy of Barth and others had a profound impact. Liberal Protestant theology was on the run, having been shown to be significantly flawed. However, there were some who were concerned that neo-orthodoxy had reacted too vigorously and gone in the opposite direction too far; the emphasis on the radical transcendence of God seemed to call into question his real immanence—he is so far "up there" that he doesn't care about what is going on "down here." These theologians were concerned that the Christianity of neo-orthodoxy would be regarded as irrelevant to the modern world, the same concern that classical liberalism had with regard to orthodoxy. So neo-orthodoxy almost immediately produced a counter-movement that could be called "new liberalism." It took into account neo-orthodoxy's valid criticisms of classical liberal Protestant theology, but wanted also to reassert God's involvement in and care for this world. It also abundantly included modern philosophical and scientific thought into theology, all in an attempt to show that Christianity can still provide answers to the questions of modern culture. Foremost of these "new liberals" was Paul Tillich.

Tillich was born in Starzeddel, Germany (now in Poland), August 20, 1886. He developed an interest in theology and philosophy at an early age and determined to prepare for ministry. His education was received at the universities of Berlin, Tübingen, Halle, and Breslau, where he completed his PhD in 1912. He was ordained in the Lutheran church the same year.

In 1914 he became an army chaplain and experienced the horrors of World War I for the next four years. "He spent as much time digging graves as he did preaching sermons."[1] Much like Karl Barth, this caused him to see the insufficiency of much of the theology and philosophy he had been taught. But it also caused an intense personal crisis of doubt and despair, which in turn caused significant rethinking of his convictions.

His teaching career began in 1919 at the University of Berlin. During this time he became very active in a radical socialist religious/political movement. Five years later he took a position at the University of Marburg; it was here that he was exposed to the neo-orthodoxy of Karl Barth as well as the existential philosophy of Martin Heidegger, who was his faculty colleague. After brief stints at Dresden and Leipzig, he joined the faculty of the University of Frankfurt.

When the Nazi party was rising to power, Tillich, like Barth, deplored the manner in which the German church yielded to the new authority. In 1932, in the style of Martin Luther's Ninety-Five Theses, he wrote *The Church and the Third Reich: Ten Theses*, in which he condemned the German church and Nazism; he even sent a copy to Hitler himself. His book *The Socialist Dilemma*, in which he expounded his socialist beliefs, was publicly burned by the Nazis in 1933. The result was to be expected: Tillich was removed from his teaching position at the University of Frankfurt

1. Hill, *The History of Christian Thought*, 296.

that same year. He claimed the honor of being the first non-Jewish professor to lose his position at the hands of the Nazis.

At that very time, Reinhold Niebuhr, an influential American theologian, was in Germany, and he arranged for Tillich to be offered a position at Union Theological Seminary in New York City. So, faced with the inevitable alternative of life in a Nazi concentration camp, Tillich moved his family to the United States in 1933. Tillich was challenged by the adjustment to a new culture and learning a new language. Apparently his German accent was so strong that his students often had a hard time understanding him. He stayed at Union until his retirement in 1955. During this time, he preached and published many sermons, wrote many books on a wide variety of cultural issues, and traveled and lectured widely. As a result, he became a public as well as an academic superstar.

After his retirement he was honored with the prestigious position of University Professor by Harvard University, which gave him great freedom to teach, lecture, travel, research, and write. His popularity and fame continued to escalate. After his "second" retirement from Harvard in 1962, he accepted the position of Nuveen Professor of Theology at the University of Chicago, also a highly prominent appointment. He remained there until his death on October 22, 1965. His ashes were scattered in a park in New Harmony, Indiana, which had been named after him.

Grenz and Olson note, "Certainly few theologians have ever received the public acclaim Tillich did. He was truly a 'legend in his own time.' However, his life as a Christian theologian was marked by great ambiguity. He was beset by doubts about his own salvation and feared death greatly. He promoted socialism while enjoying the benefits of an upper–middle class lifestyle. He was renowned as a great ecumenical Christian and yet rarely attended church and apparently lived a fairly promiscuous lifestyle."[2]

2. *20th Century Theology*, 116. They base this on the authoritative biography of Tillich: Wilhelm and Marion Pauck, *Paul Tillich: His Life and Thought* (New York: Harper & Row, 1976).

Contribution

As most influential theologians, Tillich was prolific in his writing, but his most important contribution was his three-volume *Systematic Theology*.[3] He begins by expressing his concern that both orthodoxy and neo-orthodoxy were dealing with issues that were stuck in the past and had no relevance for today; they were answering questions no one was asking. His concern with classic liberalism was that it tended to overwhelm the eternal truth of Christianity with the contemporary situation; they were answering questions from human experience or reason alone. His desire was to strike the right balance. Tillich called the method of doing this "correlation." First, theology should listen to the real questions of the contemporary cultural situation. These questions— Tillich called them "ultimate questions"—came from science, psychology, sociology, literature, the arts, etc., but were primarily posed by philosophy. Second, theology should provide answers to those questions that are consistent with the eternal truth of the Christian gospel.[4] Third, theology should offer those answers using means that come out of and therefore most effectively communicate with the contemporary situation. According to Tillich, these means were primarily philosophical, specifically existentialism. Unfortunately, when it comes to Tillich, his answers were overloaded with dense philosophical terms communicating very abstract ideas. He "can sometimes seem to be spinning off into a world of words and images of [his] own invention that do not really connect with reality."[5] Tillich's thought is a major challenge to comprehend—even in the over-simplified basics that follow. So, ready or not . . .

3. Paul Tillich, *Systematic Theology*, 3 vols (Chicago: University of Chicago Press, 1951, 1957, 1963).
4. This is to be found in divine revelation, which, for Tillich, meant something very similar to that of neo-orthodoxy. Revelation is not propositional (words and sentences), but rather any "event" by which God is made known. The Bible is not the Word of God, but merely a record of these revelation events, the greatest of which was the "Christ-event."
5. Hill, *The History of Christian Thought*, 301.

Tillich believed that the primary cultural "existential" question in his day just happened to be one of the primary tensions dealt with by existential philosophy: being versus non-being. Humans experience their own finiteness, but, having the capacity of imagination, they can think beyond finiteness to the possibility of infinity. This produces another tension: infinity versus finiteness. When one is confronted by one's own finiteness, the reality of death, that is, nonbeing, looms. Human finite existence is really an unsettling combination of being—the apparent certainty of it—and non-being—the nagging threat of it. The result is profound anxiety. So there is the most fundamental, existential, absolute question of society: How do I know I really am? Or, How do I deal with the threat of nonbeing? It sounds like Hamlet—"To be or not to be? That is the question." But you can't get more fundamental than that.

The most fundamental answer that theology offers is: God. "Only those who have experienced the shock of transitoriness, the anxiety in which they are aware of their finitude, the threat of non-being, can understand what the notion of God means."[6] That notion, according to Tillich, is that God is the "ground of being." That is, God is not *a being* but rather *being-itself*: "The being of God is being-itself. The being of God cannot be understood as the existence of a being alongside others or above others. If God is *a* being, he is subject to the categories of finitude, especially to space and substance."[7] So the threat and anxiety caused by nonbeing is answered by Being-itself—God. Tillich's doctrine of God is probably the most controversial aspect of his theology, partly because it seems to make God less than personal. Tillich would not want to say this, yet he does say this: "Our encounter with the God who is a person includes the encounter with the God who is the ground of everything personal and as such is not *a* person."[8] What exactly

6. Tillich, *Systematic Theology*, I:162.
7. Ibid., I:235.
8. As quoted by Grenz and Olson in *20th Century Theology*, 127, from Paul Tillich, *Biblical Religion and the Search for Ultimate Reality* (Chicago: University of Chicago Press, 1955), 83. Italics are original.

does this mean? Tillich's favorite terms for God—"power of being," "power of resisting nonbeing," "power of existence"—seem to imply that God is really an abstract, impersonal power source, like the "Force" of *Star Wars*.

Human existence is not only characterized by finiteness but also, due to the exercise of human freedom, "estrangement." This is what Tillich calls "sin"; it is not acts contrary to the moral nature of a holy God, but rather estrangement from God (Being-itself), as well as from oneself and others. But humans are finite and therefore cannot reconcile these divisions on their own, which brings them to sense their need for what Tillich called "New Being." This must necessarily come from outside of humans in order to reunite them with Being-itself, but it could not *be* God (as in the historic doctrine of the incarnation of Jesus Christ), only *from* God. This need for reconciliation is another fundamental problem/question of today, and the theological solution/answer is "salvation."

This is where Jesus comes in. According to Tillich, Jesus is the historical human (and only a human[9]) who lived a life without estrangement from God, self, and others. He was able to do this through the power of the "Christ," the Christian symbol of the New Being. This really sounds like a version of ancient Gnosticism, that the "Christ spirit" came upon the man Jesus, enabling him to do what he did. Interestingly, Tillich prefers the term *Jesus as the Christ* rather than *Jesus Christ*. The cross is the symbol of how Jesus fully experienced human finiteness and death/nonbeing. The resurrection is the symbol of how Jesus, with the help of the Christ/New Being, overcame estrangement and defeated death/nonbeing.[10] Those who come to benefit from this (those who are "saved") experience the New Being and are reunited with Being-itself.

9. Tillich blatantly rejected Chalcedonian Christology, that Jesus Christ is one person with two natures—divine and human. Tillich rejected the idea that Jesus was God in any sense. He also radically reinterpreted the virgin birth, resurrection, ascension, second coming, etc.

10. Tillich denied that the resurrection of Jesus was a historical, physical event.

Conclusion

Paul Tillich has been considered the most influential American theologian since Jonathan Edwards and the most influential American theologian of the twentieth century. His fame equaled that of Karl Barth in academic theology and probably surpassed it in secular culture. Many contemporary theologians would consider Tillich the single greatest influence on their own theological thinking.

Tillich's method of correlation has much to commend itself and is really what every self-respecting Christian theologian would like to think he *is* doing. But even though Tillich wanted to provide answers to contemporary questions from the eternal truth of Christianity, many critics point out that those answers seemed to be more philosophical than biblical; existential philosophy seems to trump biblical theology. Then the question becomes, if philosophy itself comes out of finite, imperfect human reason, can it be trusted to ask the right questions in the first step of correlation, provide the right answers in the next step, and even to communicate in the right terms in the last step? It seems that Tillich's intentions were good, but his follow-through was flawed. He can even be faulted for practicing the very thing that concerned him about liberalism—offering theology that is really more human than divine. In contrast to his desire to find answers in divine revelation to questions that come from human reason, he ended up finding answers in human reason that he communicated in the guise of divine revelation. In the end, his theology seems to be just a new form of the old liberalism in which the message of Christianity found in the Bible is essentially lost.

35

DIETRICH BONHOEFFER
Modern Martyr

Context

Dietrich Bonhoeffer was born February 4, 1906, in Breslau, Germany (today, Poland). His father, a professor of psychiatry, was an agnostic, as were Dietrich's brothers. Dietrich, however, developed an early interest in theology and pursued formal training in it at the Universities of Tübingen and Berlin. His doctoral dissertation, *The Communion of Saints,*[1] was praised by the likes of Karl Barth. After a short stint pastoring a German-speaking church in Barcelona, Spain, and a year of additional training at Union Theological Seminary in New York, he returned to Berlin in 1931, where he became a lecturer in systematic theology at the university. Along the way, Bonhoeffer developed an admiration for Karl Barth's thought and established a personal relationship with him. He is generally considered to be within the neo-orthodoxy of Barth

1. Later published as Dietrich Bonhoeffer, *The Communion of Saints* (New York: Harper & Row, 1963).

(although he did not hesitate to criticize and differ with Barth as well). His *Christ the Center*,[2] based on his Christology lectures at the University of Berlin, reflects this affinity with Barth—a thorough Christ-centeredness that permeates his theology.

Everything changed with the rise of Adolf Hitler in 1933. Bonhoeffer's immediate opposition to Nazism prompted him to move to London, where he briefly pastored a German-speaking church. Upon his return to Germany in 1935, Bonhoeffer aligned himself with the anti-Nazi Confessing Church, founded by Barth, and became the leader of its illegal seminary in Finkenwalde. Bonhoeffer formed this academic institution into a close-knit community that endeavored to live out their Christianity in complete dedication to Christ. Out of this experience, Bonhoeffer wrote *The Cost of Discipleship* (1937)[3] and *Life Together* (1939).[4] The Gestapo shut the seminary down in 1937.

In 1939 Bonhoeffer briefly left Germany for the United States, but soon returned, feeling that he needed to be there at that time if he was to have any constructive role in rebuilding the German Christian community later. The Nazis did not permit Bonhoeffer to speak, teach, or write, so he became involved with the underground movement and eventually a plot to assassinate Hitler.[5] Bonhoeffer's involvement was suspected, and he was arrested and imprisoned by the Gestapo on April 5, 1943. During his year-and-a-half incarceration, he wrote what was later published as *Letters and Papers from Prison*.[6] In September 1944 the Gestapo gathered sufficient evidence of Bonhoeffer's involvement in the plot. He was transferred to various prisons or concentration camps, the last being Flossenburg death

2. Dietrich Bonhoeffer, *Christ the Center*, trans. Edwin Robertson (San Francisco: Harper & Row, 1978).

3. Dietrich Bonhoeffer, *The Cost of Discipleship*, rev. ed., trans. R. H. Fuller (New York: Macmillan, 1959).

4. Dietrich Bonhoeffer, *Life Together*, trans. John W. Doberstein (New York: Harper & Row, 1976).

5. This is noteworthy because Bonhoeffer had previously been a committed pacifist.

6. Dietrich Bonhoeffer, *Letters and Papers from Prison*, ed. Eberhard Bethge (New York: Macmillan, 1971).

camp. After a late-night court-martial, he was executed by hanging, April 9, 1945, at the age of thirty-nine. The camp doctor remarked, "In the almost thirty years that I worked as a doctor, I have hardly ever seen a man die so entirely submissive to the will of God."[7] Several days later the Allies liberated Flossenburg, and Hitler committed suicide.

Contribution

One cannot really understand Bonhoeffer's contribution apart from his context—monstrous evil in the form of Nazi atrocities, and the complicity of Christianity in the form of the majority of German Christians who supported Hitler's appalling activity.

Two of his ideas that have had a lasting impact will be summarized here. Both flow from his thorough-going Christ-centeredness. The first, from *The Cost of Discipleship*, is the challenging concept of "cheap grace" versus "costly grace." The book was based on Bonhoeffer's lectures on the Sermon on the Mount at the Finkenwalde seminary. In it he accused many Christians of living according to "cheap grace." He wrote, "The essence of grace, we supposed, is that the account has been paid in advance; and, because it has been paid, everything can be had for nothing. . . . An intellectual assent to that idea is held to be of itself sufficient to secure remission of sins. . . . Cheap grace means the justification of sin without the justification of the sinner. . . . Cheap grace is grace without discipleship, grace without the cross, grace without Jesus Christ, living and incarnate."[8] Christians who practice cheap grace accept the free gift of forgiveness of sins and then "live like the rest of the world."[9] This is the Lutheran and Reformed doctrine of justification by faith alone through grace alone taken to an absolutely wrong and unbiblical conclusion.

The true calling of Jesus Christ is the practice of "costly grace," which is "costly because it calls us to follow, and it is grace because

7. Quoted by Grenz and Olson, *20th Century Theology*, 149.
8. *The Cost of Discipleship*, 45–47.
9. Ibid.

it calls us to follow Jesus Christ. It is costly because it costs a man his life, and it is grace because it gives a man the only true life. It is costly because it condemns sin, and grace because it justifies the sinner. Above all, it is costly because it cost God the life of his Son. . . . Above all, it is grace because God did not reckon his Son too dear a price to pay for our life, but delivered him up for us. Costly grace is the Incarnation of God."[10] Can you sense how explosive these words would be in the middle of Nazi Germany, being ruled by the personification of evil, Adolf Hitler, and the unrelenting pressure on Christians and churches to give their approval to unimaginable wickedness?! It is still convicting today, even for us Christians who live in times of relative peace and freedom.

The second of Bonhoeffer's ideas, from *Letters and Papers from Prison*, is the provocative concept of "religionless Christianity." He continued to be provoked by German churches that refused to stand for and with the oppressed—in this case, Jews—and rather were quick to provide Christians with a safe and easy form of Christianity, or cheap grace. A "religious" world senses its dependence upon God, at least at the "boundaries" of life (where there is weakness, need, guilt, death); a "religionless" world has no sense of dependence upon God for anything at all. It is the latter that exists today, as Bonhoeffer put it, a "world come of age." He wrote, "What is bothering me incessantly is the question of what Christianity really is, or indeed who Christ really is, for us today."[11] He analyzed the situation something like this: Due to the Enlightenment drift away from God, Christianity had grown increasingly individualistic, inward, and otherworldly, that is, concerned about one's own salvation, spiritual life, and eternal destiny. In other words, Christianity was withdrawing from the secular world into itself; Christianity was so caught up in its "religious" jargon and way of thinking that the modern world could too easily dismiss it as irrelevant and out-of-date. Bonhoeffer's solution was

10. Ibid., 47–48.
11. *Letter and Papers from Prison*, 279.

that Christianity had to become like the world in which it found itself—"religionless" and "secular."

Bonhoeffer was by no means advocating pushing God out of our lives, but rather pulling him back into the center of our lives. This was really a reaction against Barth's extreme emphasis on God's transcendence—he is "out there," beyond, distant—and an attempt to recapture his immanence—he is "down here," involved, engaged. "[God] [not 'religion'] must be recognized at the centre of life, not when we are at the end of our resources [at our 'boundaries']; it is his will to be recognized in life, and not only when death comes; in health and vigour, and not only in suffering; in our activities, and not only in sin. The ground for this lies in the revelation of God in Jesus Christ. He is the centre of life. . . ."[12] This means that Christianity has to do away with the "religious" way of expressing itself and get back to Christ himself, "the one for others," including the demanding commitment of following him, not out of the world, but into the world, even to the point of death. This is costly grace.

Bonhoeffer also made some very mysterious statements. For example, "God would have us know that we must live as men who manage our lives without him. The God who is with us is the God who forsakes us (Mark 15:34). . . . Before God and with God we live without God. God lets himself be pushed out of the world onto the cross. He is weak and powerless in the world, and that is precisely the way, the only way, in which he is with us and helps us. . . . Christ helps us, not by virtue of his omnipotence, but by virtue of his weakness and suffering [Matthew 8:17]."[13] What exactly did Bonhoeffer mean by this? He admitted, "How this religionless Christianity looks, what form it takes, is something that I am thinking about a great deal."[14] Unfortunately he died before he could more fully work out and explain this idea of "religionless Christianity."

12. Ibid., 312.
13. Ibid., 360–61.
14. Ibid., 282.

Conclusion

Even though his life and work were cut short, Dietrich Bonhoeffer had a significant and nearly immediate effect on the thinking of many people. In fact, it was probably because of the manner of his death that his publications gained worldwide popularity and appeal. His was not thought produced in a pristine theological setting—just the opposite; he was neck-deep in evil and war. Furthermore, his own actions were demonstrations of his theological convictions, even to the cost of his own life.

Bonhoeffer has been described as the "first post-Christian theologian."[15] His provocative theology was taken even further in the form of the radical theologies of the latter part of the twentieth century, for example, the radical theology of the "death-of-God" movement,[16] "secular theology,"[17] Jürgen Moltmann's "theology of hope,"[18] as well as liberation and feminist theology.[19] These, somewhat like Bonhoeffer, were revolts against the neo-orthodox emphasis on the utter transcendence of God and attempts to re-emphasize the immanence of God and his concern for this world. It is questionable, however, whether Bonhoeffer would have approved of how far some of them went in nearly writing off the transcendent and spiritual realm. As much as Bonhoeffer emphasized God's being in the world and the necessity of the church being in the world as well, he never lost sight of ultimate and eternal reality. Even this he demonstrated personally in his last words before being executed: "This is the end—for me the beginning of life."

15. Hill, *The History of Christian Thought*, 286.

16. As presented, for example, in Thomas J. J. Altizer and William Hamilton, *Radical Theology and the Death of God* (Indianapolis: Bobbs-Merrill, 1966) and Altizer, *The Gospel of Christian Atheism* (Philadelphia: Westminster, 1966).

17. For example, Harvey Cox, *The Secular City* (New York: Macmillan, 1965).

18. Chapter 36.

19. Chapters 38 and 39 respectively.

36

JÜRGEN MOLTMANN

Theologian of Hope

Context

World War II left Germany devastated, the German people defeated, and the German church humiliated. Karl Barth, Paul Tillich, and Dietrich Bonhoeffer experienced this firsthand. The next generation of German theologians, those who were trained or influenced by these three great theologians, also experienced the horrors of war, some as young soldiers and all as Germans. They also worked out their own theology in the aftermath of the war, trying to make sense of it all.

One of the most influential of the post-war German theologians was Jürgen Moltmann. He was born in Hamburg, Germany, on April 8, 1926, into what he called an "enlightened secular" family. He was encouraged to read German philosophers and poets; the Bible was not a part of his early education. He fought in World War II, and it was while he was being held a prisoner of war that he was given a Bible and personally embraced the Christian faith.

In addition to his own personal crisis, it was also the crisis of war in general, German atrocities in specific, as well as the general unwillingness of German churches to stand against Nazism that attracted him to Karl Barth and Dietrich Bonhoeffer due to their thought and actions in Nazi Germany. After the war he studied theology at the University of Göttingen under a faculty that was strongly influenced by Barth. Moltmann completed his doctorate in 1952 and entered pastoral ministry in the Reformed Church. His academic career began in 1957, first at the Confessing Church academy in Wuppertal in 1958,[1] then briefly at the University of Bonn beginning in 1963, and finally at the University of Tübingen in 1967, where he remained until his retirement in 1994.

Contribution

Moltmann's first major work was *Theology of Hope* (1964),[2] in which he introduced an approach to theology from the perspective of eschatology, that is, the doctrine of the last things or future events in the divine program. This was rather gutsy because genuine, biblical eschatology had essentially been abandoned by theologians for a century or so. Liberalism talked about the kingdom of God, but it had nothing to do with God or Jesus Christ reigning on earth in the future; it was just an ideal human society on earth. Fundamentalism talked a lot about eschatology and the future earthly reign of Christ, but often in such extreme and dogmatic ways that mainstream theologians reacted by going in the opposite direction. So *Theology of Hope* was fresh and revolutionary, and with its publication, Moltmann became an instant theological sensation.

1. Another theologian on the faculty of this school at the same time was Wolfhart Pannenberg. This chapter could have appropriately been devoted to him, as these two—Moltmann and Pannenberg—were considered among the most important Protestant theologians at the time, and both emphasized the importance of eschatology in theology (as we will see for Moltmann specifically). Pannenberg went on to teach theology at the University of Munich until his retirement.

2. Jürgen Moltmann, *Theology of Hope*, trans. James W. Leitsch (New York: Harper & Row, 1967).

In the introduction he summarized this perspective as follows:

From first to last, and not merely in the epilogue, Christianity is eschatology, is hope, forward looking and forward moving, and therefore also revolutionizing and transforming the present. The eschatological is not one element of Christianity, but it is the medium of Christian faith as such, the key in which everything in it is set, the glow that suffuses everything here in the dawn of an expected new day. . . . [3] Hence, eschatology cannot really be only a part of Christian doctrine. Rather, the eschatological outlook is characteristic of all Christian proclamation, of every Christian existence and of the whole Church.[4]

For Moltmann, divine revelation boils down to "promise." At its heart, it reveals what God has in store in the future. The Bible *itself* is not divine revelation and certainly not verbally inspired or inerrant, but it is the *witness* to divine revelation—note Barth's influence here—specifically God's promises for the future "Kingdom of Glory." So based on what Moltmann found in the Bible, he emphasizes a real, meaningful future hope for the Christian in the form of an honest-to-goodness kingdom of *God* on earth—in contrast to classical liberalism. But it is this future hope that is "also revolutionizing and transforming the *present*"[5]—in contrast to fundamentalism, which had pretty much given up all hope for contemporary society.[6] Hope for the future and transformation of the present—which were very important to Moltmann—were all dependent upon God, who alone is to be the dynamic for propelling the world into a state of perfect peace and justice, the new heaven and earth revealed in Scripture. This hope for the future, which is based on and guaranteed by the historic death and resurrection of Jesus Christ, is the theme that runs throughout Moltmann's theology.

3. What was omitted here will be quoted below.
4. *Theology of Hope*, 16.
5. Ibid.
6. See chapter 40 for more on fundamentalism's attitude toward the present world.

Moltmann's doctrine of God was also quite innovative; he began to develop it in *The Crucified God* (1972)[7] and continued in later books.[8] Like Karl Barth, he takes Christ to be the primary revelation of God, and therefore our understanding of God must come through Christ. We can know what God is like because we see God in Jesus. But in stark contrast to Barth, who describes God as profoundly distinct from the world, Moltmann finds God to be intimately involved in the world. After all, the most striking reality about Jesus is that he suffered and died, and therefore we can know that the Christian God is not a God who is immune to suffering. In fact, it is suffering that becomes a primary characteristic of God. This turns historic theological thought on its head. Theologians have characteristically believed that God is impassible, or unable to suffer. Moltmann reverses this, saying that not only can God suffer, but suffering is at the heart of who God is, just as love is at the heart of who God is. "God and suffering are no longer contradictions," indeed "God's being is in suffering and the suffering is in God's being itself, because God is love."[9] It is God's love that works itself out in his intimate involvement in the world, even to the extent of suffering with it. This does *not* call into question his sovereignty and self-sufficiency, as most theologians would claim, because the suffering God experiences is not *forced upon him* from external circumstances, as is true of human suffering. Rather, according to Moltmann, God sovereignly, freely, and lovingly chooses to *allow* himself to be affected by suffering and therefore to suffer himself. This is God's self-limitation. This is also quite revolutionary thinking.

But Christ did not *just* suffer and die; he was resurrected and conquered death. This is also a part of God's very being and makes possible a theology of hope. Note what was left out of Moltmann's statement from *Theology of Hope* as quoted above: "For

7. *The Crucified God*, trans. R. A. Wilson and John Bowden (New York: Harper & Row, 1974).

8. Such as *The Trinity and the Kingdom of God*, trans. Margaret Kohl (San Francisco: Harper & Row, 1981).

9. *The Crucified God*, 227.

Christian faith lives from the raising of the crucified Christ, and strains after the promises of the universal future of Christ. Eschatology is the passionate suffering and passionate longing kindled by the Messiah."[10]

All in all, for Moltmann it seems that God's real existence is in the future. He is the "power of the future," who reaches from the future into the present to pull the present into the future. The death and resurrection of Christ, then, are really eschatological events that are projected back into the present.

This hope for the future seems to be for more than just Christians; rather, it is for everyone, indeed even the material world itself. That is, Moltmann seems to favor universalism, that all will be saved in the end, and the world itself will be "resurrected" and transformed.

Conclusion

The eschatological theology of Moltmann[11] was appealing to many theologians because it seemed to be middle ground between historic orthodoxy, whose God seemed too remote—uninvolved in and unaffected by the world—and liberal theology, whose God was very interested in the world but also nearly identified with and trapped in it. The God of eschatological theology does not dominate his creation; he has granted genuine freedom. But neither is he uninvolved; in fact, he allows himself to be deeply affected by it. This provided a way for Moltmann to explain evil, such as World War II and the Holocaust: Evil is possible due to God-given freedom in the world, and evil is reality because the kingdom of God is yet future. But the time is coming when, due to the death and resurrection of Jesus Christ, God will come in power, defeat sin and evil, and establish his kingdom of perfect and eternal peace.

10. *Theology of Hope*, 16.
11. and Pannenberg.

37

KARL RAHNER

Contemporary Catholic

Context

After the Catholic Counter-Reformation and the Council of Trent,[1] the Roman Catholic Church remained very traditional and committed to its established doctrinal beliefs. The First Vatican Council, also known as Vatican I, was called by Pope Pius IX in 1869 out of his great concern regarding the onslaught of Enlightenment thinking and liberalism and how the Roman Catholic Church was being affected. The council reaffirmed the conclusions of the Council of Trent (1545–1563), supported the pope in his condemnation of liberalism, and went even further, decreeing,

> When the Roman pontiff speaks *ex cathedra*, that is, when, in the exercise of his office as shepherd and teacher of all Christians, in virtue of his supreme apostolic authority, he defines a doctrine concerning faith or morals to be held by the whole church, he possesses, by the

1. See Brief Interlude.

divine assistance promised to him in blessed Peter, that infallibility which the divine Redeemer willed his church to enjoy in defining doctrine concerning faith or morals.[2]

The idea of the infallibility of the pope was not new among Roman Catholics, but Vatican I elevated it to the status of church dogma.

Generally, Roman Catholicism remained very conservative and rejected any modernizing attempts and attitudes. However, there were more and more Catholics who began to reject this reactionary attitude by the Church.

Pope John XXIII was elected in 1959, and he was determined to move the Roman Catholic Church from the middle ages into the twentieth century. Almost immediately he called for another ecumenical council to reconsider these matters, and the Second Vatican Council (Vatican II) met from 1962 to 1965. Profound changes resulted. For example, the Mass could now be celebrated in the language of the people and no longer in Latin exclusively. Similarly, there were now opportunities for the laity to be involved in the affairs of the Church and no longer the clergy exclusively. Even more significantly, there was a new openness to the possibility of salvation outside of the Roman Catholic Church. There was a much more positive attitude toward Eastern Orthodoxy and Protestantism, and even more amazingly toward non-Christian religions. Vatican II brought about the most revolutionary shift in the Roman Catholic Church—regarding beliefs, attitudes, and practices—in many centuries.

Another result of Vatican II was the opportunity for Catholic theologians to be more creative and innovative in their research and scholarship, as opposed to just restating and reaffirming what the Church had been teaching for hundreds of years. One of the most influential theologians who both contributed to and benefitted from this shift was Karl Rahner. He was born into a traditional Catholic family in Freiburg, Germany, in 1904. At the age of eighteen, he joined the Jesuits and studied in various Jesuit institutions,

2. Quoted in Hill, *The History of Christian Thought*, 257.

where he was trained in traditional, conservative Vatican I theology (Vatican II had not yet taken place). While maintaining his loyalty to historic Catholicism, he also demonstrated his willingness to embrace the modern age. For example, his doctoral dissertation at the University of Freiburg was rejected because it was deemed to be too influenced by existential philosophy.[3] After this setback, he transferred to the University of Innsbruck, where he completed his doctorate.

He began his teaching career in 1937 at the University of Innsbruck until it was interrupted by World War II. After the war he returned to Innsbruck in 1948 to resume his work as professor of theology. He later held faculty positions at the universities of Munich and Münster.

Rahner also played a very influential role in Vatican II. He was appointed as a theological advisor to the council and had a significant effect upon it. Some consider him to be "the most powerful man at the Council."[4] As a result, he gained a widespread reputation outside of academic circles, and his influence was vastly multiplied.

Rahner retired from teaching in 1971, although he remained active in lecturing and writing until his death in 1984.

Contribution

Rahner's publications number over 3,500, but his two most important were *Theological Investigations*[5]—twenty-three volumes containing many of his articles and essays—and *Foundations of Christian Faith: An Introduction to the Idea of Christianity*[6]—a single-volume summary of his theology.

3. It was eventually published as *Spirit in the World*, William V. Dych, trans. (New York: Herder & Herder, 1968).
4. Quoted by Grenz and Olson, *20th Century Theology*, 239.
5. Karl Rahner, *Theological Investigations*, Cornelius Ernst, trans. (Baltimore: Helicon Press, 1961–1992).
6. Karl Rahner, *Foundations of Christian Faith: An Introduction to the Idea of Christianity*, William V. Dych, trans. (New York: Crossroad, 1989).

His theology would be considered moderate.[7] He rejected, on the one hand, the strict traditionalism of Vatican I, and on the other hand, liberalism, which was heading in the direction of outright secularism. "He interacted positively and powerfully with modern thought, while remaining doggedly faithful to the rich heritage of Catholic theology."[8]

Rahner summarized his own massive literary output as follows: "I really only want to tell the reader something very simple. Human persons in every age, always and everywhere, whether they realize it and reflect upon it or not, are in relationship with the unutterable mystery of human life that we call God. Looking at Jesus Christ the crucified and risen one, we can have the hope that now in our present lives, and finally after death, we will meet God as our own fulfillment."[9] Basically, Rahner had a very pastoral concern to help individuals understand Christianity generally, and Catholicism specifically, in the context of the modern world. His profound thoughts, however, were expressed in very philosophical and esoteric terms, making them rather challenging to grasp.

Here are a few of his interrelated themes, overly simplified to be sure: First, *all* human beings experience God in *all* of life and cannot experience life *at all* apart from God—most just don't know it. Rahner illustrated this by comparing God to light. We cannot visually perceive anything apart from light, but we are usually not aware of the light itself, just the object that we are seeing. We don't see the light itself, but rather the object that it illuminates. God, then, is the necessary "light" by which we experience the world; without him, we could experience nothing. Furthermore, *all* human beings are naturally "open" to God due to God's grace in *everyone*. Rahner calls this the "supernatural existential," that is, "the dynamic personal self-communication of God for which

---

7. A few other important twentieth-century Roman Catholic theologians are Hans Küng (who was generally more liberal than Rahner) and Hans Urs von Balthasar (who was more conservative and traditional than Rahner).

8. Grenz and Olson, *20th Century Theology*, 253.

9. Quoted by Grenz and Olson, *20th Century Theology*, 240.

humans are created."[10] It is in Jesus' humanity that we see the perfect "openness" to God. In fact, Jesus Christ is the pinnacle of God's universal grace and his ultimate self-revelation. This is why salvation is to be found only in Jesus Christ.

A second theme has to do with the nature of God. Here Rahner was loyal to traditional orthodoxy and Catholic teaching, but emphasized the need to balance God's immanence or involvement in the world (which was so emphasized in liberal theology) and transcendence or separation from the world (which was so emphasized by Karl Barth). Rahner's view is really the corollary to the first theme: as all human beings are "open" to God, God is "open" to all humans. This "openness" is a part of the very being of God; it is a part of what makes God God.

A third theme in Rahner's thought is the concept of "anonymous Christianity." The historic stance of the Roman Catholic Church going back to Cyprian[11] was that there is no salvation outside of the (Roman Catholic) Church. Even though this still remains the official doctrine of the Catholic Church, it has been "re-interpreted" and softened more recently, by Rahner and others. Rahner reasoned as follows: God's desire is that *all* should be saved (1 Timothy 2:4). God's grace is at work in *all* people (the supernatural existential), even through non-Christian religions. Therefore, *all* people can be saved in one way or another. Even atheists can be saved if they have lived consistently with their convictions and conscience, for it is through these that even atheists experience God, even though they don't recognize it.

Through Rahner's influence, Vatican II articulated the idea in this way: "All this [the accomplishment of salvation] holds true not only for Christians, bur for all men of good will in whose hearts grace works in an unseen way. For, since Christ died for all men, and since the ultimate vocation of man is in fact one, and divine, we ought to believe that the Holy Spirit in a manner known only

10. Anne Carr, "Karl Rahner" in Donald W. Musser and Joseph L. Price, eds, *A New Handbook of Christian Theologians* (Nashville: Abingdon, 1996), 377.
11. See chapter 8.

to God offers to every man the possibility of being associated with this paschal mystery."[12]

Rahner defines his unusual term as follows: "The 'anonymous Christian' in our sense of the term is the pagan after the beginning of the Christian mission, who lives in the state of Christ's grace through faith, hope and love, yet who has no explicit knowledge of the fact that his life is oriented in grace-given salvation to Jesus Christ."[13] That is, these are individuals who take full advantage of the supernatural existential in them (even though they have no idea of what that is), respond positively to God's grace (even though they do not know they are doing so), and as a result receive salvation from God (even though they may have never heard the gospel of Jesus Christ). Responding positively to God's grace basically means living according to their religion (whatever it may be) as best they can, living consistently with their conscience, and treating others in love. In fact, one must explicitly reject God's universal grace in order to be eternally lost. So "anonymous Christians" are "Christians" because they are in fact saved by Jesus Christ, who is the savior of all mankind, but are also "anonymous" because they themselves do not know or acknowledge Jesus Christ as their savior, and they do not know that they themselves are Christians.

This concept of anonymous Christianity is probably both the most famous and infamous of Rahner's theological ideas; many have eagerly adopted it and many others have vigorously attacked it. One pertinent critique of it is stated by Lane: "Perhaps the greatest weakness in Rahner's theory is the transformation of an exceptional possibility (that someone who has not heard the Gospel may be in a state of grace) into the norm—so that the church is to treat all people as if they were probably anonymous

12. *Pastoral Constitution on the Church in the Modern World* (1965), paragraph 22. The term *paschal mystery* is used often in the declarations of Vatican II. It basically refers to the accomplishment of salvation through Christ as proclaimed by the Church.

13. *Theological Investigations*, vol. 14, ch. 17, as quoted in Lane, *A Concise History of Christian Thought*, 316.

Christians, while the biblical approach is to treat them as if they were lost."[14]

Conclusion

Roger Olson says of Rahner, his "career of teaching and writing Catholic theology [was] paralleled in history only by Thomas Aquinas himself" and he "was the Catholic counterpart of Karl Barth in terms of influence and impact. He was *the* Catholic theologian of the twentieth century and perhaps of the modern era itself."[15] Many would agree with Olson's assessment. It is largely due to Karl Rahner that more recent dialogues between Catholics, Protestants, and even adherents of non-Christian religions have taken place and are even possible.

It should be noted that, even though Karl Rahner introduced into Roman Catholicism a more openness to modern thought, there has also been a more recent conservative pushback against the influences of liberalism from within the Roman Catholic Church. This started under Pope Paul VI (1963–1978) and continued under Pope John Paul II (1978–2005) and his successor, Benedict XVI. So today Roman Catholic theology is very diverse to say the least, stretching across the theological continuum from near fundamentalism to extreme liberalism.

14. Lane, *A Concise History of Christian Thought*, 316.
15. *The Story of Christian Theology*, 597. Emphasis original.

38

GUSTAVO GUTIÉRREZ

Liberation Theologian

Context

In the 1960s and '70s, out of the heightened social consciousness of liberalism, came a variety of "liberation theologies." They have in common, as the name implies, the conviction that Christianity involves redeeming a particular group from a specific form of oppression. The difference between these various liberation theologies is the specific form of oppression that is being addressed. Black liberation theology focuses on racism in the United States. Feminist liberation theology focuses on the repression of women wherever it occurs.[1] Latin American liberation theology, the "original" variety, focuses on poverty in that part of the world. Primary theologians of Latin American liberation theology include Leonardo Boff, a Brazilian; José Míguez Bonino, an Argentinean; Juan Luis Segundo, a Uruguayan; and Jon Sobrino of El Salvador; but the real founder of Latin American liberation theology is Gustavo Gutiérrez.[2]

---

1. This will be the subject of the next chapter.
2. All of these are Roman Catholics, with the sole exception of Bonino, who is a Methodist.

Gutiérrez was born into a poor family in Lima, Peru, on June 8, 1928. He was ordained as a Roman Catholic priest in 1959 after receiving his theological training at the Catholic University of Louvain, Belgium, and the University of Lyon, France. While dedicating himself to parish ministry among the poor in Lima, he also taught theology at the Pontifical Catholic University in Lima. The intersection of his personal experience of suffering and poverty in pastoral ministry and his intellectual explorations and reflections in academic pursuits began to reshape Gutiérrez's convictions into what became the first theology of liberation. In 1968 he had the opportunity to provide crucial advice at the Second Latin American Episcopal Conference (CELAM II) in Medellín, Colombia. There the bishops discussed the massive problem of poverty in Latin American countries and rocked the religious realm by concluding that it was caused by "institutionalized violence," and called for drastic changes.[3] A movement was born, even though its roots extended centuries into the past. Gutiérrez then went on to write *A Theology of Liberation*[4] in 1973, which provided the first and most influential theological explanation of the movement. It was from the title of this book that the movement took its name.

Contribution

Gutiérrez's thought illustrates the themes that are common to most liberation theologies. The first theme is that theology is not universal but contextual, meaning that Scripture can be understood and applied in different ways, by different groups, in different cultural settings. There is no such thing as "one theology fits all." Liberation theologians would also claim that this is true of *all* theology—that it is shaped by its cultural context—whether

3. This conference and its conclusions were possible only in the aftermath of Vatican II (see the previous chapter).
4. The revised edition is Gustavo Gutiérrez, *A Theology of Liberation: History, Politics, and Salvation*, trans. and ed. Sister Caridad Inda and John Eagleson (Maryknoll, NY: Orbis, 1988).

it knows it or not, whether it acknowledges it or not; liberation theology simply acknowledges it and embraces that presupposition. The all-important cultural context in Latin America is poverty—oppressive, insidious, overwhelming poverty. This unfortunate reality has been imposed upon the majority of Latin Americans by local repressive regimes (dictators and militias) who use their power to preserve their power, and by Western cultures (North American and European), which exploit Latin Americans to enhance their own economic well-being. Liberation theologians have concluded that this poverty is due to the sinful "structures" of society.

In his book entitled *The Power of the Poor in History*,[5] Gutiérrez puts it this way:

> What we are faced with is a situation that takes no account of the dignity of human beings, or their most elemental needs, that does not provide for their biological survival, or their basic right to be free and autonomous. Poverty, injustice, alienation, and the exploitation of human beings by other human beings combine to form a situation that the Medellín conference [CELAM II] did not hesitate to condemn as "institutionalized violence."[6]

What makes it worse is that the Catholic Church, which is dominant in nearly all of Latin America, has been supportive of this shameful status quo; the church "has contributed, and continues to contribute to supporting the established order."[7]

A second common theme in liberation theology is the use of Marxism to analyze the Latin American situation, especially in terms of class struggle, the exploitation of capitalism (which is characterized as inherently evil), and the necessity to change things through revolution (ideally peaceful revolution, but there is an openness to violent revolution as a means of last resort). As in Marxism, the goal is to establish a sort of socialism that, though imperfect, is the much-preferred economic system. This use of Marxism is really the

5. Gustavo Gutiérrez, *The Power of the Poor in History*, trans. Robert R. Barr (Maryknoll, NY: Orbis, 1983).

6. Ibid., 28.

7. Gutiérrez, *A Theology of Liberation*, 151.

most controversial aspect of liberation theology, and the Roman Catholic establishment took a dim view of Gutiérrez's views for this reason. In 1980 Joseph Cardinal Ratzinger (later Pope Benedict XVI), as head of the Congregation for the Doctrine of the Faith, began to investigate Gutiérrez and his thought. This culminated in the document "Instruction on Certain Aspects of the 'Theology of Liberation'" (1984), which issued stern warnings about liberation theology's use of Marxism. Gutiérrez responded in *The Truth Shall Make You Free*.[8] In part, he justified the use of Marxism by comparing it to the early theologians' use of Greek philosophy.

A third common theme is that God always sides with the poor and oppressed over the rich and powerful; he gives preference to the poor. In the preface of *A Theology of Liberation*, Gutiérrez wrote, "[T]he poor deserve preference not because they are morally or religiously better than others, but because God is God, in whose eyes 'the last are first.' This statement clashes with our narrow understanding of justice; this very preference reminds us, therefore, that God's ways are not our ways."[9] Liberation theologians see this in the exodus event when God liberated his oppressed people from Egypt; in the Old Testament prophets who routinely condemned the rich and encouraged the poor on behalf of God (e.g., Amos); and in the example of Jesus, who routinely associated with the marginalized (e.g., "tax collectors and sinners") and was soundly condemned for it by the establishment of the day. So if God takes the side of the poor and oppressed, the church must *necessarily* do the same. This is not an option; it is mandatory. And this must not take the form of shouting encouragement to the poor from the sidelines; rather, the church must identify with the disenfranchised, enter into their suffering, and support them from within. After all, isn't this what God himself did through the incarnation? He entered into history and identified with broken humanity in the person of Jesus Christ in order to bring redemption.

8. Gustavo Gutiérrez, trans. Matthew J. O'Connell, *The Truth Shall Make You Free: Confrontations* (Maryknoll, NY: Orbis, 1990).

9. *A Theology of Liberation*, xxxviii.

A fourth common theme in liberation theology is that ortho-praxy (right doing) is more important than orthodoxy (right think-ing); Christian practice trumps Christian doctrine. Specifically, this practice must involve ending oppression in its many forms and seeking justice and equality in its place. Gutiérrez defined theology as practiced by liberation theologians as "a critical re-flection on Christian praxis [as opposed to theory] in light of the word of God."[10] Because God is God, his people must do what God does—liberate the oppressed. Only then is it appropriate to do theology—to reflect on this "praxis" in light of Scripture in order to support, guide, and refine the praxis.

The priority of praxis is important because it is what leads us back to God. Gutiérrez says, "To know God is to work for justice [praxis]. There is no other path to reach God."[11] Indeed, this is what salvation is. If sin is not individual but rather "struc-tural"—that is, social, political, and economic in nature—then so must be salvation. Liberation theologians do not think in terms of individual salvation, which guarantees an eternity of spiritual bless-ing. Rather, "Salvation is the activity of God and humans working together within history to bring about the full humanization of all relationships."[12] Here liberation theology looks very much like classical liberal theology in emphasizing the here-and-now effect of Christianity rather than the hereafter expectation of Christianity.

Conclusion

Gustavo Gutiérrez and liberation theology, which he has pioneered, can be commended in several ways, but there are also concerns that should be noted. First, liberation theology's insight regarding the contextualization of theology has been helpful. More and more, theologians are coming to grips with the fact that they do not do

10. *A Theology of Liberation,* xxix.
11. Ibid., 156.
12. Grenz and Olson, *20th Century Theology,* 222.

theology in a historical or cultural vacuum.[13] On the other hand, liberation theology takes this contextualization to an extreme that brings into question whether there is really any universal theological reality at all—that which is true for all people, of all time, in all places. If they are right, it seems like an extreme cultural relativity is inevitable.

Second, liberation theology should be applauded for bringing a greater worldwide awareness of the plight of the marginalized and disenfranchised, especially the poor. They are right to point out the heart of God for the poor, which is a consistent theme throughout Scripture. On the other hand, to say that God is on the side of the poor simply because they are poor seems to be going beyond the biblical text. Is it really biblically correct to condemn the rich simply because they are rich? Didn't God himself bless some biblical characters with significant riches, like Abraham, David, and Solomon? Aren't there unrighteous poor as well as righteous rich?

Furthermore, as mentioned above, liberation theology has been highly influenced by Marxist philosophy and economics, especially in terms of solutions to poverty and powerlessness. Again, Gutiérrez justified this by comparing it to the church fathers' use of Greek philosophy. However, as we have seen over and over in previous chapters, the degree to which philosophy should influence theology—or even whether philosophy should have any role in theology at all—is very much a matter of debate. Certainly, it is always dangerous to elevate any philosophy above the teachings of Scripture.

Third, liberation theology is right in emphasizing praxis—that the Christian church should be actively living out its beliefs. But putting praxis before theology seems to be a problem. This order is diametrically opposed to the classical methodology: theology is done first, and how we live and practice Christianity flows from that. Liberation theology is encouraging an entire paradigm shift! It also seems that even liberation theologians have theological

13. That is why I have structured these chapters as I have, beginning with the "context" of these theologians so that we can better understand their theologies.

presuppositions (theories) that *precede* their praxis. For example, they would insist that *right* praxis is to be actively involved in liberating oppressed people. But how do they determine right from wrong? What is their standard of "right"? Is it just that God always sides with the poor? If so, that is a theological conviction that precedes their praxis. Giving practice priority over doctrine really seems impossible—even dangerous.

39

ROSEMARY RADFORD RUETHER

Feminist Theologian

Context

One of the burning issues of the twentieth century was feminism, which, among other things, demanded total equality among men and women. The roots of this actually go back to the abolitionist movement in the nineteenth century and the civil rights movement in the mid-twentieth century. The central concern of both was freedom and equality. In 1963 Betty Friedan published *The Feminist Mystique*, and she was one of the founders and became the first president of the National Organization for Women in 1966. The women's liberation movement was born.

It had an immediate and profound effect upon the Christian church, the result being feminist theology. This has much in common with liberation theology, including the conviction that theology and praxis go together, and the belief that the church has been guilty of faulty theology, which has worked its way out in faulty praxis, including outright oppression. Other central convictions of Christian feminist theology are these: Christianity and Christian theology have been exclusively patriarchal and virtually oblivious to women's concerns for centuries; this has had a disastrous effect on women within the church, including even misogyny or hatred of women; therefore, women themselves need to redevelop and restate theology from the perspective of women's experience, at the center of which are centuries of repression within a patriarchal society and the need for not only liberating but also empowering women in society and the church. For example, with regard to theology, the feminist critique has been that Christianity has for too long and for the wrong reasons been expressed in male-oriented terms such as "God, the *Father*" and "Jesus, the *Son of Man.*" With regard to church practice, Christian feminists have pushed hard for the ordination of women.

Some feminists have rejected Christianity as hopelessly patriarchal. For example, Mary Daly (1928–2010), a former Roman Catholic, wrote *The Church and the Second Sex*[1] and *Beyond God the Father.*[2] Many others, however, have tried to reform Christianity from within and restate Christian theology from a feminist perspective. Probably most influential in the latter category is Rosemary Radford Ruether.

She was born in 1936 and lost her father when she was twelve. Her mother was a devout Catholic but was also open to questioning the traditions of the Catholic Church as well as what non-Christian religions had to offer. She raised Rosemary to be a freethinker like herself. Rosemary was also influenced by the early feminist movement through her mother.

Her early education was largely in private Catholic institutions. She entered Scripps College to study art. There she met and married Herman Ruether, who was studying political science and who, along with Rosemary's mother and various teachers along the way, helped

---

1. Mary Daly, *The Church and the Second Sex* (Boston: Beacon Press, 1968).
2. Mary Daly, *Beyond God the Father: Toward a Philosophy of Women's Liberation* (Boston: Beacon Press, 1973).

shape her thinking and convictions. Through the influence of one of her professors, she changed her major to philosophy. In 1965 she received her PhD in Classics and Patristics at the Claremont School of Theology. She has had a long and distinguished teaching career at Garrett Theological Seminary (Illinois), Claremont School of Theology (California), and the Pacific School of Religion and Graduate Theological Union (California).

Beginning in the '60s, Ruether was also influenced by the civil rights movement and the ecological movement. As a result, along with her academic pursuits, Ruether and her husband became very socially active in these causes and others. Vatican II also gave her, as a Catholic theologian, much greater freedom to express her nontraditional views and still remain part of the Roman Catholic Church.

Contribution

Rosemary Ruether has been and continues to be a prolific author. She has written or edited over thirty books, as well as many other articles and essays. Among her more noteworthy books are *Sexism and God-Talk: Toward a Feminist Theology*,[3] *Gaia and God: An Ecofeminist Theology of Earth Healing*,[4] and *Goddesses and the Divine Feminine: A Western Religious History*.[5]

Ruether and other Christian feminist theologians share a profound distrust of Scripture, for therein they find laws regarding women's "uncleanness" during menstruation and after childbirth, a priesthood that excludes women, commands for women to be submissive to men, and even restrictions regarding women speaking in church. On the other hand, Ruether does find in Scripture the all-too-often overlooked female prophets, judges, leaders, and

3. Rosemary Ruether, *Sexism and God-Talk: Toward a Feminist Theology* (Boston: Beacon Press, 1983).

4. Rosemary Ruether, *Gaia and God: An Ecofeminist Theology of Earth Healing* (New York: HarperCollins, 1994).

5. Rosemary Ruether, *Goddesses and the Divine Feminine: A Western Religious History* (Berkeley: University of California Press, 2005).

followers of Jesus. In addition, she sees in Scripture what she calls the "prophetic-liberating tradition," practiced at its best by Jesus himself. This tradition is "the vision of a completely egalitarian, nonhierarchical society unmarked by patterns of domination and submission."[6] As Reuther herself states in *Sexism and God-Talk*, "Feminist readings of the Bible can discern a norm within Biblical faith by which the Biblical texts themselves can be criticized. . . . On this basis many aspects of the Bible are to be frankly set aside and rejected."[7] So for Ruether, the Bible is certainly not the *only* authority (*sola* scriptura) nor is it even the *primary* authority for doing theology. In addition to the Bible (critically assessed, of course), Ruether creatively integrates other sources into her theology: texts from "heretical" Christianity such as Gnosticism, traditions from Roman Catholicism as well as Eastern Orthodoxy and Protestantism, themes from non-Christian religions, and concepts from a variety of philosophies, both ancient and modern, such as ancient Greek philosophy and Marxism, along with, of course, the *primary* source—women's experience.

If feminists want to redevelop theology, they must start with the doctrine of God, and so they do. Ruether's conception of God is "the primal matrix," which is similar to Tillich's "ground of being"—that from which *all* that exists springs into existence (or, is given birth, if you will). Her unique title for this divine one is "God/ess." Ruether's goal is to reverse the dualisms of historic Christianity, such as supernatural/natural, spirit/matter, soul/body, even good/evil, and of course male/female. She believes that the male has historically been associated with the former of these distinctions, while females have been associated with the latter. All of these distinctions break down once we get back to the true nature of God/ess, and what ought to be left is a radical, comprehensive, all-inclusive unity. And she means "*all*—" : "My own assumption is that the Divine Being that generates, upholds and renews the world is truly *universal*, and is the father and mother of *all* peoples

6. Grenz and Olson, *20th Century Theology*, 230.
7. Quoted by Grenz and Olson, Ibid.

without discrimination. This means that true revelation and true relationship to the divine are to be found in *all* religions. God/ess is the ground of *all* beings, and not just human beings."[8] Critics suggest that she is very close to identifying God with nature itself, that is, pantheism, or implying that all that exists is a part of one, single operating principle, that is, monism, also known as "Gaia."

Jesus Christ is a bit of a problem for Christian feminists because, after all, he is a man. So considerable reinterpretation is again in order. Ruether does this first by rejecting the Chalcedonian understanding of Jesus as the God-man—a divine nature and a human nature in one person.[9] Beyond that, she basically resorts to the Jesus of classic liberalism, that is, merely a human but also the ideal human, or as feminists like to say, the "paradigm" of redeemed humanity. What is important about Jesus is not who he is (which certainly does not include any sort of true deity), but rather what he did. Ruether sees the Jesus of the gospels as a prophet who, in the first century, spoke against the very things that feminism speaks against now in the twenty-first century: hierarchical structures (such as patriarchalism), oppression, injustice, poverty, and so on. She says, "Once the mythology about Jesus as Messiah or divine *Logos*, with its traditional masculine imagery, is stripped off, the Jesus of the synoptic Gospels can be recognized as a figure remarkably compatible with feminism."[10] She goes on to say that Jesus is not even to be exclusively equated with Christ; he is only the paradigm of "Christ." "Christ" ultimately is the redeemed humanity pioneered by Jesus. "The Christian community continues Christ's identity."[11]

Sin, according to Ruether, is relational and social. It is relational in the sense of wrong views of what it means to be in relationship with God/ess, other humans, ourselves, ecology, and pretty much everything else. It is social in the sense that we all inherit these

8. Quoted by Mary Hembrow Snyder, "Rosemary Radford Ruether" in *A New Handbook of Christian Theologians* (Nashville: Abingdon Press, 1996), 403. Emphasis added.
9. See chapter 13.
10. *Sexism and God-Talk*, 135.
11. Ibid., 138.

wrong views from our societies. Salvation comes, then, when we commit ourselves to adopting the correct views of our "paradigm," Jesus, and practicing mutuality, justice, and compassion toward *all*. Of course, Jesus is only the "paradigm" for *Christians*; there are other valid paradigms in other religions that can lead to the same thing. Furthermore, salvation is not something that is to be accomplished in some future spiritual realm (heaven), but rather something that is to be established now on earth. That, she believes, would be the kingdom of God that Jesus envisioned and proclaimed.

Conclusion

It seems reasonable to say that the feminist movement has had some degree of effect upon most if not all traditions of Christianity. At the very least, it has brought a greater awareness of the value and contribution of women and a greater sensitivity to past less-than-Christian attitudes toward and treatment of women. The fact that more and more denominations are enthusiastically practicing the ordination of women also illustrates its continuing influence.

However, there are some profound concerns regarding Christian feminist theology in general and Rosemary Radford Ruether specifically. For example, if the primary source and authority for doing theology is women's experience, how can the resulting theology be evaluated objectively? What makes women's experience any more of a standard than men's experience, or children's, or atheists', or animals'? There really is no *objective* standard by which the theology can be critiqued.

Another concern is the degree to which the central truths of Christianity have been reformulated. If Christian feminist theology continues in its current direction, one wonders how long it can legitimately retain the title "Christian." In fact, Ruether's radical openness to all religions seems to rob Christianity of any distinctiveness or uniqueness whatsoever. A radical relativity seems to be all that is left, as long as *everything* is equal to *everything* else.

40

CARL F. H. HENRY

Evangelical Theologian

Context

As we saw in chapter 32, the orthodox or conservative reaction against liberal Protestant theology came in the form of fundamentalism and theologians like J. Gresham Machen. It was a significant and promising counterpoint to liberalism in its prime, but 1925 marked a turning point in the form of the infamous Scopes "monkey" trial. Even though the trial was decided in favor of the fundamentalist view (vehemently opposed to the theory of evolution), the American populace in general adopted a very negative opinion of the fundamentalist movement. Other factors also led to an "evolution" in the movement. First, some minor matters were given major importance (for example, creationism in contrast to evolution as a view of origins and an extremely literal interpretation of Scripture). This caused the movement to lose its helpful focus. Second, fundamentalism became very pessimistic and negative regarding culture due to its liberal bent; society was beyond hope. Therefore, fundamentalists were encouraged to disengage and withdraw from it, including nonconservative Protestant Christianity. The movement became very "separatistic," sometimes including even "secondary" separation, that is, the refusal to cooperate or fellowship with other conservative Christians who do not separate sufficiently enough from nonconservative Christians. Third, due to this pessimism regarding the present state of culture, fundamentalism became very future-oriented; the only real hope Christians can have is in the future (thus, another doctrine that came to be emphasized was the imminent return of Christ). Finally, fundamentalism became very individual-focused; the gospel was intended for the salvation of individuals only. Evangelist Dwight L. Moody's comment was typical. He compared the world to a sinking ship (beyond hope), and Christians' responsibility was to save as many "souls" as possible from going down with the ship.

However, there were some within fundamentalism who were uncomfortable with this transition in the fundamentalist movement. The concern was not regarding theology—all conservatives were pretty much in agreement doctrinally—but rather attitude—pessimism, cynicism, negativity, and the like. As a result, some conservatives began to distinguish themselves from fundamentalism. The separatistic fundamentalists retained the title "fundamentalist," and the others adopted the title "evangelical." For example, in 1941, Carl McIntire founded the very separatistic American Council of Christian Churches. The following year, those in the tradition of Machen and the early fundamentalist movement organized the National Association of Evangelicals.

Another indication of the differences between fundamentalists and evangelicals was the publication of *The Uneasy Conscience of Modern Fundamentalism* in 1947[1] by Carl F. H. Henry, which "exploded like a bombshell in the fundamentalist camp."[2] The

1. Carl F. H. Henry, *The Uneasy Conscience of Modern Fundamentalism* (Grand Rapids: Eerdmans, 1947).
2. Grenz and Olson, *20th Century Theology*, 287.

author quickly became one of the leading theologians of, and a primary spokesman for, evangelical theology and the evangelical movement.

Carl Ferdinand Howard Henry was born on January 22, 1913, in New York City. His father and mother were both immigrants from Germany—his father, Karl, a Lutheran, and his mother, Johanna, a Catholic. Somehow, Carl, the first of eight children, ended up being confirmed as an Episcopalian. However, he quickly deserted the church altogether.

At the age of twenty he had a conversion experience and decided to pursue the study of theology. At Wheaton College, where he was profoundly influenced by Gordon Clark, a leading evangelical philosopher, Henry received both a BA (1938) and an MA (1941). He also developed friendships with a number of future leaders of the evangelical movement, such as Billy Graham and Harold Lindsell. He continued his theological education at Northern Baptist Theological Seminary, receiving a BD (1941) and a ThD (1942). While serving on the faculty of his alma mater, Northern Seminary, he undertook a PhD in philosophy at Boston University, which he completed in 1949.

Beginning in 1947, Henry served as a faculty member of Fuller Theological Seminary, a brand-new evangelical institution in Pasadena, California. In 1956 he helped launch an evangelical magazine, *Christianity Today*, and served as its editor until 1968. Henry also served on the faculty of Eastern Baptist Theological Seminary and worked closely with a variety of other evangelical organizations, such as the National Association of Evangelicals and World Vision. *Time* magazine recognized Henry's accomplishments in 1978 when it named him evangelicalism's "leading spokesman." He died on December 7, 2003.

Contribution

A year before writing *The Uneasy Conscience of Modern Fundamentalism*, Carl Henry wrote *The Remaking of the Modern*

Mind,[3] and he continued to be prolific: *The Protestant Dilemma,*[4] *Christian Personal Ethics,*[5] *Evangelical Responsibility in Contemporary Theology,*[6] *Aspects of Christian Social Ethics,*[7] *Frontiers in Modern Theology,*[8] *Evangelicals at the Brink of Crisis,*[9] *Evangelicals in Search of Identity,*[10] *The Christian Mindset in a Secular Society,*[11] and *Christian Countermoves in a Decadent Culture,*[12] among many others.[13] The titles of these books indicate a primary focus of much of Henry's thought: the role and responsibility of Christianity and Christian theology in modern society as seen from an evangelical perspective.

His *magnum opus* is the six-volume *God, Revelation and Authority.*[14] These three terms also serve as a means of summarizing Henry's theology as it relates to the primary focus mentioned above.

The first part of *God, Revelation and Authority* is "God who speaks and shows," which addresses the doctrine of revelation (volumes 1–4). He begins here rather than the doctrine of God due to his conviction that we cannot know anything about God apart from God *speaking* about himself in words and propositions and *showing* himself in acts of history. Liberal theology would generally agree with the latter, which makes it possible for us to know God through human reason and experience of these divine

3. Carl F. H. Henry, *The Remaking of the Modern Mind* (Grand Rapids: Eerdmans, 1946). The second edition was published in 1948.

4. Carl F. H. Henry, *The Protestant Dilemma* (Grand Rapids: Eerdmans, 1949).

5. Carl F. H. Henry, *Christian Personal Ethics* (Grand Rapids: Eerdmans, 1957).

6. Carl F. H. Henry, *Evangelical Responsibility in Contemporary Theology* (Grand Rapids: Eerdmans, 1957).

7. Carl F. H. Henry, *Aspects of Christian Social Ethics* (Grand Rapids: Eerdmans, 1964).

8. Carl F. H. Henry, *Frontiers in Modern Theology* (Chicago: Moody, 1966).

9. Carl F. H. Henry, *Evangelicals at the Brink of Crisis* (Waco: Word, 1967).

10. Carl F. H. Henry, *Evangelicals in Search of Identity* (Waco: Word, 1976).

11. Carl F. H. Henry, *The Christian Mindset in a Secular Society* (Portland: Multnomah, 1984).

12. Carl F. H. Henry, *Christian Countermoves in a Decadent Culture* (Portland: Multnomah, 1986).

13. A complete list of his massive literary output can be found at www.henry center.org.

14. Carl F. H. Henry, *God, Revelation and Authority*, 6 vols., (Waco: Word, 1976–1983).

"showings." However, liberal theology has profoundly rejected the former conviction. So Henry felt the need to particularly emphasize that God has spoken in *words* that were *written down* and preserved in the Bible. He strongly insisted that revelation is not only personal (he shows), but also propositional (he speaks).[15] Apart from God's speaking, we cannot understand his showing. Thus, Henry also argued for the rationality of Scripture; God explains himself in a way that can be understood. One of the themes that Henry expounded on was "God's revelation is rational communication conveyed in intelligible ideas and meaningful words, that is, in conceptual-verbal form."[16] It should be no surprise to note, then, that Henry was firmly committed to the historic and orthodox doctrines of inspiration (the Bible is truly the Word of God), inerrancy (as the Word of God, the Bible has no errors), and infallibility (the inerrant Word of God will not lead anyone into error). These doctrines were jettisoned by modern, liberal theology, and Henry felt compelled to restate them and reassert their centrality to the whole of theology.

The second part of *God, Revelation and Authority* is about the "God who stands and stays," which addresses the doctrine of God (volumes 5–6). For Henry, this doctrine was the foundation and glue of all theology. An inadequate or erroneous view of God led to an inadequate or erroneous theology, and it is through the Bible that we can know and understand God. Henry's doctrine of God was consistent with historic, orthodox theology (e.g., with regard to the Trinity, the divine attributes, etc.), but with a particular emphasis on his transcendence—that he is apart from and superior to his creation. This is the "God who stands" under his creation, as its cause, sufficiency and sovereign. But God is also the one who stays involved with and a part of his creation—the immanence of God. Henry maintained the balance between these two crucial biblical truths regarding God, but his emphasis on

15. Liberal theology denies propositional revelation because it believes the Bible is only a human book. Neo-orthodoxy denies propositional revelation in favor of personal revelation (see chapter 33).

16. *God, Revelation and Authority*, 3:248. He covers this in pp. 248–487.

transcendence was necessary due to liberal theology's tendency to overemphasize God's immanence nearly to the complete neglect of his transcendence. He wrote, "If Christianity is to win intellectual respectability in the modern world, the reality of the transcendent God must indeed be proclaimed by the theologians—and proclaimed on the basis of man's rational competence to know the transempirical [supernatural] realm."[17]

So if God is truly transcendent, then he is the ultimate authority. If the Bible is truly God's Word, then it is our ultimate written authority. One of Henry's primary critiques of twentieth-century theology is that it had forsaken its heritage of being rooted in Scripture, which is divine revelation and therefore authoritative. *God, Revelation and Authority* is not a systematic theology, but rather an attempt to lay a foundation upon which a valid, evangelical, systematic theology can be built, namely, the Bible recognized as the divinely inspired, totally inerrant, completely authoritative Word of God.

Henry critiqued not only liberal theology but also conservative theology, both fundamentalist and evangelical, and this critique necessarily flowed out of the concepts of God, revelation, and authority. With regard to fundamentalism, his charge was that it had overreacted against liberalism in its withdrawing from culture and Christian responsibility to society. "Whereas once the redemptive gospel was a world-changing message, now it was narrowed to a world-resisting message."[18] God did indeed purpose to change individuals through the work of Christ, but also to change society through redeemed individuals who were "salt and light" in the world. Henry agreed with liberalism that society needed to be and could be transformed, and he disagreed with fundamentalism that society was beyond help and should be abandoned. But he agreed with fundamentalists (and disagreed with liberalism) that individual transformation was the priority; only through transformed individuals could society be transformed.[19] He did agree

17. Henry, *Frontiers in Modern Theology*, 154–55, as quoted by Grenz and Olson, *20th Century Theology*, 295.
18. *The Uneasy Conscience of Modern Fundamentalism*, 30.
19. He argues this in *Aspects of Christian Social Ethics*.

with fundamentalism that the kingdom of God is indeed "then" in the future, but he also agreed with liberalism in that it can (and must) be "now" in the present.[20] This reflects the God who "stays." His challenge to his fellow evangelical Christian and scholars, then, was to even further engage with modern society to help bring about this transformation by getting back to the true God who is known through the truthful Word of God.

Conclusion

As a result of Carl F. H. Henry and many others, the evangelical movement has grown in size and influence—*Newsweek* magazine declared 1976 to be the "year of the evangelical"—while fundamentalism has declined, but certainly not deceased. Evidence of evangelicalism's vitality includes socially oriented organizations such as Focus on the Family and Prison Fellowship, educational institutions such as Wheaton College and Biola University, and scholarly societies such as the Evangelical Theological Society and the Institute for Biblical Research. Evangelicalism is not without its faults and challenges, but it continues in the twenty-first century to be a viable and attractive alternative to liberal theology and mainstream Protestantism.

20. *The Uneasy Conscience*, 48–57.

CONCLUSION

We have covered a lot in these chapters—people, ideas, movements, denominations, councils, creeds, heresies—all of which fit into a vast sweep of time—two millennia. It is easy to get lost in all the details and decades, so let me try to draw a few conclusions—some broad, sweeping observations that I think are important to keep in mind.

First, these theologians lived in certain historical/cultural/theological contexts that most certainly affected their thought—Greek or existential philosophy, national or ecclesiastical politics, feudalism, the Enlightenment, world wars, poverty, etc. As even some of them have appropriately reminded us (notably Gustavo Gutiérrez), this is unavoidable; it is impossible to think unaffected by our setting. It is not ideal, but it is reality.

This, in connection with these theologians being limited, fallible human beings, means that none of their theological systems were flawless, perfect representations of spiritual reality. Just because Augustine, Aquinas, Calvin, Edwards, or Barth believed something does not necessarily mean anything. And they would certainly be the first to admit it—at least most of them. So we should guard against putting any of these great thinkers on such a pedestal that anything they write is just assumed to be God's truth. Rather, their thought should always be measured against an objective, universal standard of truth. It is my personal conviction that we have such a standard in the Bible, the written Word of God. Of course, not all of these influential Christians would agree with that.

An implication here is that none of the rest of us are unaffected by our life setting. As objective as we would like to think we are, we grew up in certain families, experienced certain life situations, went to certain churches, learned the Bible and theology from certain pastors and teachers . . . and all of this has become a part of us. Even as we try to assess the thinking of these theologians against the standard of Scripture, we need to acknowledge that our understanding of Scripture has significant subjective elements. We need to own up to this. We need to be humbled by this. We need to be open to different perspectives—which is one of the reasons for doing historical theology. And most certainly, we need to be dependent upon God's Spirit to lead us into God's truth.

A second conclusion is really the flip side of the first: Just because these theologians are not perfect is no reason to dismiss their ideas. Just because Origen was very affected by Greek philosophy does not mean that he had no valid biblical insight to offer. Just because Arminius contradicted Calvin on important issues does not mean that Calvinists can flippantly dismiss him (and vice versa). Just because Schleiermacher, Ritschl, and Tillich are labeled as liberals does not mean they have no legitimate challenges for conservatives. In fact, isn't it usually the case that we grow in our understanding of things when we are challenged by beliefs contrary to our own, as opposed to just having those who agree with us constantly assuring us that we (and they) are right?

Third, even though these theologians and their theologies are far from perfect and even contain significant errors, there has been a consistency of truth and belief among Christians for two thousand years—the historic Christian consensus. This has been called the "apostolic teaching," or "orthodoxy." Some refer to it as the "great tradition." In one sense, this is rather remarkable. In light of the great amount of time since the closing of the biblical canon, the great number of people involved in interpreting it, and the great number of threats against it, it is amazing that Christian belief today has any similarity at all to what Christians believed in the first century. Remember the old game of telephone?

On the other hand, this just makes sense. This is *God's* truth, and therefore *God* is working to protect it (Matthew 5:17–18). An implication is that we should have great confidence that divinely revealed truth has not and will not be lost in the shuffle.

Another equally amazing aspect of this is that God has chosen to protect and propagate biblical truth through very imperfect people. But this is also exactly what we see in Scripture—God doing very remarkable things through very unremarkable humans. None of these theologians have done the job perfectly, but each has done a piece of it. As a result, we have a multitude of perspectives and aspects of theology. As pure, white light is diffracted by a prism into a variety of colors, so God's truth is diffracted through people into a myriad of traditions.

A final conclusion is that there will always be more theology to do and more progress to make. After all, the subject matter is God, who said, "For my thoughts are not your thoughts, neither are your ways my ways. As the heavens are higher than the earth, so are my ways higher than your ways and my thought than your thoughts" (Isaiah 55:8–9). These great Christian thinkers of the past have not completed the task; they haven't even scratched the surface. So much more reflective probing needs to be done into the stratosphere of spiritual truth. Just as there have been influential Christian thinkers in the past, so there will be influential Christian thinkers in the future, those who are called by God to help the rest of us know him better and better.

But even as we look forward to this progress, we should not neglect the past. As one historical theologian put it, "The way for us to move ahead in theology is to move back—to the greats of the past."[1] So in closing, I commend to you the very influential Christians discussed in the previous chapters and so many more on whose shoulders we stand today in order to better view the greatest sight to behold—God.

1. McDermott, *The Great Theologians*, 208.

THE CREED OF NICEA

We believe in one God,
the Father, Almighty,
maker of all things visible and invisible;

and in the one Lord Jesus Christ,
the Son of God,
begotten of the Father,
only-begotten, that is, from the substance of the Father;
God from God, Light from Light,
very God from very God,
begotten not made,
of one substance with the Father,
through whom all things were made,
both in heaven and in earth;
who for us men and for our salvation came down and was
     incarnate,
was made man, suffered, and rose again on the third day,
ascended into heaven,
and is coming to judge the living and the dead;

And in the Holy Spirit.

The catholic and apostolic church places under a curse those who
say: "There was a time when he was not" and "Before he was begotten he was not" and "He came into being from nothing," and
those who pretend that the Son of God is "of another substance"
[than the Father] or "created" or "alterable" or "mutable."

THE NICENO-CONSTANTINOPOLITAN CREED

We believe in one God,
the Father, the Almighty,
maker of heaven and earth,
of all that is, seen and unseen.
We believe in one Lord, Jesus Christ,
the only Son of God,
eternally begotten of the Father,
God from God, Light from Light,
true God from true God,
begotten, not made,
of one being with the Father;
through him all things were made.
For us and for our salvation
he came down from heaven,
was incarnate of the Holy Spirit and the Virgin Mary
and became truly human.
For our sake he was crucified under Pontius Pilate;
he suffered death and was buried.
On the third day he rose again
in accordance with the Scriptures;

he ascended into heaven
and is seated at the right hand of the Father.
He will come again in glory to judge the living and the
  dead,
and his kingdom will have no end.
We believe in the Holy Spirit, the Lord, the giver of life,
who proceeds from the Father [and the Son*],
who with the Father and the Son is worshiped and
  glorified,
who has spoken through the prophets.
We believe in one holy, catholic and apostolic Church.
We acknowledge one baptism for the forgiveness of sins.
We look for the resurrection of the dead,
and the life of the world to come. Amen.

*The phrase "and the Son" was added later.

RESOURCES

Primary Sources

Lay, Robert F. *Readings in Historical Theology: Primary Sources of the Christian Faith*. Grand Rapids, MI: Kregel Publications, 2009.

McGrath, Alister E. *The Christian Theology Reader*. Third Edition. Oxford: Blackwell Publishing, 2007.

Placher, William C. *Readings in the History of Christian Theology, Volume 1: From Its Beginnings to the Eve of the Reformation*. Louisville: Westminster John Knox Press, 1988.

_____. *Readings in the History of Christian Theology, Volume 2: From the Reformation to the Present*. Louisville: Westminster John Knox Press, 1988.

Secondary Sources

Allison, Gregg R. *Historical Theology: An Introduction to Christian Doctrine*. Grand Rapids, MI: Zondervan, 2011.

Anderson, William P. *A Journey Through Christian Theology: With Texts from the First to the Twenty-first Century*. Second Edition. Minneapolis: Fortress Press, 2010.

Benedict XVI, *Great Christian Thinkers: From the Early Church Through the Middle Ages*. Minneapolis: Fortress Press, 2011.

Bromiley, Geoffrey W. *Historical Theology: An Introduction*. Grand Rapids, MI: Wm. B. Eerdmans Publishing Company, 1978.

Foster, Paul, ed. *Early Christian Thinkers: The Lives and Legacies of Twelve Key Figures*. Downers Grove, IL: InterVarsity Press, 2010.

Green, Bradley G. *Shapers of Christian Orthodoxy: Engaging with Early and Medieval Theologians*. Downers Grove, IL: InterVarsity Press, 2010.

Hannah, John. *Our Legacy: The History of Christian Doctrine*. Colorado Springs: NavPress, 2001.

Haykin, Michael A. G. *Rediscovering the Church Fathers: Who They Were and How They Shaped the Church*. Wheaton: Crossway, 2011.

Hill, Jonathan. *The History of Christian Thought*. Downers Grove, IL: InterVarsity Press, 2003.

Lane, Tony. *A Concise History of Christian Thought*. Revised Edition. Grand Rapids, MI: Baker Academic, 2006.

McDermott, Gerald R. *The Great Theologians: A Brief Guide*. Downers Grove, IL: InterVarsity Press, 2010.

McGrath, Alister E. *Historical Theology: An Introduction to the History of Christian Thought*. Oxford: Blackwell Publishing, 1998.

Olson, Roger E. *The Story of Christian Theology: Twenty Centuries of Tradition and Reform*. Downers Grove, IL: InterVarsity Press, 1999.

Daryl Aaron earned his MA at the University of Texas at Dallas, his ThM at Dallas Theological Seminary, his DMin at Bethel Theological Seminary, and his PhD at Graduate Theological Foundation. He spent fourteen years in pastoral ministry and now teaches at Northwestern College, where he is Professor of Biblical and Theological Studies. Dr. Aaron lives in Mounds View, Minnesota, with his wife, Marilyn. They have one daughter, Kimberly, who is a graduate of Northwestern College. After completing a master's program at Minnesota State University–Mankato, she has joined her (very proud) father on the faculty of Northwestern College, teaching Spanish.

An Easy-to-Use Guide to Christian Theology

ALSO FROM DARYL AARON

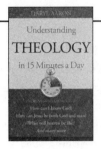

Theology can be intimidating, even overwhelming. Where do you start? How is it important to the Christian life? What are the key topics that you need to understand? How do you make time to study something so complex without going to Bible college or seminary?

In *Understanding Theology in 15 Minutes a Day*, professor and former pastor Daryl Aaron answers forty critical questions about the Christian faith. Arranged by topic, you can choose the areas that interest you, or systematically read through the book. Each section is short and easy to understand. You'll come away with a deeper faith as you learn about the nature of God, heaven, the Bible, church, and even yourself.

Understanding Theology in 15 Minutes a Day by Daryl Aaron